中国残疾人事业统计年鉴

China Statistical Yearbook on the Work for Persons with Disabilities

2021

（总第20期 No.20）

中国残疾人联合会 编

Compiled By China Disabled Persons' Federation

图书在版编目（CIP）数据

中国残疾人事业统计年鉴. 2021：汉英对照 / 中国残疾人联合会编. -- 北京 ：中国统计出版社, 2021.9
ISBN 978-7-5037-9638-8

Ⅰ. ①中… Ⅱ. ①中… Ⅲ. ①残疾人－社会福利事业－统计资料－中国－2021－年鉴－汉、英 Ⅳ. ①D669.69-66

中国版本图书馆 CIP 数据核字(2021)第 178203 号

中国残疾人事业统计年鉴—2021
China Statistical Yearbook on the Work for Persons with Disabilities-2021

作　　者/中国残疾人联合会
责任编辑/冯燕玲
封面设计/张　然
出版发行/中国统计出版社
通信地址/北京市丰台区西三环南路甲 6 号　邮政编码/100073
电　　话/邮购（010）63376909　书店（010）68783171
网　　址/http://www.zgtjcbs.com
印　　刷/河北鑫兆源印刷有限公司
经　　销/新华书店
开　　本/880×1230mm　1/16
印　　张/14.25　彩页 0.5
字　　数/472 千字
版　　别/2021 年 9 月第 1 版
版　　次/2021 年 9 月第 1 次印刷
定　　价/180.00 元

如有印装差错，由本社发行部调换。

《中国残疾人事业统计年鉴-2021》
编委会和编辑工作人员

编者说明

《中国残疾人事业统计年鉴—2021》系统收录了全国和各省、自治区、直辖市 2020 年残疾人工作各方面的统计数据，是一部全面反映中国残疾人事业发展的资料性年鉴。

本年鉴内容由六部分组成：第一部分为主要指标数据图；第二部分为 2020 年中国残疾人事业发展统计公报；第三部分为综合统计资料，是历年统计情况的综合反映；第四部分为 2020 年度分省统计资料，记录 2020 年各省（自治区、直辖市）任务指标执行情况和全国汇总情况；第五部分为分省统计报告，包括全国 31 个省（自治区、直辖市）和新疆生产建设兵团的残疾人事业统计公报；第六部分为附录，介绍中国残疾人事业统计有关的政策法规文件。

本年鉴涉及的全国性统计数据均不包括香港、澳门特别行政区和台湾省数据。

本年鉴是根据各地残联报送的统计年报和部分专项业务项目统计结果编制而成。表格中“空格”表示该项统计指标数据不足本表最小单位数、数据不详或无该项数据。

2021 年 9 月

目　录
Contents

第一部分　主要数据图
Part Ⅰ　Charts

第二部分　统计公报
Part Ⅱ　Statistical Communique

第三部分　综合统计资料
Part Ⅲ　Overall Statistics

第四部分　分省统计资料
Part Ⅳ　Provincial Statistics

一、康复
Rehabilitation

二、教育
Education

三、就业
Employment

四、扶贫
Poverty Alleviation

五、社会保障
Social Security

六、专门协会
Specialized Associations

七、盲人按摩
Massage by the Blind

八、宣传文化
Publicity and Cultural Activities

九、体育
Sports

十、维权
Rights Protection

第六部分 附 录
Part Ⅵ Appendix

主要数据图

Charts

图-1 “十三五”期间得到基本康复服务的残疾人

Chart1 Rehabilitation Services Received by Persons with Disabilities during 2016-2020

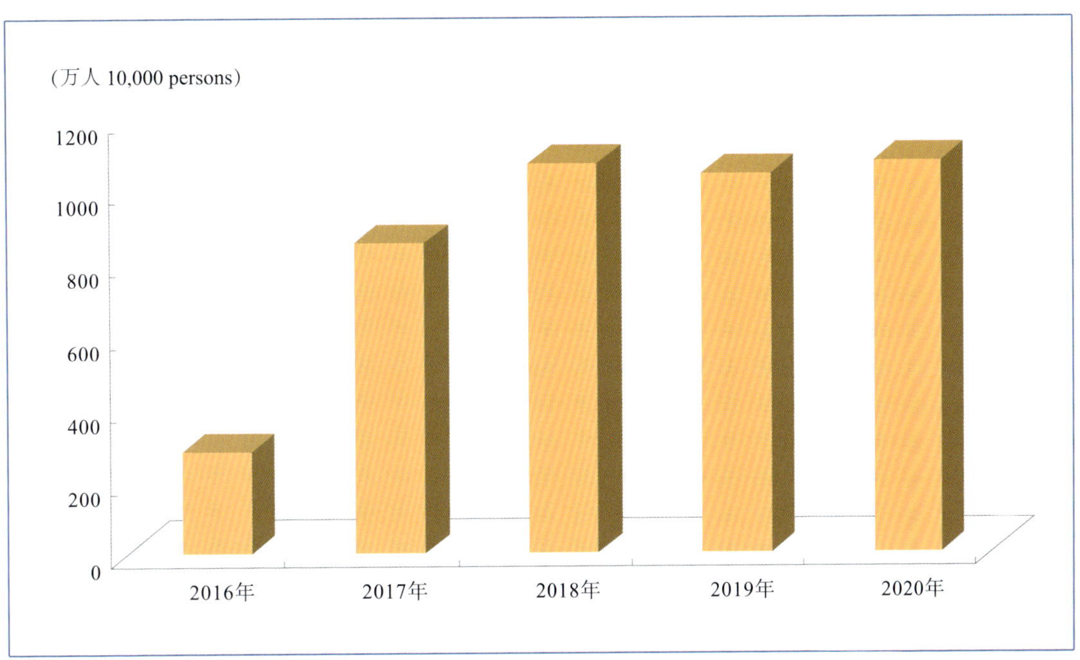

图-2 “十三五”期间残疾人康复机构建设情况

Chart 2 Development of Rehabilitation Facilities of Persons with Disabilities during 2016-2020

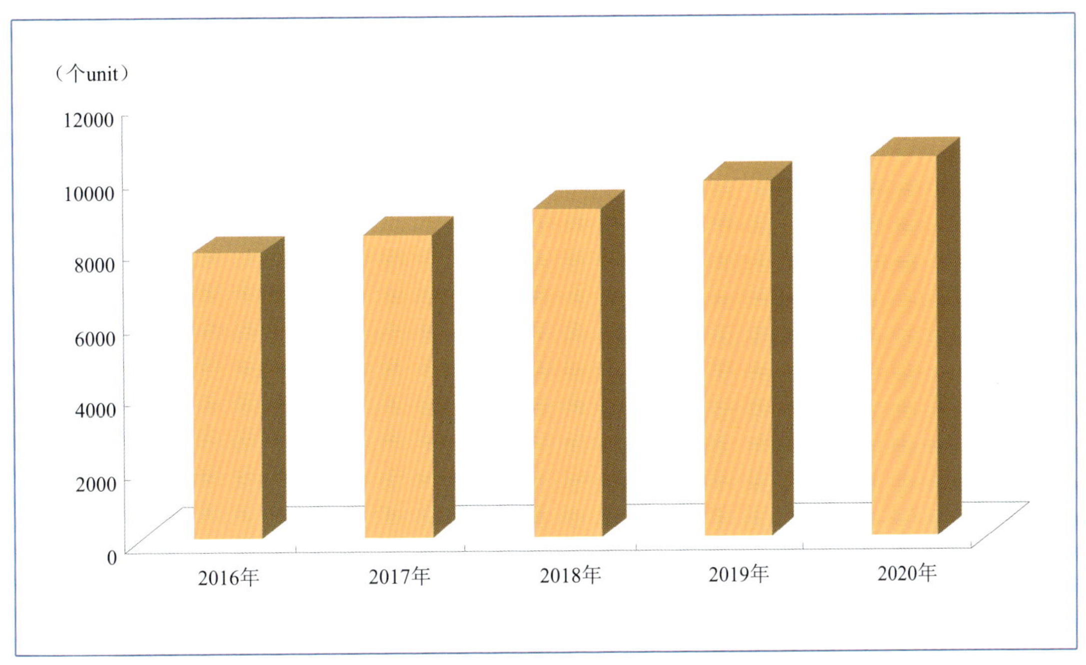

图-3 “十三五”期间高等院校录取残疾考生情况

Chart 3 Admission of Disabled Students to Higher Education Institutions during 2016-2020

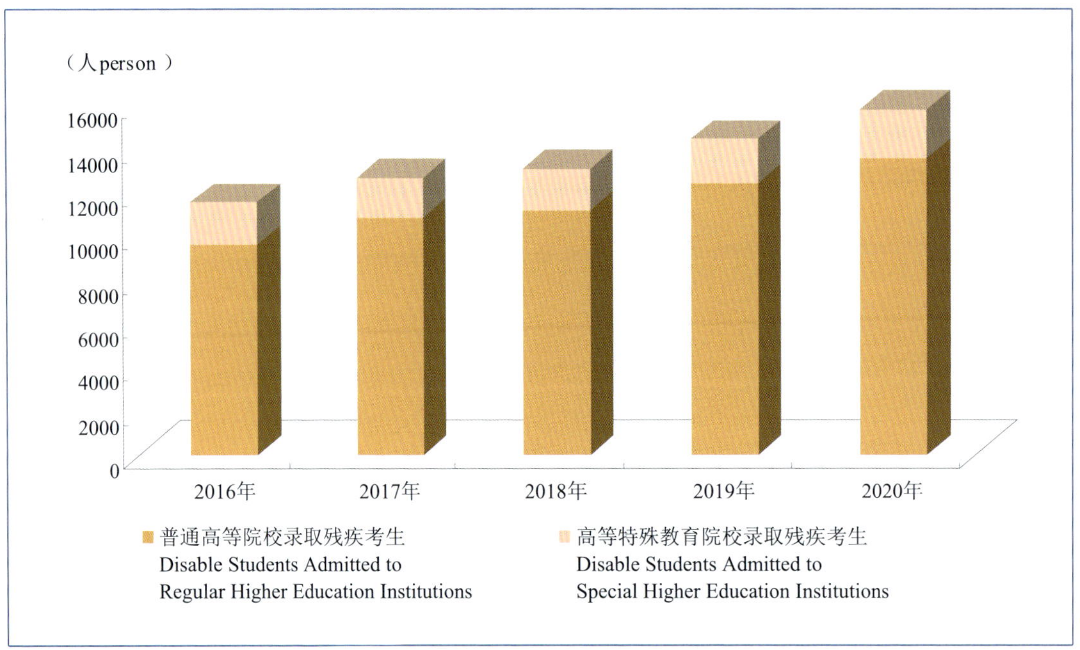

图-4 “十三五”期间持证残疾人就业情况

Chart 4 Employment of registered persons with Disabilities in Urban and Rural Areas during 2016-2020

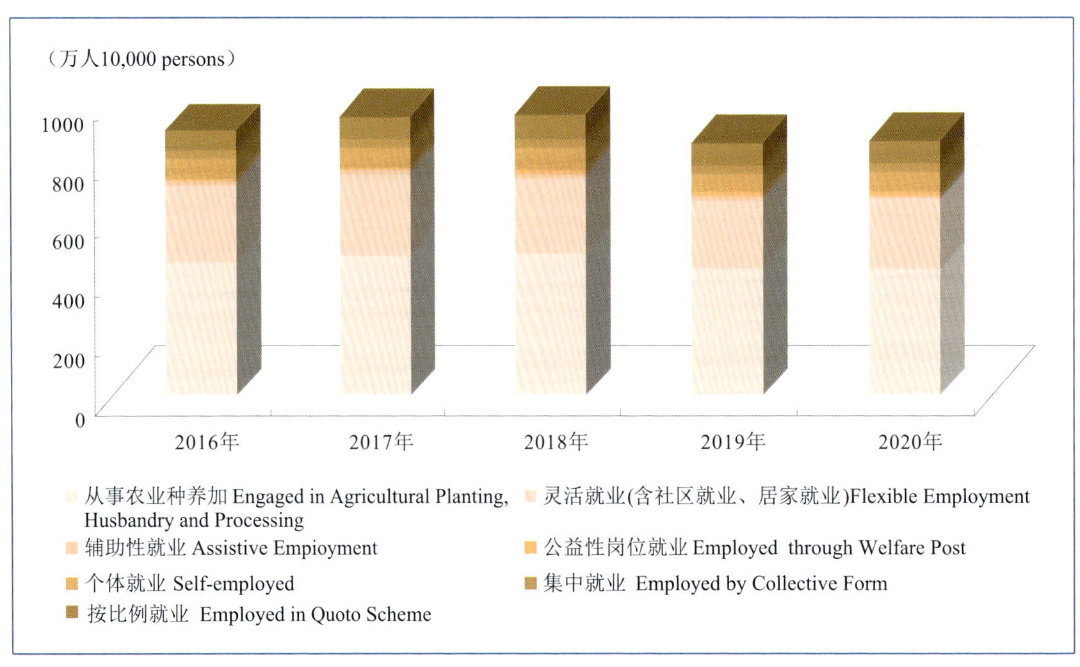

图-5 “十三五”期间农村贫困残疾人危房改造情况

Chart 5 House Renovation for Financially Difficult Persons with Disabilities in Rural Areas during 2016-2020

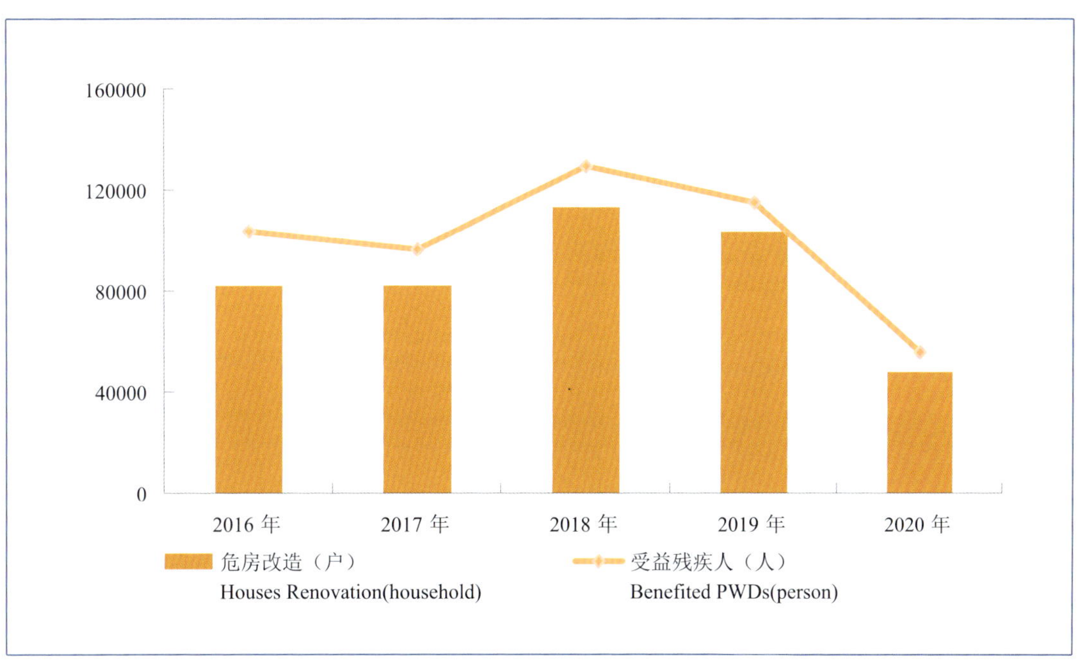

图-6 “十三五”期间农村贫困残疾人扶持情况

Chart 6 Poverty Alleviation for Financially Difficult Persons with Disabilities in Rural Areas during 2016-2020

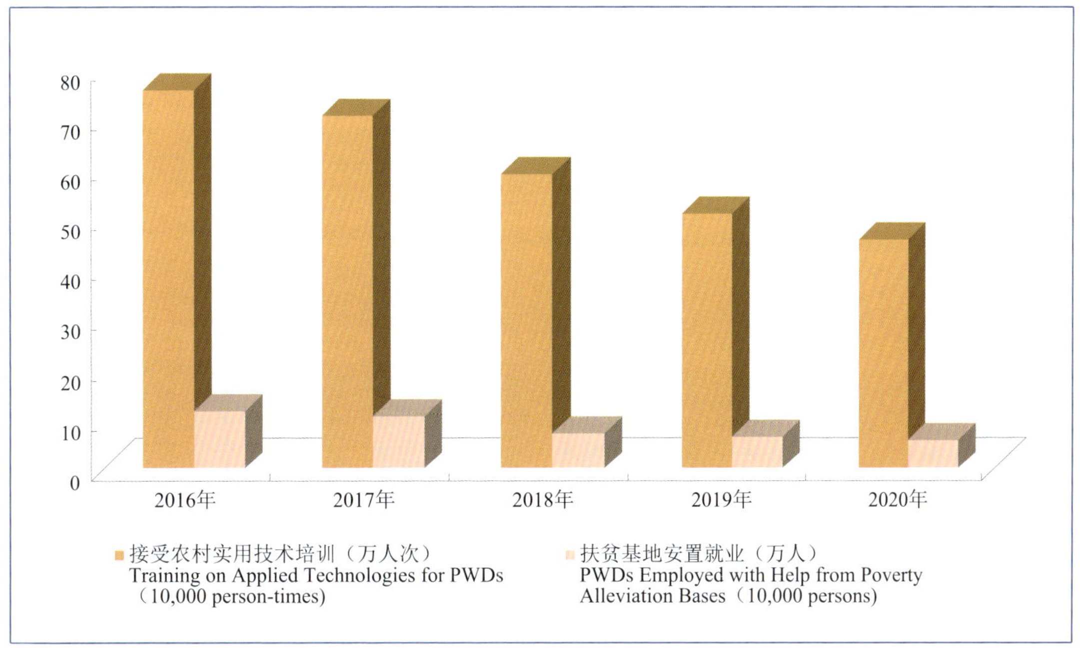

图-7 “十三五”期间残疾人接受托养服务情况

Chart7 Persons with Disabilities Receiving Fostering Service during 2016-2020

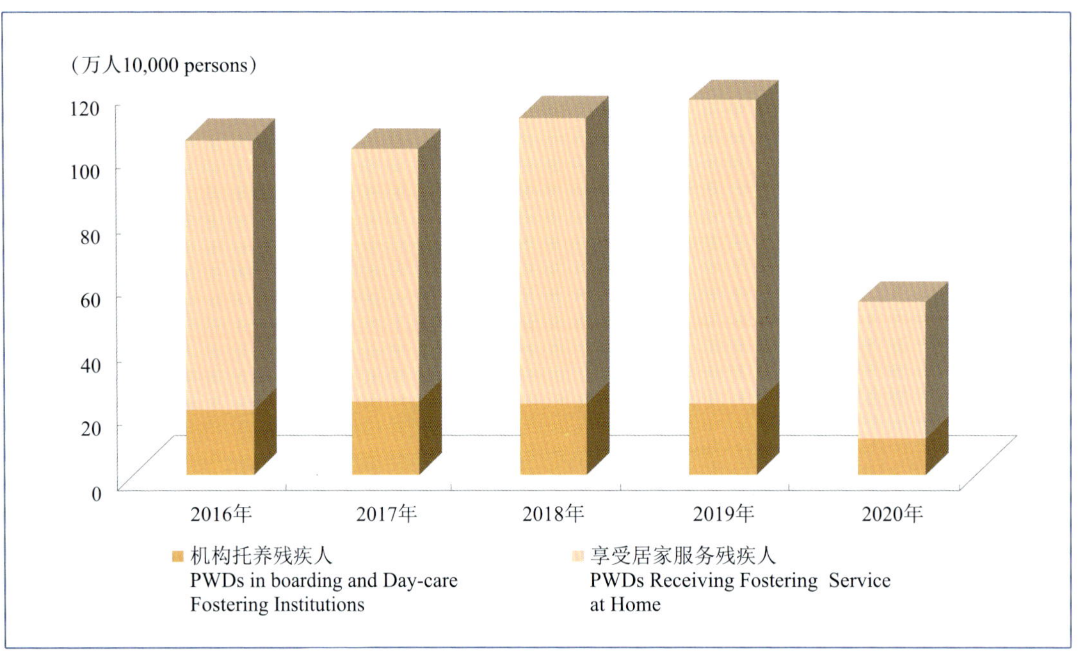

图-8 “十三五”期间省、市级电视手语栏目播出情况

Chart 8 Sign Language Displayed in Provincial and Municipal TV Programs during 2016- 2020

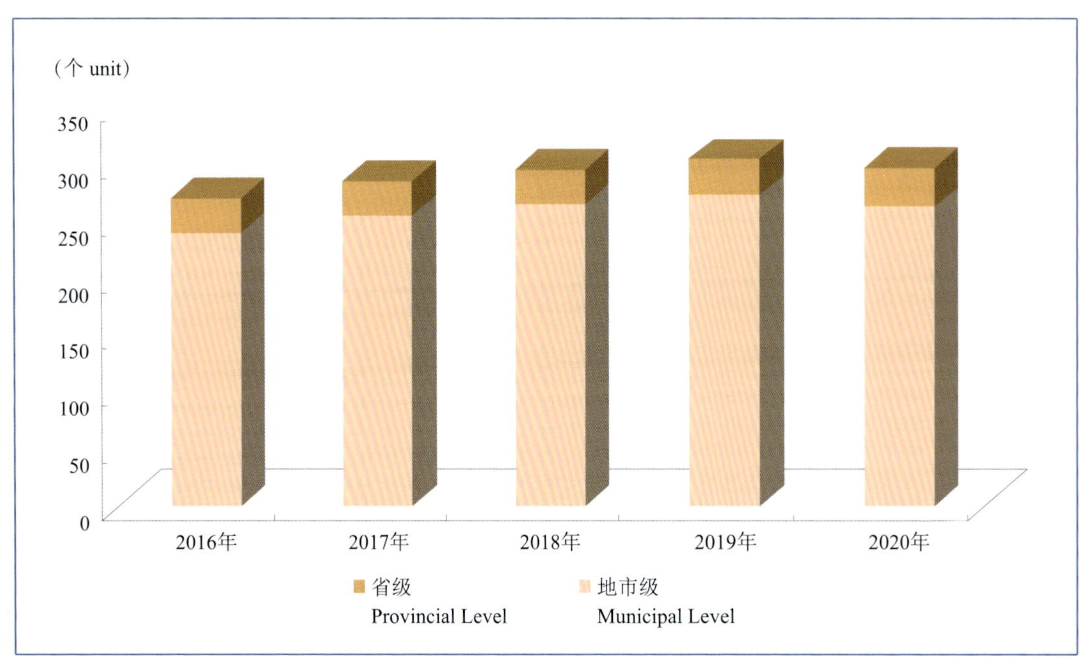

图-9 “十三五”期间系统开展无障碍环境建设地市、县

Chart 9 Accessible Environments Building in Cities and Counties during 2016-2020

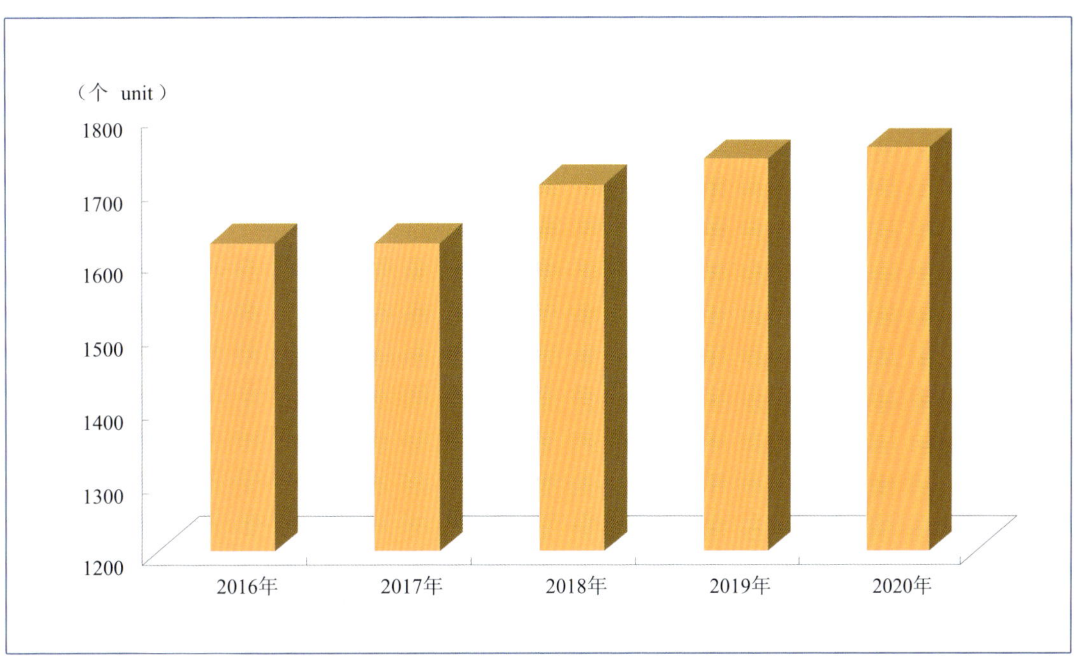

图-10 “十三五”期间残疾人专职委员选聘情况

Chart 10 Appointment of Commissioners for Disability Issuses at Grass-roots during 2016-2020

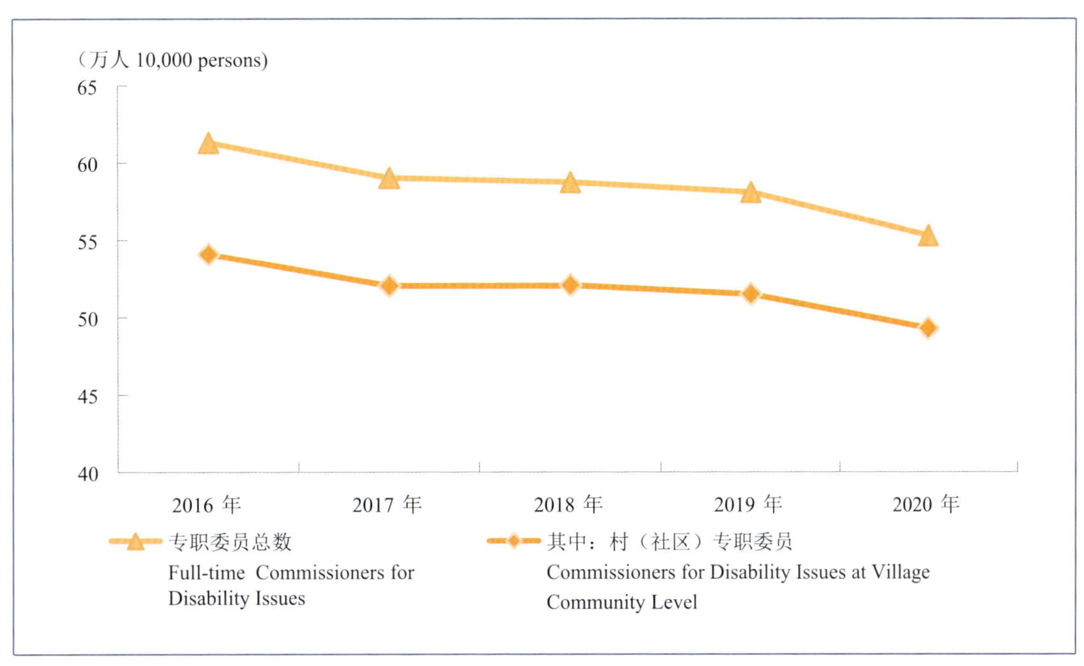

图-11 2020年残疾人服务设施建设情况

Chart 11 Development of Service Facilities for Persons with Disabilities in 2020

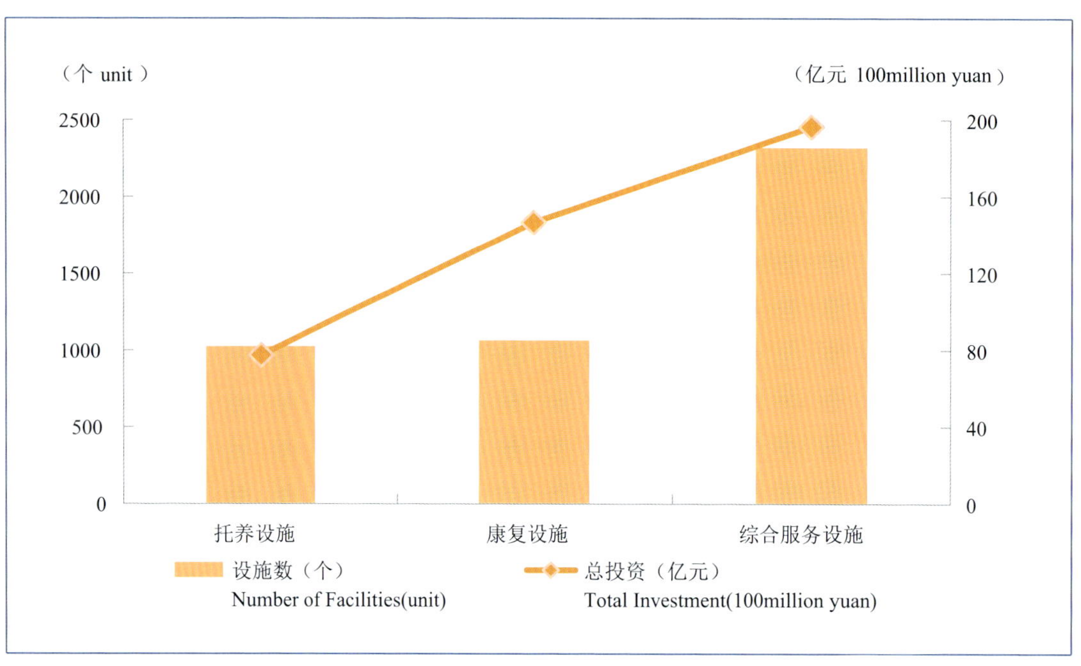

图-12 "十三五"期间残疾人持证情况

Chart 12 Persons with Disabilities holding certificates during 2016-2020

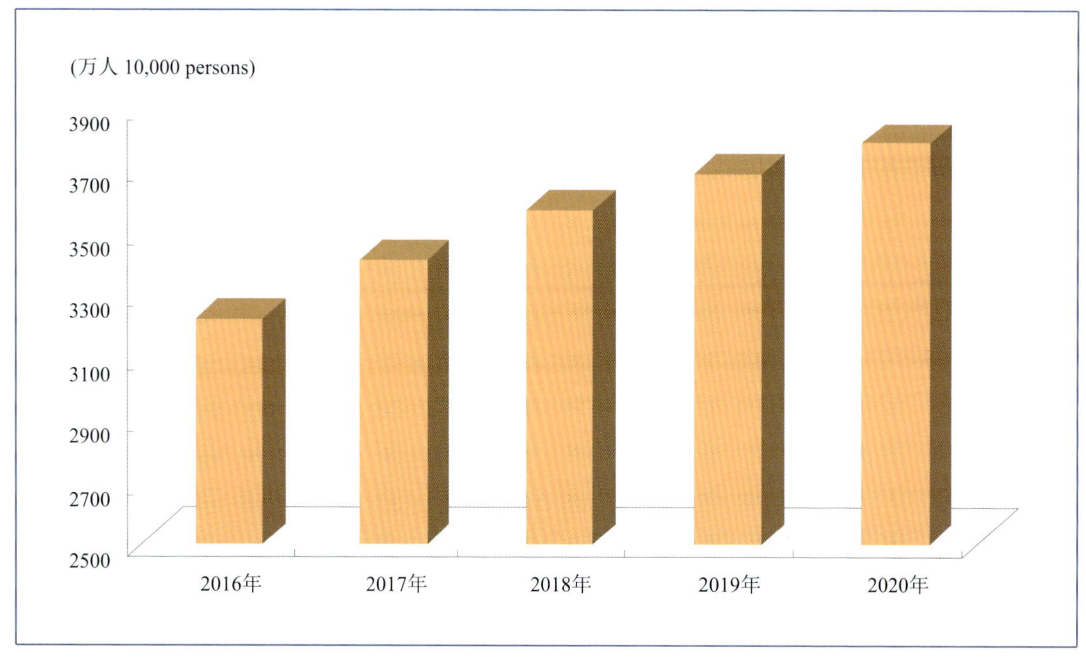

统计公报

Statistical Communique

2020年残疾人事业发展统计公报

2020年，各级残联坚持以习近平新时代中国特色社会主义思想为指导，深入学习贯彻习近平总书记关于残疾人事业的重要论述和指示批示精神，全面贯彻党的十九大和十九届二中、三中、四中、五中全会精神，按照党中央、国务院决策部署，残疾人脱贫攻坚、全面小康和疫情防控等重点工作成绩显著，残疾人工作上了一个新台阶。

一、康复

2020年，全面落实《国务院关于建立残疾儿童康复救助制度的意见》，全国普遍建立残疾儿童康复救助工作体系和服务网络。以贫困残疾人为重点，持续组织实施残疾人精准康复服务行动，1077.7万持证残疾人及残疾儿童得到基本康复服务，其中0-6岁残疾儿童23.7万人。得到康复服务的持证残疾人中，有视力残疾人114.6万、听力残疾人81.6万、言语残疾人5.1万、肢体残疾人542.8万、智力残疾人86.4万、精神残疾人178.4万、多重残疾人54.7万。全年共为242.6万残疾人提供各类辅助器具。积极维护残疾人健康，保障贫困残疾人基本医疗。协调国家卫健委共同印发《关于进一步做好建档立卡贫困残疾人家庭医生签约服务工作的通知》，推进贫困残疾人家庭医生签约服务。

加强残疾人康复机构规范化建设，持续深化社区康复工作。与民政部、国家卫健委共同开展残疾儿童康复救助定点服务机构管理试点工作，制定出台《精神障碍社区康复服务规范》。开展全国残联系统康复人才实名制培训。截至2020年底，全国有残疾人康复机构10440个，其中残联系统康复机构2550个。康复机构在岗人员达29.5万人，其中，管理人员3.1万人，业务人员21.3万人，其他人员5.1万人。贯彻落实《国家残疾预防行动计划（2016-2020年）》，组织开展以“残疾预防，从儿童早期干预做起”为主题的第四次残疾预防日宣传教育活动。

二、教育

以普及适龄残疾儿童少年义务教育、推广国家通用手语和国家通用盲文为重点，进一步改善残疾人教育支持保障条件。配合教育部实现2020年底适龄残疾儿童少年义务教育入学率达到95%的目标。会同教育部修订《残疾人中等职业学校设置标准》，推动修订《普通高等学校招生体检工作指导意见》。《〈中华人民共和国国歌〉国家通用手语方案》作为语言文字规范发布实施。组织研制国家通用手语和国家通用盲文水平等级标准、手语翻译资格（水平）标准，研建国家通用盲文测试大纲和题库。实施残疾人事业专项彩票公益金助学项目，为1.5万名家庭经济困难残疾儿童享受普惠性学前教育提供资助，带动各地对5409名残疾儿童给予学前教育资助。

2020年，全国共有特殊教育普通高中（部、班）104个，在校生10173人，其中聋生6034人、盲生1491人、其他2648人。残疾人中等职业学校（班）147个，在校生17877人，毕业生4281人，毕业生中1461人获得职业资格证书。全国有13551名残疾人被普通高等院校录取，2253名残疾人进入高等特殊教育学院学习。

4.6万名残疾青壮年文盲接受了扫盲教育。

三、就业

2020年城乡持证残疾人新增就业38.1万人，其中，城镇新增就业13.2万人，农村新增就业24.9万人；城乡新增残疾人实名培训38.2万人。

全国城乡持证残疾人就业人数为861.7万人，其中按比例就业78.4万人，集中就业27.8万人，个体就业63.4万人，公益性岗位就业14.7万人，辅助性就业14.3万人，灵活就业（含社区、居家就业）238.8万人，从事农业种养加424.3万人。

全国共培训盲人保健按摩人员12761名、盲人医疗按摩人员7820名。现有保健按摩机构17313个，医疗按摩机构873个。621人获得盲人医疗按摩人员初级职务任职资格，138人获得中级职务任职资格。

四、社会保障

截至2020年底，残疾居民参加城乡社会养老保险人数2699.2万；680.1万60岁以下参保重度残疾人中，657.9万享受了参保个人缴费资助政策，占比

96.7%。303.7 万非重度残疾人享受了个人缴费资助政策。1140.5 万人领取养老金。

残疾人托养服务工作稳步推进，残疾人托养服务机构 8370 个，其中寄宿制托养服务机构 1945 个，日间照料机构 3615 个，综合性托养服务机构 1369 个，为 11.7 万残疾人提供了托养服务。42 万残疾人接受居家服务。3.6 万名托养服务管理和服务人员接受了各级各类专业培训。

五、扶贫开发

圆满完成贫困残疾人脱贫攻坚任务。全国有 45.7 万人次农村残疾人接受了实用技术培训，4158 名贫困残疾人获得康复扶贫贴息贷款扶持，4581 个残疾人扶贫基地安置 5.6 万名残疾人就业，辐射带动 9.6 万户残疾人家庭增收。

全国共完成 4.8 万户农村贫困残疾人家庭危房改造，投入资金 6.3 亿元，5.6 万名残疾人受益。

六、宣传文化

2020 年，以“助残脱贫・决胜小康”为主题，组织第三十次全国助残日活动，精心组织开展“决胜全面小康、决战脱贫攻坚”主题宣传活动，以“残疾人脱贫攻坚中的奋进力量”为题，在国务院新闻办公室举行残疾人脱贫攻坚基层代表中外记者见面会，开展第 15 届残疾人事业好新闻奖评选，发布全国助残日主题歌曲《一个也不能少》；全年组织记者采访 500 多人次，进行 60 多次专题新闻发布，拍摄制作发布《残疾人小康故事》视频纪录片，组织拍摄微视频 5 部。各大媒体大力宣传残疾人事业，新华社发表文章 288 篇，中央电视台播发新闻 80 条，《人民日报》发表文章 138 篇。“两微一端”关注、订阅人数 462 万人。截至 2020 年底，全国共有省级残疾人专题广播节目 25 个、电视手语栏目 34 个；地级残疾人专题广播节目 209 个、电视手语栏目 262 个。扶持地县级公共图书馆盲人阅览室建设，实施文化残疾人进家庭“五个一”项目。组织第二批“十三五”全国残疾人文创产业基地申报评选工作。截至 2020 年底，全国省地县三级公共图书馆共设立盲文及盲文有声读物阅览室 1258 个，共开展残疾人文化周活动 8000 多场次；全国省地两级残联艺术团 249 个。

七、体育

备战北京冬残奥会和东京残奥会，组织冬残奥 6 个项目 5 支队伍、夏残奥 14 个项目 17 支队伍开展训练，举办残奥单板滑雪、越野滑雪、亚洲杯比赛，参赛获得 30 枚金牌，参加 2020 年自行车、羽毛球国际赛事获得 17 枚金牌，经过努力，残疾人体育领域实现疫情“零感染”。全国新增设立社区残疾人健身示范点 1320 处，为 10.9 万户重度残疾人提供康复体育进家庭服务，培养残疾人社会体育指导员 1 万名，新增设立 13 个国家残疾人体育训练基地，开展健身周、特奥日、冰雪季活动。全国残疾人社区文体活动参与率由 2019 年的 14.6%上升至 2020 年的 17.8%。

八、维权

各级残联维权组织建设进一步加强，残疾人事业法律法规体系进一步完善，无障碍环境建设取得新突破，残疾人维权工作全面开展。

2020 年，制定或修改省级关于残疾人的专门法规、规章 4 个，地级 5 个；制定或修改保障残疾人权益的省级规范性文件 22 个，地级 64 个，县级 163 个。全国县级以上人大开展《中华人民共和国残疾人保障法》执法检查和专题调研 318 次；政协开展视察和专题调研 282 次。全国开展省级普法宣传教育活动 500 多次，近 40 万人参加；举办省级法律培训班 44 个，4800 多人参加。

截至 2020 年底，全国成立残疾人法律救助工作协调机构 2881 个，建立残疾人法律救助工作站 2795 个。

残疾人参政议政工作稳步开展，各地残联协助人大代表、政协委员提出议案、建议、提案 735 件，办理议案、建议、提案 1109 件。

无障碍环境建设法规、标准进一步完善。全国共出台了 674 个省、地、县级无障碍环境建设与管理法规、政府令和规范性文件；1753 个地市、县系统开展无障碍环境建设；全国开展无障碍环境建设检查 8000 多次，无障碍培训 5.6 万人次；2020 年度为 167.3 万残疾人家庭实施了无障碍改造，其中包括近 10 万贫困重度残疾人；为 34.1 万残疾人发放了残疾人机动轮椅车燃油补贴。

九、组织建设

2020 年，全国省地县乡（除新疆生产建设兵团外）共有残联 4 万个，各省（区、市）、市（地、州、盟）、县（市、区、旗）全部成立残联，96.4%的乡镇（街道）已建立残联；95.5%的社区（村）建立残协，共 53.9 万个。

地方各级残联工作人员10.8万人，乡镇（街道）残联、村（社区）残协专职委员总计55.3万人。全部省级残联、65.8%的地级残联配备了残疾人领导干部，48.7%的县级残联配备了残疾人干部。

地方各级残疾人专门协会1.5万个，其中省、地、县级各类专门协会已建比例分别为98.8%、97.1%和91.3%。全国助残社会组织3004个。

十、服务设施

残疾人服务设施建设得到全面发展。截至2020年底，全国已竣工的各级残疾人综合服务设施2318个，总建设规模612.3万平方米，总投资196.2亿元；已竣工各级残疾人康复设施1063个，总建设规模462.7万平方米，总投资146.4亿元；已竣工的各级残疾人托养服务设施1024个，总建设规模285.4万平方米，总投资77.3亿元。

十一、信息化建设

截至2020年底，全国31个省级、256个地级、760个县级残联开通网站，全国残疾人人口基础数据库入库持证残疾人3780.7万人。与公安部、民政部、教育部、人力资源社会保障部等部门建立共享机制，并向31个省、地级残联提供残疾人数据接口和数据推送服务。基于残疾人人口基础数据库，落实残联重点业务应用建设，推动“一网通办”。

Statistical Communique on the Development of the Work for Persons with Disabilities in 2020

In 2020, Disabled Persons' Federation (DPFs) at all levels, under the guidance of Xi Jinping Thought on Socialism with Chinese Characteristics for a New Era, studied and implemented the important statements, instructions and principles of President Xi Jinping on the work for persons with disabilities (PWDs), and fully implemented the guiding principles of the 19th National Congress of the Communist Party of China (CPC) and the second, third, fourth and fifth plenary sessions of the 19th CPC Central Committee. In accordance with the deployments of the CPC Central Committee and the State Council, DPFs at all levels focused on empowering PWDs to shake off poverty, live a well-off life, and prevent and contain the COVID-19 pandemic. So far, remarkable achievements have been made and the work related to PWDs has reached a new level.

I.Rehabilitation

In 2020, DPFs at all levels fully implemented the Opinion of the State Council on Establishing Rehabilitation Assistance System for Children with Disabilities and set up a nationwide working system and service network for providing rehabilitation assistance to children with disabilities. In the year, we focused on poverty-stricken PWDs and continued to organize and provide targeted rehabilitation services for them, with 10,777 thousand registered PWDs and children with disabilities receiving basic rehabilitation services. Among them, 237 thousand were children aged between 0 and 6 years. Of the registered PWDs who received rehabilitation services, there were 1,146 thousand with visual impairments, 816 thousand with hearing impairments, 51 thousand with speech impairments, 5,428 thousand with physical disabilities, 864 thousand with intellectual disabilities, 1,784 thousand with psycho-social disabilities, and 547 thousand with multiple disabilities. A total of 2,426 thousand PWDs were provided with various assistive devices throughout the year. We actively protected the health of PWDs, ensured that poor PWDs can get access to basic medical services. We collaborated with the National Health Commission and jointly issued the Notice on Further Improving Contracted Services of Family Doctors for Registered Poor Persons with Disabilities to advance relevant work.

In this year, China Disabled Persons' Federation (CDPF) strengthened the building of rehabilitation facilities for PWDs in accordance with relevant standards and continued enhancing community-based rehabilitation. In collaboration with the Ministry of Civil Affairs and the National Health Commission, CDPF carried out pilot work for the management of designated service agencies providing rehabilitation assistance for children with disabilities, formulated and issued the Code of Community-based Rehabilitation Services for Persons with Psycho-social Disabilities, and conducted training for rehabilitation professionals within DPFs at all levels. By the end of 2020, the number of rehabilitation institutions in China reached 10,440, including 2,550 affiliated to DPFs at all levels. Staff in those rehabilitation institutions reached 295 thousand, including 31 thousand administrative personnel, 213 thousand professional personnel, and 51 thousand other staff. In the year, CDPF implemented the National Disability Prevention Action Plan (2016-2020) and organized the publicity and educational activity themed "Disability Prevention, Starting from Early Childhood Intervention" for the Fourth Disability Prevention Day.

II.Education

We focused on popularizing compulsory education for school-age children and adolescents with disabilities and promoting the use of general sign language and braille, so as to further improve the educational conditions for PWDs. In cooperation with the Ministry of Education, we achieved the goal of enabling 95% of the school-age children and adolescents with disabilities to get access to compulsory education by the end of 2020, revised the Standards for the Establishment of Secondary Vocational Schools for PWDs, and promoted the revision of the Guiding Opinions on Physical Examination for Admission to Regular Institutions of Higher Education. The National Scheme of General Sign Language of the National Anthem of the People's Republic of China was issued and implemented as a standardized scheme. We developed the standards for certifying one's general sign language and braille level, as well as the standards for accrediting one's proficiency in sign language translation, and built national general braille test syllabus and test bank. We carried out a lottery-based student-assistance program for PWDs which provided financial support for 15 thousand children with disabilities from financially difficult families to receive inclusive preschool education, and mobilized provinces to provide pre-school education subsidies to 5,409 children with disabilities.

In 2020, there were 104 senior high schools (departments, classes) nationwide for special education, with a total of 10,173 students. Among them, 6,034 were deaf, 1,491 were blind, and 2,648 had other disabilities. There were 147 secondary vocational schools (classes) nationwide, with 17,877 students in school and 4,281 graduates. Among these graduates, 1,461 obtained vocational certificates. Throughout the country, 13,551 students with disabilities were admitted to regular higher education institutions and 2,253 entered special higher education institutions.

Altogether 46 thousand young adults with disabilities received literacy education.

III. Employment

In 2020, 381 thousand registered PWDs were newly employed, including 132 thousand in urban areas and 249 thousand in rural areas. In addition, 382 thousand PWDs received vocational training.

A total of 8,617 thousand registered PWDs were in employment, among whom 784 thousand were employed through the employment quota scheme, 278 thousand through concentrated employment, 634 thousand through self-employment, 147 thousand through welfare job posts, 143 thousand through supportive employment, 2,388 thousand through flexible employment (including community and household employment), and 4,243 thousand through agricultural planting, breeding and food processing.

Among persons with visual disabilities nationwide, 12,761 healthcare masseurs and 7,820 medical masseurs received professional training. The number of healthcare massage institutions reached 17,313, and medical massage institutions 873. As many as 621 masseurs obtained elementary professional qualification and 138 masseurs obtained intermediate qualification .

IV. Social Security

By the end of 2020, 26,992 thousand PWDs in rural and urban areas were covered by the pension scheme. Of the 6,801 thousand insured persons with severe disabilities under the age of 60, 6,579 thousand (accounting for 96.7% of the total) received government ' s subsidies in paying the pension premium. Another 3,037 thousand persons with slight or moderate disabilities were also fully or partially subsidized by the government to join in the pension scheme. Meanwhile, 11,405 thousand PWDs received their pensions.

The work of nursing care services for PWDs progressed steadily. By the end of 2020, China had 8,370 care centers serving 117 thousand PWDs. Among them, 1,945 were boarding institutions, 3,615 were daycare facilities, and 1,369 were comprehensive services institutions. 420 thousand PWDs received care services at home. Throughout the year, 36 thousand managerial and service personnel received professional trainings of different types.

V. Poverty Alleviation

In 2020, the task of poverty alleviation for impoverished PWDs was successfully fulfilled. 457 thousand PWDs in rural areas received practical technical training, 4,158 impoverished PWDs were granted interest-subsidized loans. A total of 4,581 poverty alleviation centers provided jobs to 56 thousand PWDs and created income sources for 96 thousand households with disabled members.

A total of 630 million yuan was invested to renovate dilapidated houses for 48 thousand households with PWDs in financial difficulties, to the benefit of 56 thousand persons with disabilities.

VI. Publicity and Cultural Activities

In 2020, we organized the 30th National Day of Persons with Disabilities with the theme of "Empowering Persons with Disabilities in Overcoming Poverty and Building a Moderately Prosperous Society", and carried out publicity activities themed "Achieving Moderate Prosperity in All Respects and Winning the Battle against Poverty". We also held a press conference featuring grassroots level representatives in poverty elimination for persons with disabilities at the Information Office of the State Council, which was themed "The Driving Force in Empowering PWDs to Overcome Poverty". The 15th Award for Good News on Disability Work was presented. The theme song for the National Day of Persons with Disabilities "No One Shall Be Left Behind" was released. Throughout the year, we invited journalists for more than 500 interviews, organized more than 60 news releases, produced and released the video documentary titled "PWDs in Achieving Moderate Prosperity", and made five micro videos. Major media vigorously publicized the cause for PWDs. Among them, Xinhua News Agency published 288 articles, CCTV broadcast 80 news articles, and People's Daily published 138 articles. The publications at Wechat, Microblog and CDPF APP were followed or subscribed by 4.62 million people. By the end of 2020, there were 25 broadcasting programs for PWDs and 34 sign language TV programs at the provincial level; 209 broadcasting programs for PWDs and 262 sign language TV programs at the prefectural level. In the year, we supported the construction of reading rooms for people with visual impairments in prefectural and county-level public libraries and implemented a project that brought cultural resources into families with disabled members. We organized the application evaluation of the second batch of the National Cultural & Creative Industrial Bases for PWDs during the 13th Five-year Plan period. By the end of 2020, 1,258 braille and audiobook reading rooms had been set up in the public libraries of provinces, prefectures and counties in China, and over 8,000 activities had been held during the cultural week of PWDs. There are 249 performing art troupes of PWDs in provincial and prefectural Disabled Persons' Federations.

VII. Sports

In preparations for Beijing 2022 Paralympic Winter Games and the 2020 Tokyo Paralympic Games, we organized five teams for the six events of the Paralympic Winter Games and 17 teams for the 14 events of the Paralympic Summer Games to conduct training. We hosted and won 30 gold medals in Paralympic snowboarding competition, cross country skiing competition and the Asian Cup, and obtained 17 gold medals from international bicycle and badminton competitions in 2020. Thanks to our efforts, no PWD was infected with the COVID-19 in sports. 1,320 new community fitness demonstration sites for PWDs were set up across the country, 109 thousand families with members with severe disabilities were provided to door with sports rehabilitation services, about 10,000 social sports instructors for PWDs were trained, 13 new national sports training bases for PWDs were built, and activities such as "Fitness Week", "Special Olympics Day" and "Ice and Snow Season" were organized. In the year, the ratio of PWDs nationwide participating in recreational and sports activities of the community rose from 14.6% in 2019 to 17.8% in 2020.

VIII. Rights Protection

DPFs at various levels continued to strengthen the rights protection of PWDs. The legal and regulatory system regarding disability affairs was further improved, new breakthroughs were made in building accessible environments, and the work on rights protection of PWDs was carried out in an all-round way.

In 2020, four provincial-level and five prefectural-level specific laws and regulations concerning PWDs were formulated or amended; 22 provincial-level, 64 prefectural-level and 163 county-level normative documents on rights protection of PWDs were formulated or amended. The People's Congresses at and above the county level carried out 318 inspections and specialized researches on the enforcement of the Law of the People's Republic of China on Protection of Persons with Disabilities. The People's Political Consultative Conferences at all levels carried out 282 inspections and specialized researches on disability issues. Moreover, over 500 events were held at the provincial level to publicize disability-related laws and regulations, attracting nearly 400 thousand participants, while 44 legal training sessions were organized at the provincial level for over 4,800 trainees.

By the end of 2020, 2,881 coordinating agencies and 2,795 workstations were established to render legal assistance to PWDs. The participation of PWDs in the deliberation and administration of state affairs has been steadily carried out. With assistance from DPFs, deputies of the People's Congresses and members of the People's Political Consultative Conferences submitted 735 and handled 1,109 motions and proposals. Legislation and standardization on building accessible environments were further improved. As many as 674 provincial-level, prefectural-level and county-level regulations, government decrees and normative documents on the construction and management of barrier-free environments were issued, and 1,753 prefectures, cities and counties were in the process of building accessible environments systematically. Over 8,000 accessibility inspections were carried out, and 56 thousand persons received accessibility-related training. The homes of 1,673 thousand households with PWDs were renovated to improve their accessibility, of which nearly 100 thousand were financially difficult families with severely disabled members. Meanwhile, 341 thousand PWDs received fuel subsidies for their motorized wheelchairs.

IX. Organizational Building

By the end of 2020, there were about 4,000 DPFs at provincial, prefectural, county and township levels (not including Xinjiang Production and Construction Corps), and all provinces (autonomous regions, municipalities), cities (prefectures) and counties (county-level cities and districts) had established DPFs; 96.4% of the townships (sub-districts) had DPFs; 95.5% of the communities (and villages) had disabled persons' associations, amounting to 539 thousand.

There were about 108 thousand staff in local DPFs at all levels, and 553 thousand people were designated as full-time disability commissioners in townships, sub-districts, villages and communities. All provincial and 65.8% of the prefectural DPFs had staff with disabilities and 48.7% of the county-level DPFs had staff with disabilities.

There were 15 thousand local specialized associations for/of PWDs at all levels, of which 98.8% were established at the provincial level, 97.1% at the prefectural level, and 91.3% at the county level. Meanwhile, there were 3,004 social organizations nationwide dedicated to assisting PWDs.

X. Service Facilities

Service facilities for PWDs saw extensive development. By the end of 2020, 2,318 comprehensive service facilities for PWDs had been completed nationwide, with a construction area of 6,123 thousand square meters and a total investment of 19.62 billion yuan. 1,063 rehabilitation facilities for PWDs had been completed, with a construction area of 4,627 thousand square meters and a total investment of 14.64 billion yuan. And there were 1,024 day care facilities for PWDs at various levels, with a construction area of 2,854 thousand square meters and an investment of 7.73 billion yuan.

XI. Application of Information Technology

By the end of 2020, 31 provincial-level, 256 prefectural-level and 760 county-level DPFs had established websites, and the National Basic Database of Disabled Population covered 37,807 thousand registered PWDs. CDPF has established a sharing mechanism with the Ministry of Public Security, the Ministry of Civil Affairs, the Ministry of Education, the Ministry of Human Resources and Social Security and other departments to provide 31 provincial DPFs and prefecture-level DPFs with PWDs' data interfaces and daily information access. Based on the basic database of PWDs, we have enhanced the development of applications for key business and promoted unified online service.

3

综合统计资料

Overall Statistics

3-1 中国残疾人事业主要业务进展情况 (2016－2020)

指 标 名 称		Item	
康 复		**Rehabilitation**	
1. 残疾人精准康复服务		**Provision of Targeted Rehabilitation Service**	
视力残疾人	(万人)	Visual Disability	(10,000 persons)
听力残疾人	(万人)	Hearing Disability	(10,000 persons)
言语残疾人	(万人)	Speech Disability	(10,000 persons)
肢体残疾人	(万人)	Physical Disability	(10,000 persons)
智力残疾人	(万人)	Intellectual Disability	(10,000 persons)
精神残疾人	(万人)	Mental Disability	(10,000 persons)
多重残疾人	(万人)	Multiple Disabilities	(10,000 persons)
2. 残疾人辅助器具供应服务		**Provision of Assistive Devices**	
辅助器具供应	(万人)	Assistive Devices Provided	(10,000 persons)
3. 康复机构建设		**Construction of Rehabilitation Institution**	
残疾人康复机构	(个)	Rehabilitation Institutions for PWDs	(unit)
康复机构在岗人员	(万人)	Staff of Rehabilitation Institutions	(10,000 persons)
4. 社区康复		**Community-Based Rehabilitation (CBR)**	
开展社区康复服务的县(市、区)*	(个)	Counties and Districts Providing CBR	(unit)
社区康复协调员	(万人)	CBR Coordinators	(10,000 persons)
教 育		**Education**	
1. 学前教育		**Pre-school Education**	
残疾人事业专项彩票公益金助学项目资助	(人)	Students Supported by Educational Projects Funded by Welfare Lottery Fund for PWDs	(person)
其他残疾儿童学前教育助学项目资助	(人)	Students supported by Other Pre-School Educational Projects for Disabled Children	(person)
2. 残疾人高级中等教育		**Senior Secondary Education for PWDs**	
特教普通高中	(个)	Special Education Senior High Schools	(unit)
特教普通高中在校学生	(人)	Students in Special Education Senior High Schools	(person)
中等职业教育机构	(个)	Secondary Vocational Schools	(unit)
中等职业教育在校学生	(人)	Students in Secondary Vocational Schools	(person)
3. 残疾人高等教育		**Higher Education for PWDs**	
高等特殊教育院校	(个)	Special Higher Education Institutions	(unit)
高等特殊教育院校录取残疾考生	(人)	Disable Students Admitted to Special Higher Education Institutions	(person)
普通高等院校录取残疾考生	(人)	Disable Students Admitted to Regular Higher Education Institutions	(person)
4. 扫盲教育	**(人)**	**Anti-Illiteracy Education**	**(person)**

注：*"开展社区康复服务的县(市、区)"包含正式行政区划单位和开发区、管委会等非正式行政区划，以及新疆兵团下属县级单位。
Counties (cities and districts) providing community rehabilitation service include formal administrative divisions and development zones, informal administrative divisions such as management committees, and county-level units subordinate to the Xinjiang Production and Construction Corps .

Summary on the Development of the Work for Persons with Disabilities (2016 – 2020)

2016–2020年完成情况 Implementation (2016-2020)				
2016	2017	2018	2019	2020
40.0	88.3	120.5	112.2	114.6
18.5	40.7	66.1	73.1	81.6
-	4.3	7.5	4.4	5.1
135.7	484.6	592.3	553.5	542.8
23.1	71.3	83.8	82.3	86.4
62.6	125.9	150.8	161.5	178.4
-	35.5	48.2	46.8	54.7
132.2	244.4	319.1	314.5	242.6
7858	8334	9036	9775	10440
22.3	24.6	25.0	26.4	29.5
2962	2988	2750	2731	2726
45.4	47.9	47.8	47.8	47.8
14412	18685	17216	15393	14694
2607	2971	4993	7489	5409
111	112	102	103	104
7686	8466	7666	8676	10173
118	132	133	145	147
11209	12968	19475	17319	17877
21	21	23	23	23
1942	1845	1873	2053	2253
9592	10818	11154	12362	13551
43408	42782	52462	36461	45755

3-1 续表 1

指 标 名 称		Item	
就 业		**Employment**	
1. 城乡持证残疾人就业状况		**Employment of PWDs in Urban and Rural Areas**	
按比例就业	(万人)	Employed through Quota Scheme	(10,000 persons)
集中就业	(万人)	Employed through PWDs-Oriented Post	(10,000 persons)
个体就业	(万人)	Self-Employed	(10,000 persons)
公益性岗位就业	(万人)	Employed through Welfare Post	(10,000 persons)
辅助性就业	(万人)	Assistive Employment	(10,000 persons)
灵活就业(含社区就业、居家就业)	(万人)	Flexible Employment	(10,000 persons)
从事农业种养加	(万人)	Engaged in Agricultural Planting, Husbandry and Processing	(10,000 persons)
2. 盲人按摩		**Massage by the Blind**	
按摩人员培训		Massage Training	
保健按摩人员	(人)	Training for Health-Care Masseurs	(person)
医疗按摩人员	(人)	Training for Therapeutical Masseurs	(person)
按摩机构		Institutions of Blind Massage	
医疗按摩机构	(个)	Therapeutical Massage Clinics	(unit)
保健按摩机构	(个)	Health-Care Massage Houses	(unit)
社会保障		**Social Security**	
1. 社会保险		**Social Insurance**	
残疾居民参加城乡社会养老保险	(万人)	PWDs Covered by Pension Scheme	(10,000 persons)
2. 托养服务		**Institutional Care Services**	
托养服务机构	(个)	Institutional Care Service Facilities	(unit)
托养残疾人	(万人)	PWDs Receiving Institutional Care Service	(10,000 persons)
扶 贫		**Poverty Alleviation**	
1. 实用技术培训	(万人次)	**Training on Practical Skills and Technologies for PWDs**	**(10,000 person-times)**
2. 残疾人扶贫资金落实情况		**Poverty Alleviation Fund for PWDs**	
贷款实际落实	(亿元)	Actual Implementation of The Loan	(100 million yuan)
项目贷款扶持贫困残疾人	(人)	Financially Difficult Disabled Persons Supported by Loans for Project	(person)
到户贷款扶持贫困残疾人	(人)	Financially Difficult Disabled Persons Supported by Loans to Households	(person)
3. 残疾人扶贫基地建设		**Poverty Alleviation Bases for PWDs in Rural Areas**	
残疾人扶贫基地	(个)	Poverty Alleviation Bases for PWDs	(unit)
安置残疾人就业	(万人)	PWDs Provided with Employment Opportunities	(10,000 persons)
扶持带动贫困残疾人	(万户)	Benefited PWDs with Financial Difficult	(10,000 households)
4. 农村贫困残疾人危房改造		**House Renovation for Financially Difficult PWDs in Rural Areas**	
危房改造	(万户)	Houses Renovated for PWDs	(10,000 households)
受益残疾人	(万人)	Benefited PWDs	(10,000 persons)
宣传文化		**Publicity and Cultural Activities**	
1. 宣传		**Publicity at Provincial and Municipal Level**	
省、市级广播电台残疾人专题节目	(个)	Radio Programs on Disability	(unit)

Continued 1

2016–2020年完成情况 Implementation(2016-2020)				
2016	2017	2018	2019	2020
66.9	72.7	81.3	74.9	78.4
29.3	30.2	33.1	29.1	27.8
63.9	70.6	71.4	64.2	63.4
7.9	9.0	13.1	14.4	14.7
13.9	14.4	14.8	14.3	14.3
262.9	272.6	254.6	228.2	238.8
451.2	472.5	480.1	430.1	424.2
18997	20796	19732	14678	12761
5267	7217	10160	7318	7820
1211	1255	1126	894	873
18605	19257	16776	13181	17313
2370.6	2614.7	2561.2	2630.7	2699.2
6740	7923	8435	9941	8370
104.2	101.1	111.1	116.2	53.7
75.6	70.6	58.8	50.9	45.7
6.6	4.1	3.1	1.8	1.4
8633	12155	6605	3451	2394
13866	9041	6720	2739	1764
7111	6692	5490	4662	4581
11.6	10.5	7.0	6.2	5.6
24.9	21.8	13.5	10.0	9.6
8.2	8.2	11.3	10.4	4.8
10.4	9.6	13.0	11.5	5.6
223	223	230	244	234

3−1 续表 2

指 标 名 称		Item	
省、市级电视手语栏目	(个)	TV Programmes with Sign Language	(unit)
2. 文化		**Cultural Activities at Provincial and Municipal Level**	
省、市级盲文及盲人有声读物阅览室	(个)	Reading Rooms with Braille and Audio Reading Materials	(unit)
省、市级残疾人文化周	(场次)	Cultural Week for PWDs	(session)
省、市级残疾人文化艺术类比赛及展览	(次)	Cultural or Artistic Competitions and Exhibitions for PWDs	(time)
体 育			
省、地市级残疾人体育健身示范点(累计)	(个)	**Sports Activity Demonstration Sites for PWDs**	**(unit)**
省、地市级残疾人社会体育指导员(累计)	(万人)	**Coaches for Fitness Activity for PWDs**	**(1,0000 persons)**
残疾人康复体育关爱家庭服务(累计)	(万户)	**Sports and Caring Family Services for PWDs**	**1,0000 households)**
维 权		**Rights Protection**	
1. 法规体系和政策文件		**Legal System**	
制定或修改关于残疾人的专门法规、规章	(个)	Disability-Specific Laws and Regulations Formulated or Amended	(unit)
制定或修改保障残疾人权益的规范性文件	(个)	Normative Documents on Rights of PWDs Formulated or Amended	(unit)
2. 执法检查		**Inspections on Law Enforcement**	
人大执法检查或专题调研	(次)	Inspections and Researches by People's Congresses	(time)
政协视察或专题调研	(次)	Inspections and Researches by Political Consultative Conferences	(time)
3. 法律救助		**Legal Aid**	
残疾人法律救助工作协调机构		Coordinating Agency for Legal Assistance Work for PWDs	(unit)
残疾人法律救助工作站	(个)	Legal Assistance Stations for PWDs	(unit)
4. 参政议政		**PWDs Participating in Administration and Discussion of State Affairs**	
协助人大代表、政协委员提出议案、建议、提案	(件)	Bills, Suggestions and Proposals Submitted with Assistance of Disabled Persons' Federations	(case)
办理人大、政协交办的议案、建议、提案	(件)	Suggestions and Proposals Handled by Disabled Persons' Federations	(case)
5. 无障碍环境建设		**Accessible Environments Building**	
无障碍环境建设与管理法规、政府令	(个)	Regulations and Decrees on Accessible Environments Building and Management	(unit)
残疾人家庭无障碍改造	(万人)	Accessibility Renovation for Homes of PWDs	(10,000 persons)
6. 残疾人机动轮椅车燃油补贴	**(万人)**	**Gas Subsidy for Motorized Wheelchairs of PWDs**	**(10,000 persons)**

Continued 2

2016-2020年完成情况 **Implementation (2016-2020)**				
2016	2017	2018	2019	2020
269	285	295	304	296
267	282	301	312	317
1002	1037	940	1072	1072
719	640	663	799	690
5433	7707	9080	9956	10675
6.8	9.5	11.4	12.0	12.5
8.9	22.2	27.4	32.4	43.4
19	21	24	21	9
285	217	228	255	249
392	290	294	293	318
370	267	280	229	282
1921	1987	1988	2201	2881
1670	1746	1814	2021	2795
956	753	833	733	735
988	993	1081	1113	1109
451	451	475	537	674
93.6	89.2	115.8	136.0	167.3
75.3	74.9	65.1	47.4	34.1

3-1 续表 3

指标名称		Item	
组织建设		**Organizational Structure**	
1. 省市县乡残联实有人员	**（万人）**	**Staff of Disabled Persons' Federations at Provincial, Municipal, County and Township Level**	**(10,000 persons)**
2. 市级残联		**Disabled Persons' Federations at Municipal Level**	
配备残疾人领导干部的残联	(个)	Disabled Persons' Federations Whose Leadership Include PWDs	(unit)
残疾人干部	(人)	Staff with Disability	(person)
3. 县级残联		**Disabled Persons' Federations at County Level**	
配备残疾人干部的残联	(个)	Disabled Persons' Federations Whose Leadership Include PWDs	(unit)
残疾人干部	(人)	Staff with Disability	(person)
4. 乡级残联与村级残疾人协会		**Disabled Persons' Federations in Township (Town, Sub-district) and Villages (Communities)**	
已建乡、镇、街道残联	(万个)	Disabled Persons' Federation Established	(10,000 units)
其中：已配专兼职理事长	(万人)	Disabled Persons' Federation with Full-Time (Part-Time) President	(10,000 persons)
已建村(社区)残疾人协会	(万个)	Associations of Disabled Persons Established in Villages (Communities)	(10,000 units)
选聘残疾人专职委员	(万人)	Full-time Commissioners for Disability Issues	(10,000 persons)
5. 省级以下各类专门协会		**Special Associations below Provincial Level**	
盲人协会	(个)	Associations of Persons with Visual Disability	(unit)
聋人协会	(个)	Associations of Persons with Hearing Disability	(unit)
肢残人协会	(个)	Associations of Persons with Physical Disability	(unit)
智力残疾人及亲友协会	(个)	Associations of Persons with Intellectual Disability and Their Relatives and Friends	(unit)
精神残疾人及亲友协会	(个)	Associations of Persons with Psychosocial Disability and Their Relatives and Friends	(unit)
智力残疾人及亲友协会和精神残疾人及亲友协会合一的协会	(个)	Joint Associations of Persons with Intellectual or Psychosocial Disability and Their Relatives and Friends	(unit)
残疾人服务设施建设		**Service Facilities for PWDs**	
1. 残疾人综合服务设施		**Comprehensive Service Facilities for PWDs**	
已竣工	(个)	Completed Projects	(unit)
总建设规模	(万平米)	Construction Area	(10,000 sq.m)
2. 残疾人康复设施		**Rehabilitation Service Facilities for PWDs**	
已竣工	(个)	Completed Projects	(unit)
总建设规模	(万平米)	Construction Area	(10,000 sq.m)
3. 残疾人托养设施		**Institutional Care Service Facilities for PWDs**	
已竣工	(个)	Completed Projects	(unit)
总建设规模	(万平米)	Construction Area	(10,000 sq.m)
信息化建设		**Application of IT**	
1. 残疾人人口基础库数据	**（万人）**	**Data of the National Basic Database of Persons with Disabilities**	**(10,000 persons)**
2. 省、市、县各级残联网站	**（个）**	**Websites at Provincial, Municipal, and County Levels**	**(unit)**

Continued 3

2016–2020年完成情况 Implementation (2016-2020)				
2016	2017	2018	2019	2020
11.3	11.3	11.1	11.1	10.8
235	229	236	240	223
409	418	429	432	491
1584	1572	1499	1450	1456
2180	2165	2195	2133	2313
4.0	4.0	3.9	3.8	3.7
2.4	2.4	2.1	2.1	1.9
58.4	58.6	54.9	54.0	53.9
61.3	59	58.7	58.1	55.3
3147	3145	3140	3018	3024
3133	3130	3121	3006	3013
3159	3155	3154	3035	3044
2986	3003	2991	2873	2870
2982	3003	2992	2868	2870
169	117	128	128	136
2294	2340	2364	2341	2318
504.7	533	578.3	584.5	612.3
762	833	914	1006	1063
213.4	261.4	344.9	414.2	462.7
566	649	791	887	1024
129.6	161.2	214.8	251.3	285.4
3219.4	3404	3566.2	3681.7	3780.7
1634	1504	1155	1051	1047

3-2 全国残疾人人口基础库主要数据
Statistics of the National Basic Information Database of Persons with Disabilities

单位：人 (截止时间：2020年12月31日) (person)

地 区	Region	已办理残疾人证 Registered Persons with Disabilities	0-14岁 Aged 0-14	15-59岁 Aged 15-59	60岁及以上 Aged 60 and above
全 国	**Nationwide**	**37806899**	**1109123**	**19925672**	**16772104**
北 京	Beijing	542181	7005	223929	311247
天 津	Tianjin	369010	4739	163791	200480
河 北	Hebei	1923862	54875	993271	875716
山 西	Shanxi	1012923	23169	552337	437417
内蒙古	Inner Mongolia	783049	15427	439041	328581
辽 宁	Liaoning	1095550	17481	617657	460412
吉 林	Jilin	867135	14809	497076	355250
黑龙江	Heilongjiang	1103374	15886	674209	413279
上 海	Shanghai	596550	3385	178642	414523
江 苏	Jiangsu	1698585	43609	886547	768429
浙 江	Zhejiang	1353086	28280	616308	708498
安 徽	Anhui	1953002	54930	1041435	856637
福 建	Fujian	867276	31869	433382	402025
江 西	Jiangxi	1222762	48718	741719	432325
山 东	Shandong	2586368	79095	1244319	1262954
河 南	Henan	2933993	101319	1491120	1341554
湖 北	Hubei	1635095	35865	909753	689477
湖 南	Hunan	1952089	57795	1064913	829381
广 东	Guangdong	1716984	86108	928884	701992
广 西	Guangxi	1451184	57906	716767	676511
海 南	Hainan	196588	9023	116757	70808
重 庆	Chongqing	905030	27490	502621	374919
四 川	Sichuan	2839152	72621	1417145	1349386
贵 州	Guizhou	1321343	50167	759213	511963
云 南	Yunnan	1499626	49357	869076	581193
西 藏	Tibet	109881	9172	69175	31534
陕 西	Shaanxi	1381697	24546	645126	712025
甘 肃	Gansu	893343	27624	502357	363362
青 海	Qinghai	180002	9071	110889	60042
宁 夏	Ningxia	230570	7617	128913	94040
新 疆	Xinjiang	519918	38557	341742	139619
新疆兵团	Xinjiang Production and Construction Corps	65691	1608	47558	16525

3−2 续表 1 Continued 1

单位：人 (person)

地 区	Region	已办理证件残疾人 Registered Persons with Disabilities					
		性 别 Gender		残疾等级 Disability Grading			
		男 性 Male	女 性 Female	残疾一级 Grade-1	残疾二级 Grade-2	残疾三级 Grade-3	残疾四级 Grade-4
全 国	**Nationwide**	**21923008**	**15883891**	**4925371**	**11625057**	**9720761**	**11535710**
北 京	Beijing	289335	252846	66221	117036	133583	225341
天 津	Tianjin	200251	168759	36926	108507	103844	119733
河 北	Hebei	1113028	810834	245281	592422	428441	657718
山 西	Shanxi	617158	395765	131768	302044	243566	335545
内蒙古	Inner Mongolia	457454	325595	81297	231942	217927	251883
辽 宁	Liaoning	667525	428025	135055	333986	304052	322457
吉 林	Jilin	519363	347772	96037	283543	245114	242441
黑龙江	Heilongjiang	675141	428233	125695	311957	317952	347770
上 海	Shanghai	301684	294866	80168	112287	144132	259963
江 苏	Jiangsu	933450	765135	208324	551561	495969	442731
浙 江	Zhejiang	778184	574902	178593	273846	405804	494843
安 徽	Anhui	1095722	857280	223723	814187	488856	426236
福 建	Fujian	503374	363902	142942	284533	198736	241065
江 西	Jiangxi	739291	483471	128670	363161	335198	395733
山 东	Shandong	1516238	1070130	370959	881922	633778	699709
河 南	Henan	1667118	1266875	341669	1019472	768108	804744
湖 北	Hubei	954913	680182	238104	572282	390260	434449
湖 南	Hunan	1175876	776213	242546	728752	433960	546831
广 东	Guangdong	995193	721791	299221	653684	394942	369137
广 西	Guangxi	821007	630177	187916	437046	330356	495866
海 南	Hainan	115115	81473	66761	48495	44177	37155
重 庆	Chongqing	540889	364141	102071	255610	229288	318061
四 川	Sichuan	1644446	1194706	383572	831757	712446	911377
贵 州	Guizhou	810020	511323	159124	261817	330533	569869
云 南	Yunnan	880835	618791	184314	350581	348394	616337
西 藏	Tibet	56276	53605	13470	22750	27687	45974
陕 西	Shaanxi	775252	606445	168297	322642	512838	377920
甘 肃	Gansu	506268	387075	158084	252790	231983	250486
青 海	Qinghai	99923	80079	26255	60441	46287	47019
宁 夏	Ningxia	126979	103591	27607	81981	56365	64617
新 疆	Xinjiang	306525	213393	67656	143465	148301	160496
新疆兵团	Xinjiang Production and Construction Corps	39175	26516	7045	18558	17884	22204

3-2 续表 2 Continued 2

单位：人 (person)

地区	Region	已办理证件残疾人 Registered Persons with Disabilities				
		残疾类别 Disability Category				
		视力残疾人 Persons with Visual Disability	听力残疾人 Persons with Hearing Disability	言语残疾人 Persons with Speech Disability	肢体残疾人 Persons with Physical Disability	智力残疾人 Persons with Intellectual Disability
全国	**Nationwide**	**4189456**	**3200358**	**618150**	**20459869**	**3368959**
北京	Beijing	57719	42642	3164	305753	50488
天津	Tianjin	30285	27041	4362	241772	30333
河北	Hebei	170807	139729	33944	1164781	171733
山西	Shanxi	106890	96574	21451	577689	95787
内蒙古	Inner Mongolia	79334	73853	13865	437310	67976
辽宁	Liaoning	113378	88522	10906	603775	117572
吉林	Jilin	93410	78672	13459	481778	78515
黑龙江	Heilongjiang	114469	90527	13789	656877	96069
上海	Shanghai	96497	80482	5492	288189	57708
江苏	Jiangsu	200438	112882	9017	907795	216137
浙江	Zhejiang	132371	211753	17132	632274	132986
安徽	Anhui	211618	132335	29345	1007878	182788
福建	Fujian	87227	118679	12003	402610	95534
江西	Jiangxi	129657	89911	18170	634004	120969
山东	Shandong	194285	188650	25466	1531962	229078
河南	Henan	276993	231025	68553	1700324	292302
湖北	Hubei	214038	130020	36682	796063	136651
湖南	Hunan	246920	133763	37175	1010310	174598
广东	Guangdong	141812	155351	29587	780443	184933
广西	Guangxi	165127	110897	26349	766997	115138
海南	Hainan	18442	13853	3298	98836	19067
重庆	Chongqing	135117	63003	15183	474581	83679
四川	Sichuan	422573	236283	45069	1564362	195625
贵州	Guizhou	151962	84959	31814	797615	79568
云南	Yunnan	187962	126033	32312	828016	93052
西藏	Tibet	17760	12796	5191	55179	2991
陕西	Shaanxi	164206	135437	23372	732220	89285
甘肃	Gansu	96631	88837	12407	472956	74854
青海	Qinghai	23815	24820	3710	93738	15963
宁夏	Ningxia	29331	24563	3919	122154	19966
新疆	Xinjiang	70236	51589	11180	258497	41026
新疆兵团	Xinjiang Production and Construction Corps	8146	4877	784	33131	6588

3-2 续表 3 Continued 3

单位：人 (person)

地 区	Region	已办理证件残疾人 Registered Persons with Disabilities			
		残疾类别 Disability Category		户口性质 Registered Permanent Residence	
		精神残疾人 Persons with Mental Disability	多重残疾人 Persons with Multiple Disabilities	农业 Rural	非农业 Urban
全 国	**Nationwide**	**4036805**	**1933302**	**29985629**	**7821270**
北 京	Beijing	53576	28839	207414	334767
天 津	Tianjin	27205	8012	136751	232259
河 北	Hebei	134662	108206	1669805	254057
山 西	Shanxi	69856	44676	816860	196063
内蒙古	Inner Mongolia	71100	39611	537800	245249
辽 宁	Liaoning	117744	43653	619212	476338
吉 林	Jilin	87024	34277	509332	357803
黑龙江	Heilongjiang	96609	35034	577661	525713
上 海	Shanghai	54145	14037	96685	499865
江 苏	Jiangsu	195200	57116	1328042	370543
浙 江	Zhejiang	168309	58261	1081197	271889
安 徽	Anhui	263613	125425	1666370	286632
福 建	Fujian	101743	49480	727532	139744
江 西	Jiangxi	161524	68527	990841	231921
山 东	Shandong	271334	145593	2282938	303430
河 南	Henan	251324	113472	2632449	301544
湖 北	Hubei	225537	96104	1328158	306937
湖 南	Hunan	247833	101490	1686349	265740
广 东	Guangdong	318558	106300	1294718	422266
广 西	Guangxi	183284	83392	1316452	134732
海 南	Hainan	34448	8644	147441	49147
重 庆	Chongqing	96852	36615	681176	223854
四 川	Sichuan	264746	110494	2393203	445949
贵 州	Guizhou	89626	85799	1189653	131690
云 南	Yunnan	157571	74680	1329856	169770
西 藏	Tibet	6294	9670	101440	8441
陕 西	Shaanxi	135111	102066	1206611	175086
甘 肃	Gansu	74825	72833	765098	128245
青 海	Qinghai	6218	11738	141979	38023
宁 夏	Ningxia	17885	12752	162142	68428
新 疆	Xinjiang	43965	43425	358495	161423
新疆兵团	Xinjiang Production and Construction Corps	9084	3081	1969	63722

3-2 续表 4 Continued 4

单位：人 (person)

地区	Region	已办理证件残疾人 Registered Persons with Disabilities 受教育程度 Education 文盲 Illiterate	小学 Primary School	初中 Junior High School	高中及中专 Senior High or Vocational School	大学专科及以上 Junior College and Above	其他 Others
全国	**Nationwide**	**7075436**	**14989785**	**11256656**	**3141812**	**697821**	**645389**
北京	Beijing	56496	93011	210750	120896	53875	7153
天津	Tianjin	31839	85563	147079	77402	24387	2740
河北	Hebei	238407	785938	664544	161103	30915	42955
山西	Shanxi	128197	347119	406980	95143	20667	14817
内蒙古	Inner Mongolia	129672	283709	264286	79452	17885	8045
辽宁	Liaoning	111551	347152	484989	114667	26976	10215
吉林	Jilin	98636	279919	344390	122210	16781	5199
黑龙江	Heilongjiang	89083	378250	465164	135143	24420	11314
上海	Shanghai	46173	117491	249493	136451	46941	1
江苏	Jiangsu	538872	528920	463133	131955	35633	72
浙江	Zhejiang	267715	606263	350294	81559	25501	21754
安徽	Anhui	584065	759569	466327	92080	23849	27112
福建	Fujian	151399	410439	208607	57777	12201	26853
江西	Jiangxi	158481	529811	387874	91610	14817	40169
山东	Shandong	514768	960340	796896	219469	36283	58612
河南	Henan	786630	1006958	844286	205292	33860	56967
湖北	Hubei	339091	540764	527154	177844	29158	21084
湖南	Hunan	253820	848262	599819	195492	23341	31355
广东	Guangdong	247987	722947	502710	144017	30738	68585
广西	Guangxi	171921	733071	398409	81870	13796	52117
海南	Hainan	36088	62626	71808	19118	3077	3871
重庆	Chongqing	92356	463482	256011	58234	12366	22581
四川	Sichuan	452118	1489753	690349	144958	32100	29874
贵州	Guizhou	381984	580355	280334	49620	15888	13162
云南	Yunnan	389464	723055	279871	66291	22377	18568
西藏	Tibet	63537	37525	5020	1329	809	1661
陕西	Shaanxi	271167	514703	443406	119586	21174	11661
甘肃	Gansu	275202	343666	187559	65660	13442	7814
青海	Qinghai	45538	89354	27596	11222	3816	2476
宁夏	Ningxia	57944	84882	58921	18840	6894	3089
新疆	Xinjiang	60598	216825	146196	53988	20023	22288
新疆兵团	Xinjiang Production and Construction Corps	4637	18063	26401	11534	3831	1225

4

分省统计资料

Provincial Statistics

一、康复
Rehabilitation

4−1−1 社区康复
Community-Based Rehabilitation(CBR)

地 区	Region	开展社区康复服务的市辖区* Districts Delivering CBR Services	开展社区康复服务的县(市)* Counties Delivering CBR Services	社区康复协调员 CBR Coordinators
		个 unit	个 unit	人 person
全 国	**Nationwide**	**1014**	**1712**	**477532**
北 京	Beijing	16		5961
天 津	Tianjin	16		4141
河 北	Hebei	49	107	45540
山 西	Shanxi	24	87	23703
内蒙古	Inner Mongolia	25	83	12262
辽 宁	Liaoning	67	42	14345
吉 林	Jilin	33	39	10957
黑龙江	Heilongjiang	58	67	6726
上 海	Shanghai	16		4882
江 苏	Jiangsu	62	37	19581
浙 江	Zhejiang	43	52	23454
安 徽	Anhui	51	60	17402
福 建	Fujian	29	57	14444
江 西	Jiangxi	36	73	13537
山 东	Shandong	62	71	45748
河 南	Henan	62	103	47176
湖 北	Hubei	43	57	10158
湖 南	Hunan	36	75	24888
广 东	Guangdong	71	57	24286
广 西	Guangxi	35	55	14296
海 南	Hainan	4	9	2194
重 庆	Chongqing	29	12	11372
四 川	Sichuan	43	101	20260
贵 州	Guizhou	10	80	10235
云 南	Yunnan	14	90	13123
西 藏	Tibet	4	10	758
陕 西	Shaanxi	32	79	14317
甘 肃	Gansu	17	69	12828
青 海	Qinghai	7	38	2874
宁 夏	Ningxia	8	13	2341
新 疆	Xinjiang	12	84	3182
新疆兵团	Xinjiang Production and Construction Corps		5	561

注：*“开展社区康复服务的县(市、区)”包含正式行政区划单位和开发区、管委会等非正式行政区划，以及新疆兵团下属县级单位。

The data in "Counties Delivering CBR Services" covered formal administrative units and informal administrative units such as development zones, as well as county-level units under the jurisdiction of Xinjiang Production and Construction Corps .

4-1-2 残疾人接受基本康复服务总体情况
Basic Rehabilitation Services Received by Persons with Disabilities

地 区	Region	合 计 Total	其中：0-6岁残疾儿童 Disabled Children Aged 0-6	视力残疾 Persons with Visual Disability	听力残疾 Persons with Hearing Disability	言语残疾 Persons with Speech Disability	肢体残疾 Persons with Physical Disability
		人 person	人 person	人 person	人 person	人 person	人 person
全 国	**Nationwide**	**10776506**	**237253**	**1146128**	**815856**	**51030**	**5428217**
北 京	Beijing	330394	1784	34805	29070	1277	179941
天 津	Tianjin	46309	1869	3215	2946	141	26934
河 北	Hebei	266186	7722	17809	15095	1807	157963
山 西	Shanxi	139403	5175	9092	9337	110	81714
内蒙古	Inner Mongolia	69701	2748	4954	5664	263	38802
辽 宁	Liaoning	177239	4550	17929	10744	573	86582
吉 林	Jilin	147041	2651	12616	9461	317	83992
黑龙江	Heilongjiang	105950	2496	9526	5068	72	63861
上 海	Shanghai	166895	1606	28825	18996	1150	83629
江 苏	Jiangsu	277075	21122	22622	9981	123	114041
浙 江	Zhejiang	640858	8322	59686	82075	8255	189889
安 徽	Anhui	488078	12742	36846	22505	2222	185097
福 建	Fujian	286181	13874	15192	28615	404	120519
江 西	Jiangxi	199934	6551	17595	11331	170	90073
山 东	Shandong	1219592	19002	89599	76124	9965	729604
河 南	Henan	405181	24471	32676	29126	1306	238498
湖 北	Hubei	449303	11567	50474	29862	2980	198727
湖 南	Hunan	350110	13888	42184	20650	940	168388
广 东	Guangdong	343930	16830	16129	19405	3116	101573
广 西	Guangxi	209031	9515	18052	12229	303	102462
海 南	Hainan	40146	2127	1983	1649	83	11399
重 庆	Chongqing	283731	4897	37150	16380	1179	124074
四 川	Sichuan	2719672	14995	411309	227467	306	1521706
贵 州	Guizhou	251815	5122	28859	14869	3334	148891
云 南	Yunnan	254086	4086	25550	19981	1703	114669
西 藏	Tibet	12890	324	1635	1778	330	7279
陕 西	Shaanxi	534398	6747	58902	49042	7107	275153
甘 肃	Gansu	127675	3711	13427	13244	292	64200
青 海	Qinghai	58256	1355	7298	7760	791	32528
宁 夏	Ningxia	61144	1677	7416	6007	223	30121
新 疆	Xinjiang	104133	3591	12122	8778	183	52513
新疆兵团	Xinjiang Production and Construction Corps	10169	136	651	617	5	3395

4-1-2 续表 Continued

地 区	Region	智力残疾 Persons with Intellectual Disability	精神残疾 Persons with Mental Disability	多重残疾 Persons with Multiple Disabilities	0-17岁未持证残疾儿 Unregistered Disabled Children Aged 0-17
		人 person	人 person	人 person	人 person
全 国	**Nationwide**	**863966**	**1784257**	**546948**	**140104**
北 京	Beijing	28285	36869	19920	227
天 津	Tianjin	3169	6589	1525	1790
河 北	Hebei	15251	37636	15925	4700
山 西	Shanxi	9701	19578	6536	3335
内蒙古	Inner Mongolia	2870	11664	3781	1703
辽 宁	Liaoning	14484	32220	11357	3350
吉 林	Jilin	10586	21998	6348	1723
黑龙江	Heilongjiang	9104	12575	3831	1913
上 海	Shanghai	12081	15405	4581	2228
江 苏	Jiangsu	24618	77608	7823	20259
浙 江	Zhejiang	108803	145625	43566	2959
安 徽	Anhui	33463	170613	30511	6821
福 建	Fujian	32882	63303	14734	10532
江 西	Jiangxi	13732	53371	11202	2460
山 东	Shandong	114185	140397	54486	5232
河 南	Henan	28752	41098	16822	16903
湖 北	Hubei	35538	100803	22242	8677
湖 南	Hunan	19234	72821	16429	9464
广 东	Guangdong	28247	146788	21363	7309
广 西	Guangxi	17647	39767	12693	5878
海 南	Hainan	1965	20371	1623	1073
重 庆	Chongqing	21847	67408	12713	2980
四 川	Sichuan	189730	256066	107892	5196
贵 州	Guizhou	14101	19600	20015	2146
云 南	Yunnan	15597	59352	15792	1442
西 藏	Tibet	116	287	1460	5
陕 西	Shaanxi	34128	71497	32803	5766
甘 肃	Gansu	9078	13838	11245	2351
青 海	Qinghai	4036	2117	3316	410
宁 夏	Ningxia	3905	8866	3746	860
新 疆	Xinjiang	6232	13785	10127	393
新疆兵团	Xinjiang Production and Construction Corps	599	4342	541	19

4-1-3 辅助器具适配服务
Provision of Assistive Devices

地　区	Region	接受辅助器具适配服务的残疾人 Persons with Disablities Fitted with Assistive Devices	接受盲杖及助视器适配服务 Persons with Disablities Fitted with Tactile Sticks and Visual Aids	接受人工耳蜗及助听器适配服务 Persons with Disablities Fitted with Cochlears and Hearing Aids	接受假肢、矫形器、轮椅等主要肢体残疾辅助器具适配服务 Persons with Disablities Fitted with Prosthetics, Orthotics, Wheelchairs, and Other Mobility Aids	接受其他各类辅助器具适配服务 Persons with Disablities Fitted with Other Assistive Devices
		人 person	人 person	人 person	人 person	人 person
全　国	**Nationwide**	**2426176**	**323148**	**323737**	**1700296**	**89762**
北　京	Beijing	51442	1789	16661	27000	6094
天　津	Tianjin	16198	1076	1141	13902	92
河　北	Hebei	74374	6311	7187	60854	66
山　西	Shanxi	64421	5898	7343	51026	196
内蒙古	Inner Mongolia	37893	3542	5445	28914	13
辽　宁	Liaoning	39848	6305	2853	29729	999
吉　林	Jilin	44804	5187	4637	34949	50
黑龙江	Heilongjiang	35284	4437	3136	27706	7
上　海	Shanghai	70873	15014	8492	45807	1580
江　苏	Jiangsu	72952	9405	3821	59704	71
浙　江	Zhejiang	69697	11135	23096	35221	369
安　徽	Anhui	93213	12692	6946	73338	323
福　建	Fujian	56977	4269	18463	32638	1697
江　西	Jiangxi	68298	10436	6597	51244	80
山　东	Shandong	252214	27342	21308	176027	27804
河　南	Henan	148941	13630	15098	118056	2238
湖　北	Hubei	99195	17314	12325	69468	163
湖　南	Hunan	168174	29670	17656	120835	100
广　东	Guangdong	57054	5704	10731	40153	548
广　西	Guangxi	69996	5802	6311	49953	7998
海　南	Hainan	6826	808	1011	5009	2
重　庆	Chongqing	49090	7546	4957	36565	61
四　川	Sichuan	317264	60107	31785	228754	450
贵　州	Guizhou	75591	10614	7748	56759	575
云　南	Yunnan	52784	6880	9205	36640	133
西　藏	Tibet	10741	1325	2076	7162	222
陕　西	Shaanxi	182595	18924	43382	88181	37126
甘　肃	Gansu	48328	5852	9044	33227	299
青　海	Qinghai	28245	3876	5306	19100	66
宁　夏	Ningxia	21518	3050	3805	14389	321
新　疆	Xinjiang	38177	6782	5608	25803	18
新疆兵团	Xinjiang Production and Construction Corps	3169	426	563	2183	1

4-1-4 康复机构
Rehabilitation Institutions

地区	Region	残疾人康复机构 Rehabilitation Institutions for Persons with Disabilities	各类康复机构 Specialized Rehabilitation Institutions		
			视力残疾康复机构 Rehabilitation Institution for Visual Disabilities	听力言语残疾康复机构 Rehabilitation Institutions for Hearing and Speech Disabilities	肢体残疾康复机构 Rehabilitation Institutions for Physical Disabilities
		个 unit	个 unit	个 unit	个 unit
全国	**Nationwide**	**10440**	**1457**	**1819**	**4749**
北京	Beijing	151	8	27	48
天津	Tianjin	95	13	8	19
河北	Hebei	444	52	92	216
山西	Shanxi	317	33	43	156
内蒙古	Inner Mongolia	272	64	77	156
辽宁	Liaoning	416	59	53	197
吉林	Jilin	286	59	25	158
黑龙江	Heilongjiang	279	47	37	175
上海	Shanghai	1083	100	66	326
江苏	Jiangsu	473	97	83	170
浙江	Zhejiang	252	17	50	102
安徽	Anhui	295	13	75	109
福建	Fujian	350	23	69	107
江西	Jiangxi	293	21	71	115
山东	Shandong	870	68	91	503
河南	Henan	498	65	151	286
湖北	Hubei	254	10	38	95
湖南	Hunan	444	53	81	119
广东	Guangdong	859	158	158	382
广西	Guangxi	416	68	76	238
海南	Hainan	42	1	9	13
重庆	Chongqing	305	73	62	113
四川	Sichuan	320	46	63	162
贵州	Guizhou	257	66	57	108
云南	Yunnan	297	59	78	119
西藏	Tibet	11	1	1	5
陕西	Shaanxi	342	59	45	217
甘肃	Gansu	208	65	63	114
青海	Qinghai	59	12	15	43
宁夏	Ningxia	42	8	12	34
新疆	Xinjiang	176	23	26	116
新疆兵团	Xinjiang Production and Construction Corps	34	16	17	28

4−1−4 续表 Continued

地 区	Region	各类康复机构 Specialized Rehabilitation Institutions			
		智力残疾康复机构 Rehabilitation Institutions for Intellectual Disabilities	精神残疾康复机构 Rehabilitation Institutions for Mental Disabilities	孤独症儿童康复机构 Rehabilitation Institutions for Children with Autism	辅助器具服务机构 Assistive Technology Institutions Providing
		个 unit	个 unit	个 unit	个 unit
全 国	**Nationwide**	**3974**	**2109**	**2681**	**2027**
北 京	Beijing	72	25	39	8
天 津	Tianjin	19	9	35	23
河 北	Hebei	151	125	90	69
山 西	Shanxi	153	52	80	62
内蒙古	Inner Mongolia	111	63	59	64
辽 宁	Liaoning	137	84	100	90
吉 林	Jilin	77	66	47	53
黑龙江	Heilongjiang	81	41	58	21
上 海	Shanghai	334	286	75	262
江 苏	Jiangsu	143	64	153	73
浙 江	Zhejiang	134	36	127	49
安 徽	Anhui	155	21	145	48
福 建	Fujian	154	50	156	75
江 西	Jiangxi	117	60	82	37
山 东	Shandong	301	132	232	100
河 南	Henan	235	76	140	93
湖 北	Hubei	73	58	54	64
湖 南	Hunan	155	74	119	123
广 东	Guangdong	377	252	310	127
广 西	Guangxi	208	89	138	76
海 南	Hainan	16	5	17	6
重 庆	Chongqing	119	74	53	47
四 川	Sichuan	147	77	80	82
贵 州	Guizhou	74	91	47	58
云 南	Yunnan	107	67	43	116
西 藏	Tibet	2		1	10
陕 西	Shaanxi	95	53	59	48
甘 肃	Gansu	100	36	68	70
青 海	Qinghai	36	8	25	14
宁 夏	Ningxia	31	10	24	10
新 疆	Xinjiang	49	17	21	43
新疆兵团	Xinjiang Production and Construction Corps	11	8	4	6

4-1-5　康复人才
Rehabilitation Professionals

地　区	Region	康复机构在岗人员 Staff in Rehabilitation Institutions	业务人员 Professionals	管理人员 Managerial Personnel	其他人员 Other Staff
		人 person	人 person	人 person	人 person
全　国	**Nationwide**	**294658**	**212238**	**31103**	**51317**
北　京	Beijing	4014	2731	451	832
天　津	Tianjin	2441	1627	248	566
河　北	Hebei	12364	9217	1307	1840
山　西	Shanxi	11009	8483	954	1572
内蒙古	Inner Mongolia	6104	4127	620	1357
辽　宁	Liaoning	11623	8294	1304	2025
吉　林	Jilin	9145	6221	1246	1678
黑龙江	Heilongjiang	5913	4355	668	890
上　海	Shanghai	8808	4609	1369	2830
江　苏	Jiangsu	13973	10572	1363	2038
浙　江	Zhejiang	8822	6243	1068	1511
安　徽	Anhui	8570	6945	765	860
福　建	Fujian	10123	7717	1145	1261
江　西	Jiangxi	7905	5199	1014	1692
山　东	Shandong	31264	24158	2651	4455
河　南	Henan	17562	13902	1695	1965
湖　北	Hubei	8403	5820	1155	1428
湖　南	Hunan	14109	10019	1563	2527
广　东	Guangdong	30771	21247	2568	6956
广　西	Guangxi	10349	6815	1083	2451
海　南	Hainan	1550	925	241	384
重　庆	Chongqing	9188	6435	1026	1727
四　川	Sichuan	10116	6840	1047	2229
贵　州	Guizhou	9958	6687	1215	2056
云　南	Yunnan	10235	7814	976	1445
西　藏	Tibet	75	47	20	8
陕　西	Shaanxi	8948	6840	1041	1067
甘　肃	Gansu	4695	3561	539	595
青　海	Qinghai	2161	1552	292	317
宁　夏	Ningxia	986	722	106	158
新　疆	Xinjiang	2564	1971	300	293
新疆兵团	Xinjiang Production and Construction Corps	910	543	63	304

4－1－5 续表 1 Continued 1

地 区	Region	康复机构在岗人员 Staff in Rehabilitation Institutions			
		视力残疾康复在岗人员 Staff for Vision Rehabilitation	业务人员 Professionals	管理人员 Managerial Personnels	其他人员 Other Staff
		人 person	人 person	人 person	人 person
全 国	**Nationwide**	**20302**	**13108**	**2844**	**4350**
北 京	Beijing	68	52	14	2
天 津	Tianjin	294	221	37	36
河 北	Hebei	285	140	35	110
山 西	Shanxi	959	705	118	136
内蒙古	Inner Mongolia	649	493	76	80
辽 宁	Liaoning	1495	1040	169	286
吉 林	Jilin	1519	1008	262	249
黑龙江	Heilongjiang	255	161	62	32
上 海	Shanghai	615	351	88	176
江 苏	Jiangsu	1177	764	188	225
浙 江	Zhejiang	90	56	20	14
安 徽	Anhui	239	192	37	10
福 建	Fujian	223	115	47	61
江 西	Jiangxi	233	162	26	45
山 东	Shandong	1247	742	188	317
河 南	Henan	879	560	182	137
湖 北	Hubei	183	96	18	69
湖 南	Hunan	2086	1188	241	657
广 东	Guangdong	1897	1298	186	413
广 西	Guangxi	649	339	95	215
海 南	Hainan	7	2	2	3
重 庆	Chongqing	1208	786	157	265
四 川	Sichuan	492	325	75	92
贵 州	Guizhou	934	518	181	235
云 南	Yunnan	1283	944	112	227
西 藏	Tibet	3	2	1	
陕 西	Shaanxi	466	268	97	101
甘 肃	Gansu	494	319	75	100
青 海	Qinghai	211	161	22	28
宁 夏	Ningxia	29	16	4	9
新 疆	Xinjiang	101	66	21	14
新疆兵团	Xinjiang Production and Construction Corps	32	18	8	6

4-1-5 续表 2 Continued 2

地 区	Region	康复机构在岗人员 Staff in Rehabilitation Institutions			
		听力言语康复在岗人员 Staff for Hearing and Speech Rehabilitation	业务人员 Professionals	管理人员 Managerial Personnel	其他人员 Other Staff
		人 person	人 person	人 person	人 person
全 国	**Nationwide**	**18310**	**11766**	**2268**	**4276**
北 京	Beijing	461	270	61	130
天 津	Tianjin	59	29	5	25
河 北	Hebei	1040	761	130	149
山 西	Shanxi	504	346	70	88
内蒙古	Inner Mongolia	786	177	59	550
辽 宁	Liaoning	550	339	64	147
吉 林	Jilin	334	252	52	30
黑龙江	Heilongjiang	248	186	30	32
上 海	Shanghai	376	112	51	213
江 苏	Jiangsu	1092	835	94	163
浙 江	Zhejiang	502	345	60	97
安 徽	Anhui	623	479	74	70
福 建	Fujian	607	473	68	66
江 西	Jiangxi	673	409	108	156
山 东	Shandong	1079	805	112	162
河 南	Henan	1803	1312	231	260
湖 北	Hubei	450	309	61	80
湖 南	Hunan	906	593	122	191
广 东	Guangdong	1738	944	158	636
广 西	Guangxi	552	319	87	146
海 南	Hainan	196	105	44	47
重 庆	Chongqing	470	271	78	121
四 川	Sichuan	590	398	70	122
贵 州	Guizhou	631	368	84	179
云 南	Yunnan	639	401	93	145
西 藏	Tibet	8	7	1	
陕 西	Shaanxi	385	260	62	63
甘 肃	Gansu	521	334	71	116
青 海	Qinghai	172	123	25	24
宁 夏	Ningxia	132	93	6	33
新 疆	Xinjiang	143	88	27	28
新疆兵团	Xinjiang Production and Construction Corps	40	23	10	7

4-1-5 续表 3 Continued 3

地区	Region	康复机构在岗人员 Staff in Rehabilitation Institutions			
		肢体残疾康复在岗人员 Staff for Physical Rehabilitation	业务人员 Professionals	管理人员 Managerial Personnel	其他人员 Other Staff
		人 person	人 person	人 person	人 person
全国	**Nationwide**	**90170**	**71532**	**7113**	**11525**
北京	Beijing	918	735	80	103
天津	Tianjin	468	325	30	113
河北	Hebei	3644	2954	337	353
山西	Shanxi	3682	3144	225	313
内蒙古	Inner Mongolia	1918	1377	192	349
辽宁	Liaoning	2730	2225	194	311
吉林	Jilin	2495	1895	335	265
黑龙江	Heilongjiang	2385	1950	226	209
上海	Shanghai	3645	2178	306	1161
江苏	Jiangsu	4029	3415	255	359
浙江	Zhejiang	2650	2026	249	375
安徽	Anhui	2654	2313	155	186
福建	Fujian	1797	1563	115	119
江西	Jiangxi	1695	1297	167	231
山东	Shandong	13331	10978	790	1563
河南	Henan	6730	5855	432	443
湖北	Hubei	2605	1817	514	274
湖南	Hunan	2496	2041	217	238
广东	Guangdong	8746	6372	607	1767
广西	Guangxi	3349	2683	244	422
海南	Hainan	403	180	23	200
重庆	Chongqing	2016	1574	152	290
四川	Sichuan	2294	1876	176	242
贵州	Guizhou	3126	2368	267	491
云南	Yunnan	2615	2129	131	355
西藏	Tibet	23	21	2	
陕西	Shaanxi	3570	3025	315	230
甘肃	Gansu	1457	1225	127	105
青海	Qinghai	763	539	96	128
宁夏	Ningxia	310	262	35	13
新疆	Xinjiang	1304	1091	109	104
新疆兵团	Xinjiang Production and Construction Corps	322	99	10	213

4-1-5 续表 4 Continued 4

地 区	Region	康复机构在岗人员 Staff in Rehabilitation Institutions			
		智力残疾康复在岗人员 Staff for Intellectual Rehabilitation	业务人员 Professionals	管理人员 Managerial Personnel	其他人员 Other Staff
		人 person	人 person	人 person	人 person
全 国	**Nationwide**	**51775**	**38992**	**4946**	**7837**
北 京	Beijing	1247	764	147	336
天 津	Tianjin	368	300	34	34
河 北	Hebei	2231	1670	243	318
山 西	Shanxi	2263	1842	187	234
内蒙古	Inner Mongolia	935	765	77	93
辽 宁	Liaoning	1697	1149	160	388
吉 林	Jilin	937	591	62	284
黑龙江	Heilongjiang	941	785	85	71
上 海	Shanghai	1540	527	334	679
江 苏	Jiangsu	1865	1468	157	240
浙 江	Zhejiang	1578	1024	188	366
安 徽	Anhui	2133	1716	201	216
福 建	Fujian	1982	1369	284	329
江 西	Jiangxi	1742	1244	211	287
山 东	Shandong	5429	4225	463	741
河 南	Henan	4120	3458	283	379
湖 北	Hubei	1262	935	104	223
湖 南	Hunan	2356	1880	213	263
广 东	Guangdong	4362	3117	354	891
广 西	Guangxi	2210	1637	206	367
海 南	Hainan	438	325	65	48
重 庆	Chongqing	1364	970	154	240
四 川	Sichuan	1501	1228	134	139
贵 州	Guizhou	1185	921	121	143
云 南	Yunnan	2086	1750	156	180
西 藏	Tibet	4	3	1	
陕 西	Shaanxi	1681	1404	120	157
甘 肃	Gansu	1067	912	88	67
青 海	Qinghai	536	426	48	62
宁 夏	Ningxia	200	164	23	13
新 疆	Xinjiang	424	340	39	45
新疆兵团	Xinjiang Production and Construction Corps	91	83	4	4

4-1-5 续表 5 Continued 5

地 区	Region	康复机构在岗人员 Staff in Rehabilitation Institutions			
		精神残疾康复在岗人员 Staff for Mental Rehabilitation	业务人员 Professionals	管理人员 Managerial Personnel	其他人员 Other Staff
		人 person	人 person	人 person	人 person
全 国	**Nationwide**	**71809**	**48485**	**7758**	**15566**
北 京	Beijing	821	557	90	174
天 津	Tianjin	737	387	54	296
河 北	Hebei	3865	2835	355	675
山 西	Shanxi	2817	1934	218	665
内蒙古	Inner Mongolia	1085	842	84	159
辽 宁	Liaoning	3669	2613	485	571
吉 林	Jilin	3069	2000	428	641
黑龙江	Heilongjiang	1319	729	162	428
上 海	Shanghai	1481	915	288	278
江 苏	Jiangsu	2899	1956	330	613
浙 江	Zhejiang	2201	1614	279	308
安 徽	Anhui	840	679	61	100
福 建	Fujian	2048	1430	288	330
江 西	Jiangxi	2491	1409	337	745
山 东	Shandong	5946	4310	575	1061
河 南	Henan	2387	1672	270	445
湖 北	Hubei	2664	1812	284	568
湖 南	Hunan	4125	2922	406	797
广 东	Guangdong	8060	5405	564	2091
广 西	Guangxi	1775	998	194	583
海 南	Hainan	63	32	20	11
重 庆	Chongqing	3123	2192	309	622
四 川	Sichuan	4424	2502	433	1489
贵 州	Guizhou	3103	1982	378	743
云 南	Yunnan	3124	2345	347	432
西 藏	Tibet				
陕 西	Shaanxi	1886	1163	311	412
甘 肃	Gansu	587	429	65	93
青 海	Qinghai	311	210	63	38
宁 夏	Ningxia	168	87	13	68
新 疆	Xinjiang	315	212	40	63
新疆兵团	Xinjiang Production and Construction Corps	406	312	27	67

4-1-5 续表 6 Continued 6

地区	Region	康复机构在岗人员 Staff in Rehabilitation Institutions			
		孤独症儿童康复在岗人员 Staff for Rehabilitation of Children with Autism	业务人员 Professionals	管理人员 Managerial Personnel	其他人员 Other Staff
		人 person	人 person	人 person	人 person
全　国	**Nationwide**	**31973**	**23069**	**3864**	**5040**
北　京	Beijing	414	299	46	69
天　津	Tianjin	433	323	61	49
河　北	Hebei	1020	739	135	146
山　西	Shanxi	534	384	70	80
内蒙古	Inner Mongolia	529	380	67	82
辽　宁	Liaoning	1151	790	134	227
吉　林	Jilin	626	405	62	159
黑龙江	Heilongjiang	671	511	83	77
上　海	Shanghai	349	237	62	50
江　苏	Jiangsu	2390	1811	249	330
浙　江	Zhejiang	1651	1107	234	310
安　徽	Anhui	1913	1484	187	242
福　建	Fujian	1982	1454	242	286
江　西	Jiangxi	927	632	123	172
山　东	Shandong	3579	2687	394	498
河　南	Henan	1192	799	180	213
湖　北	Hubei	970	714	87	169
湖　南	Hunan	1490	1061	190	239
广　东	Guangdong	4996	3652	528	816
广　西	Guangxi	1046	722	137	187
海　南	Hainan	419	266	82	71
重　庆	Chongqing	697	505	79	113
四　川	Sichuan	501	352	82	67
贵　州	Guizhou	736	471	102	163
云　南	Yunnan	216	146	37	33
西　藏	Tibet	2	1	1	
陕　西	Shaanxi	748	587	89	72
甘　肃	Gansu	382	266	57	59
青　海	Qinghai	109	57	24	28
宁　夏	Ningxia	117	87	14	16
新　疆	Xinjiang	172	133	25	14
新疆兵团	Xinjiang Production and Construction Corps	11	7	1	3

4-1-5 续表 7 Continued 7

地区	Region	康复机构在岗人员 Staff in Rehabilitation Institutions				培训康复管理人员 Rehabilitation Managerial Staff Trained	培训康复业务人员 Rehabilitation Professionals Trained
		辅助器具残疾康复在岗人员 Staff for Rehabilition with Assistive Devices	业务人员 Professionals	管理人员 Managerial Personnel	其他人员 Other Staff		
		人 person	人 person	人 person	人 person	人次 person-time	人次 person-time
全 国	**Nationwide**	**10319**	**5286**	**2310**	**2723**	**87122**	**415948**
北 京	Beijing	85	54	13	18	2400	16634
天 津	Tianjin	82	42	27	13	364	1831
河 北	Hebei	279	118	72	89	2733	7554
山 西	Shanxi	250	128	66	56	1866	13722
内蒙古	Inner Mongolia	202	93	65	44	589	4194
辽 宁	Liaoning	331	138	98	95	4382	18655
吉 林	Jilin	165	70	45	50	1850	8745
黑龙江	Heilongjiang	94	33	20	41	691	1660
上 海	Shanghai	802	289	240	273	3141	14401
江 苏	Jiangsu	521	323	90	108	5467	25711
浙 江	Zhejiang	150	71	38	41	3434	20484
安 徽	Anhui	168	82	50	36	1267	6423
福 建	Fujian	1484	1313	101	70	3496	16558
江 西	Jiangxi	144	46	42	56	4877	14587
山 东	Shandong	653	411	129	113	7053	51292
河 南	Henan	451	246	117	88	3688	16838
湖 北	Hubei	269	137	87	45	9432	33720
湖 南	Hunan	650	334	174	142	3345	14737
广 东	Guangdong	972	459	171	342	6318	44640
广 西	Guangxi	768	117	120	531	2381	11748
海 南	Hainan	24	15	5	4	121	519
重 庆	Chongqing	310	137	97	76	3440	13328
四 川	Sichuan	314	159	77	78	7281	14012
贵 州	Guizhou	243	59	82	102	1397	10014
云 南	Yunnan	272	99	100	73	1847	7805
西 藏	Tibet	35	13	14	8	6	112
陕 西	Shaanxi	212	133	47	32	2251	10576
甘 肃	Gansu	187	76	56	55	718	5692
青 海	Qinghai	59	36	14	9	334	1643
宁 夏	Ningxia	30	13	11	6	179	3227
新 疆	Xinjiang	105	41	39	25	667	3111
新疆兵团	Xinjiang Production and Construction Corps	8	1	3	4	107	1775

二、教育
Education

4-2-1 学前教育阶段
Pre-School Education

地 区	Region	残疾人事业专项彩票公益金助学项目资助 Students Supported by Educational Projects Funded by Welfare Lottery Fund for PWDs	视力残疾 Children with Visual Disability	听力残疾 Children with Hearing Disability	言语残疾 Children with Speech Disability	肢体残疾 Children with Physical Disability
		人 person	人 person	人 person	人 person	人 person
全 国	**Nationwide**	**14694**	**274**	**2490**	**772**	**2323**
北 京	Beijing	6				
天 津	Tianjin					
河 北	Hebei	818	10	216	39	26
山 西	Shanxi	509	2	77	18	84
内蒙古	Inner Mongolia	46	3	4		18
辽 宁	Liaoning	1472	14	168	30	204
吉 林	Jilin	221	2	11	6	22
黑龙江	Heilongjiang					
上 海	Shanghai					
江 苏	Jiangsu	217	13	61	5	39
浙 江	Zhejiang					
安 徽	Anhui	920	12	226	27	173
福 建	Fujian	517	12	109	18	123
江 西	Jiangxi	1279	9	121	23	112
山 东	Shandong	226	1	34	4	37
河 南	Henan	1325	28	308	91	220
湖 北	Hubei	759	31	106	50	92
湖 南	Hunan	1320	3	254	63	88
广 东	Guangdong	895	33	113	52	207
广 西	Guangxi	1104	22	170	53	83
海 南	Hainan	347	6	51	9	34
重 庆	Chongqing	301	4	31	28	38
四 川	Sichuan	107	2	16	6	9
贵 州	Guizhou	960	41	92	141	356
云 南	Yunnan	575	9	155	53	120
西 藏	Tibet	6	1			4
陕 西	Shaanxi	10		1	1	3
甘 肃	Gansu	283	3	60	22	76
青 海	Qinghai	168	6	36	8	62
宁 夏	Ningxia	226	6	47	24	71
新 疆	Xinjiang	39	1	16		8
新疆兵团	Xinjiang Production and Construction Corps	38		7	1	14

4-2-1 续表 Continued

地 区	Region	智力残疾 Chidren with Intellectual Disability	精神残疾 Children with Mental Disability	多重残疾 Children with Multiple Disabilities	其他残疾儿童学前教育助学项目资助 Students Supported by Other Pre-School Educational Projects for Disabled Children
		人 person	人 person	人 person	人 person
全 国	**Nationwide**	**4996**	**1805**	**2034**	**5409**
北 京	Beijing	5		1	125
天 津	Tianjin				162
河 北	Hebei	298	97	132	
山 西	Shanxi	174	38	116	1
内蒙古	Inner Mongolia	7	10	4	681
辽 宁	Liaoning	527	415	114	142
吉 林	Jilin	75	58	47	16
黑龙江	Heilongjiang				
上 海	Shanghai				
江 苏	Jiangsu	47	32	20	578
浙 江	Zhejiang				706
安 徽	Anhui	284	117	81	100
福 建	Fujian	148	42	65	262
江 西	Jiangxi	485	235	294	715
山 东	Shandong	89	31	30	117
河 南	Henan	432	97	149	242
湖 北	Hubei	311	78	91	29
湖 南	Hunan	630	137	145	18
广 东	Guangdong	241	101	148	634
广 西	Guangxi	443	65	268	8
海 南	Hainan	101	133	13	165
重 庆	Chongqing	142	23	35	89
四 川	Sichuan	24	17	33	446
贵 州	Guizhou	215	34	81	42
云 南	Yunnan	151	10	77	5
西 藏	Tibet			1	3
陕 西	Shaanxi	4		1	53
甘 肃	Gansu	55	22	45	27
青 海	Qinghai	39	1	16	12
宁 夏	Ningxia	55	11	12	4
新 疆	Xinjiang	3		11	16
新疆兵团	Xinjiang Production and Construction Corps	11	1	4	11

4-2-2　高中教育阶段
Senior High Education

地区	Region	特殊教育普通高中学校(班) Special Education Senior High Schools/Classes	盲普通高中 Senior High Schools for Blind Students	聋普通高中 Senior High Schools for Deaf Students	其他 Others	学生 Students 招生 Newly Enrolled Students with Disabilities	盲 Students with Visual Disability	聋 Students with Hearing Disability
		个 unit	个 unit	个 unit	个 unit	人 person	人 person	人 person
全　国	**Nationwide**	**104**	**11**	**43**	**50**	**2369**	**394**	**1975**
北　京	Beijing	2	1	1		47	13	34
天　津	Tianjin	2	1	1		43	14	29
河　北	Hebei	10	1	5	4	533	62	471
山　西	Shanxi	9	1	2	6	160	11	149
内蒙古	Inner Mongolia	4		3	1	41		41
辽　宁	Liaoning	6		2	4	15		15
吉　林	Jilin	5		4	1	34		34
黑龙江	Heilongjiang							
上　海	Shanghai	1	1			7	7	
江　苏	Jiangsu	4		1	3	145	11	134
浙　江	Zhejiang	6	1	1	4	106	40	66
安　徽	Anhui	1			1	4	1	3
福　建	Fujian	4			4	47	12	35
江　西	Jiangxi	1			1	13	6	7
山　东	Shandong	7	2	2	3	90	38	52
河　南	Henan	5		3	2	107		107
湖　北	Hubei	6	1	3	2	150	25	125
湖　南	Hunan	5			5	65	1	64
广　东	Guangdong	7	1	4	2	96	5	91
广　西	Guangxi	3		2	1	45	5	40
海　南	Hainan							
重　庆	Chongqing	2	1	1		66	36	30
四　川	Sichuan	4		2	2	235	50	185
贵　州	Guizhou	6		4	2	239	55	184
云　南	Yunnan							
西　藏	Tibet							
陕　西	Shaanxi							
甘　肃	Gansu	1			1	2	1	1
青　海	Qinghai	1		1		11		11
宁　夏	Ningxia	1			1	21	1	20
新　疆	Xinjiang	1		1		47		47
新疆兵团	Xinjiang Production and Construction Corps							

4-2-2 续表 1 Continued 1

地 区	Region	学生 Students					
		在校生 Students in School	盲 Students with Visual Disability	聋 Students with Hearing Disability	毕业生 Graduates	盲 Students with Visual Disability	聋 Students with Hearing Disability
		人 person	人 person	人 person	人 person	人 person	人 person
全 国	**Nationwide**	**10173**	**1491**	**6034**	**2534**	**379**	**1670**
北 京	Beijing	187	30	157	70	23	47
天 津	Tianjin	183	109	74	45	19	26
河 北	Hebei	1175	187	694	601	54	479
山 西	Shanxi	1215	50	476	236	15	116
内蒙古	Inner Mongolia	374		362	40		40
辽 宁	Liaoning	278	4	238	36		33
吉 林	Jilin	234		138	43		28
黑龙江	Heilongjiang						
上 海	Shanghai	33	33		8	8	
江 苏	Jiangsu	534	27	465	122	6	102
浙 江	Zhejiang	784	286	279	170	30	94
安 徽	Anhui	40	1	9	11		6
福 建	Fujian	187	34	76	90	16	35
江 西	Jiangxi	30	6	24	13		13
山 东	Shandong	889	263	382	236	86	114
河 南	Henan	271	1	268	98		93
湖 北	Hubei	692	84	483	66	22	44
湖 南	Hunan	801		332	147		53
广 东	Guangdong	390	5	250	90		51
广 西	Guangxi	159	5	128	40		29
海 南	Hainan						
重 庆	Chongqing	196	102	94	70	37	33
四 川	Sichuan	331	50	249	46	2	44
贵 州	Guizhou	569	193	366	195	56	139
云 南	Yunnan						
西 藏	Tibet						
陕 西	Shaanxi						
甘 肃	Gansu	195	16	69	20	1	14
青 海	Qinghai	151		151	11		11
宁 夏	Ningxia	66	5	61	30	4	26
新 疆	Xinjiang	209		209			
新疆兵团	Xinjiang Production and Construction Corps						

4-2-2　续表 2　Continued 2

地　区	Region	残疾人中等职业学校(班) Secondary Vocational Schools/Classes for PWDs	教育部门办 Supervised by Educational Departments	残联部门办 Supervised by Disabled Persons' Federations	其他 Others
		个 unit	个 unit	个 unit	个 unit
全　国	**Nationwide**	**147**	**134**	**9**	**4**
北　京	Beijing	3	3		
天　津	Tianjin				
河　北	Hebei	4	3		1
山　西	Shanxi	2	2		
内蒙古	Inner Mongolia	4	3	1	
辽　宁	Liaoning	15	15		
吉　林	Jilin	2	1	1	
黑龙江	Heilongjiang	5	5		
上　海	Shanghai	17	16		1
江　苏	Jiangsu	10	9	1	
浙　江	Zhejiang	16	15		1
安　徽	Anhui	4	3	1	
福　建	Fujian	8	8		
江　西	Jiangxi	7	6		1
山　东	Shandong	10	9	1	
河　南	Henan	5	5		
湖　北	Hubei	4	4		
湖　南	Hunan	1		1	
广　东	Guangdong	9	9		
广　西	Guangxi	1	1		
海　南	Hainan	1	1		
重　庆	Chongqing	1	1		
四　川	Sichuan	2	2		
贵　州	Guizhou	1		1	
云　南	Yunnan	5	5		
西　藏	Tibet				
陕　西	Shaanxi	5	4	1	
甘　肃	Gansu	2	2		
青　海	Qinghai	1	1		
宁　夏	Ningxia				
新　疆	Xinjiang	2	1	1	
新疆兵团	Xinjiang Production and Construction Corps				

4-2-2 续表 3 Continued 3

地区	Region	残疾人中等职业学校(班)学生 Students of Secondary Vocational Schools/Classes for PWDs				
		招生 Newly Enrolled Students	盲 Students with Visual Disability	聋 Students with Hearing Disability	肢残 Students with Physical Disability	其他 Others
		人 person	人 person	人 person	人 person	人 person
全国	**Nationwide**	**5967**	**954**	**1631**	**1005**	**2377**
北京	Beijing	66		8		58
天津	Tianjin					
河北	Hebei	525	50	57	300	118
山西	Shanxi	26	4	22		
内蒙古	Inner Mongolia	70	10	13	12	35
辽宁	Liaoning	250	57	43		150
吉林	Jilin	95	13	17	32	33
黑龙江	Heilongjiang	65		54		11
上海	Shanghai	240		14	5	221
江苏	Jiangsu	418	122	136	20	140
浙江	Zhejiang	428	2	34	6	386
安徽	Anhui	364	67	152	50	95
福建	Fujian	171	14	27	2	128
江西	Jiangxi	472	24	147	10	291
山东	Shandong	271	85	60	92	34
河南	Henan	242	102	111		29
湖北	Hubei	211	50	53	23	85
湖南	Hunan	176	45	56		75
广东	Guangdong	492	50	147	93	202
广西	Guangxi	63	2	31	13	17
海南	Hainan	46	6	32		8
重庆	Chongqing	34		27	1	6
四川	Sichuan	61	5	9	3	44
贵州	Guizhou	90	30	30	30	
云南	Yunnan	326	31	153	83	59
西藏	Tibet					
陕西	Shaanxi	480	100	108	150	122
甘肃	Gansu	47	1	36		10
青海	Qinghai	40	26	14		
宁夏	Ningxia					
新疆	Xinjiang	198	58	40	80	20
新疆兵团	Xinjiang Production and Construction Corps					

4-2-2 续表 4 Continued 4

地 区	Region	残疾人中等职业学校(班)学生 Students of Secondary Vocational Schools/classes for PWDs				
		在校学生 Students in Schools	盲 Students with Visual Disability	聋 Students with Hearing Disability	肢残 Students with Physical Disability	其他 Others
		人 person	人 person	人 person	人 person	人 person
全 国	**Nationwide**	**17877**	**2868**	**5809**	**2241**	**6959**
北 京	Beijing	264		74		190
天 津	Tianjin					
河 北	Hebei	289	9	63	141	76
山 西	Shanxi	68	4	63		1
内蒙古	Inner Mongolia	237	41	39	14	143
辽 宁	Liaoning	955	190	169	1	595
吉 林	Jilin	432	41	60	132	199
黑龙江	Heilongjiang	131	2	70	2	57
上 海	Shanghai	812		69	15	728
江 苏	Jiangsu	1694	401	781	118	394
浙 江	Zhejiang	1124	10	103	10	1001
安 徽	Anhui	1240	236	513	281	210
福 建	Fujian	503	28	85	2	388
江 西	Jiangxi	1299	73	368	79	779
山 东	Shandong	859	255	298	146	160
河 南	Henan	1001	331	641		29
湖 北	Hubei	602	148	172	45	237
湖 南	Hunan	442	186	122		134
广 东	Guangdong	1693	143	537	313	700
广 西	Guangxi	196	7	108	46	35
海 南	Hainan	133	13	96		24
重 庆	Chongqing	34		27	1	6
四 川	Sichuan	250	42	43	5	160
贵 州	Guizhou	180	60	60	60	
云 南	Yunnan	1039	124	491	250	174
西 藏	Tibet					
陕 西	Shaanxi	1143	308	280	400	155
甘 肃	Gansu	325	23	237		65
青 海	Qinghai	333	79	120		134
宁 夏	Ningxia					
新 疆	Xinjiang	599	114	120	180	185
新疆兵团	Xinjiang Production and Construction Corps					

4-2-2 续表 5 Continued 5

地区	Region	残疾人中等职业学校(班)学生 Students of Secondary Vocational Schools/Classes for PWDs				
		毕业生 Graduates	盲 Students with Visual Disability	聋 Students with Hearing Disability	肢残 Students with Physical Disability	其他 Others
		人 person	人 person	人 person	人 person	人 person
全 国	**Nationwide**	**4281**	**810**	**1452**	**682**	**1337**
北 京	Beijing	38		4	3	31
天 津	Tianjin					
河 北	Hebei	189	9	23	115	42
山 西	Shanxi	8	1	4	1	2
内蒙古	Inner Mongolia	29	14	7	1	7
辽 宁	Liaoning	229	41	35	6	147
吉 林	Jilin	86	9	14	39	24
黑龙江	Heilongjiang	33	2	20		11
上 海	Shanghai	65		20	1	44
江 苏	Jiangsu	333	73	122	42	96
浙 江	Zhejiang	249		50	2	197
安 徽	Anhui	327	69	149	79	30
福 建	Fujian	109	5	29	1	74
江 西	Jiangxi	247	15	102	22	108
山 东	Shandong	228	79	114	25	10
河 南	Henan	79	56	23		
湖 北	Hubei	193	57	67	22	47
湖 南	Hunan	191	51	78		62
广 东	Guangdong	394	33	122	35	204
广 西	Guangxi	55	1	43	9	2
海 南	Hainan	36		28		8
重 庆	Chongqing					
四 川	Sichuan	31	7	8		16
贵 州	Guizhou	90	30	30	30	
云 南	Yunnan	245	35	130	58	22
西 藏	Tibet					
陕 西	Shaanxi	525	164	90	153	118
甘 肃	Gansu	82	10	72		
青 海	Qinghai	50	12	23		15
宁 夏	Ningxia					
新 疆	Xinjiang	140	37	45	38	20
新疆兵团	Xinjiang Production and Construction Corps					

4-2-2　续表 6　Continued 6

地 区	Region	残疾人中等职业学校(班)学生 Students of Secondary Vocational Schools/Classes for PWDs				
		毕业生获得职业资格证书 Graduates Granted Professional Qualification Certificates	盲 Students with Visual Disability	聋 Students with Hearing Disability	肢残 Students with Physical Disability	其他 Others
		人 person	人 person	人 person	人 person	人 person
全　国	**Nationwide**	**1461**	**375**	**395**	**369**	**322**
北　京	Beijing					
天　津	Tianjin					
河　北	Hebei	186	9	20	115	42
山　西	Shanxi	7	1	4	1	1
内蒙古	Inner Mongolia					
辽　宁	Liaoning	92	25	19	6	42
吉　林	Jilin					
黑龙江	Heilongjiang					
上　海	Shanghai	7			1	6
江　苏	Jiangsu	98	8	54	20	16
浙　江	Zhejiang	82		39		43
安　徽	Anhui	39	27	12		
福　建	Fujian	9			1	8
江　西	Jiangxi	93	15	50	11	17
山　东	Shandong	49	24		25	
河　南	Henan					
湖　北	Hubei	117	43	43	12	19
湖　南	Hunan					
广　东	Guangdong	24		24		
广　西	Guangxi					
海　南	Hainan					
重　庆	Chongqing					
四　川	Sichuan	15	5	5		5
贵　州	Guizhou	60	20	20	20	
云　南	Yunnan	79	35	44		
西　藏	Tibet					
陕　西	Shaanxi	469	138	60	153	118
甘　肃	Gansu					
青　海	Qinghai					
宁　夏	Ningxia					
新　疆	Xinjiang	35	25	1	4	5
新疆兵团	Xinjiang Production and Construction Corps					

4-2-3 高等教育
Higher Education

地 区	Region	高等特殊教育学院 Special Higher Education Institutions							
		机构 Institutions	录取残疾考生 Newly Enrolled Students	研究生 Postgraduates	盲 Students with Visual Disability	聋 Students with Hearing Disability	本科 Under-graduates	盲 Students with Visual Disability	聋 Students with Hearing Disability
		个 unit	人 person	人 person	人 person	人 person	人 person	人 person	人 person
全 国	**Nationwide**	**23**	**2253**	**9**		**8**	**835**	**163**	**579**
北 京	Beijing	1	94				94	30	64
天 津	Tianjin	1	130	9		8	121		83
河 北	Hebei								
山 西	Shanxi								
内蒙古	Inner Mongolia								
辽 宁	Liaoning	1	75						
吉 林	Jilin	1	204				204	87	117
黑龙江	Heilongjiang	1	100				100		100
上 海	Shanghai	1	10				10		10
江 苏	Jiangsu	3	94				94	20	50
浙 江	Zhejiang	1	475						
安 徽	Anhui								
福 建	Fujian	1							
江 西	Jiangxi								
山 东	Shandong	2	386				36	26	10
河 南	Henan	3	340				132		115
湖 北	Hubei								
湖 南	Hunan	1	78						
广 东	Guangdong	2	72						
广 西	Guangxi								
海 南	Hainan								
重 庆	Chongqing	1	30				30		24
四 川	Sichuan	1	65				14		6
贵 州	Guizhou								
云 南	Yunnan	1	100						
西 藏	Tibet								
陕 西	Shaanxi	1							
甘 肃	Gansu								
青 海	Qinghai								
宁 夏	Ningxia								
新 疆	Xinjiang								
新疆兵团	Xinjiang Production and Construction Corps								

4-2-3 续表 1 Continued 1

地区	Region	专科(高职) Students of Vocational College	盲 Students with Visual Disability	聋 Students with Hearing Disability	普通高等院校 Regular Higher Education Institutions 残疾考生达到录取分数线 Students above Admission Line	录取人数 Students Enrolled	研究生 Postgraduates	盲 Students with Visual Disability
		人 person	人 person	人 person	人 person	人 person	人 person	人 person
全国	**Nationwide**	**1409**	**405**	**604**	**14446**	**13551**	**278**	**41**
北京	Beijing				118	118	1	
天津	Tianjin				193	69	1	
河北	Hebei				415	414	10	
山西	Shanxi				468	459		
内蒙古	Inner Mongolia				331	331	10	
辽宁	Liaoning	75	40	12	296	296	2	
吉林	Jilin				392	360	33	8
黑龙江	Heilongjiang				181	181	3	
上海	Shanghai				77	75	2	
江苏	Jiangsu				438	428	25	4
浙江	Zhejiang	475	184	115	473	436		
安徽	Anhui				781	616	28	5
福建	Fujian				214	212	1	
江西	Jiangxi				536	536	9	3
山东	Shandong	350	62	222	1144	1105	83	11
河南	Henan	208	103	82	972	972	12	3
湖北	Hubei				470	469	10	
湖南	Hunan	78		78	721	671	15	2
广东	Guangdong	72	12	26	772	714	6	
广西	Guangxi				371	358	1	
海南	Hainan				82	66		
重庆	Chongqing				577	403	1	
四川	Sichuan	51		28	733	709	15	4
贵州	Guizhou				907	857		
云南	Yunnan	100	4	41	1118	1098		
西藏	Tibet				48	37		
陕西	Shaanxi				210	194	1	
甘肃	Gansu				576	560	4	
青海	Qinghai				182	178	1	
宁夏	Ningxia				201	196	2	
新疆	Xinjiang				414	398	2	1
新疆兵团	Xinjiang Production and Construction Corps				35	35		

4-2-3 续表 2 Continued 2

地区	Region	普通高等院校 Regular Higher Education Institutions					
		聋 Students with Hearing Disability	肢残 Students with Physical Disability	本科 Under-graduates	盲 Students with Visual Disability	聋 Students with Hearing Disability	肢残 Students with Physical Disability
		人 person	人 person	人 person	人 person	人 person	人 person
全国	**Nationwide**	**37**	**181**	**5611**	**717**	**1052**	**3350**
北京	Beijing		1	92	6	24	51
天津	Tianjin		1	44		16	28
河北	Hebei	2	8	148	12	37	86
山西	Shanxi			193	15	34	136
内蒙古	Inner Mongolia	2	8	149	22	21	90
辽宁	Liaoning		2	149	19	47	76
吉林	Jilin	3	18	186	27	56	72
黑龙江	Heilongjiang	2	1	93	18	19	49
上海	Shanghai		2	37	7	12	16
江苏	Jiangsu	2	18	215	31	71	99
浙江	Zhejiang			184	19	53	106
安徽	Anhui	7	15	273	27	45	167
福建	Fujian	1		116	15	40	54
江西	Jiangxi		5	177	32	28	100
山东	Shandong	12	52	401	45	95	216
河南	Henan	1	7	450	41	73	310
湖北	Hubei	1	9	184	26	51	89
湖南	Hunan	3	9	238	26	45	138
广东	Guangdong		6	206	18	51	122
广西	Guangxi		1	146	19	14	103
海南	Hainan			29	3	5	21
重庆	Chongqing		1	211	40	25	125
四川	Sichuan		10	316	67	39	185
贵州	Guizhou			382	51	34	260
云南	Yunnan			365	45	28	265
西藏	Tibet			7	1		5
陕西	Shaanxi		1	134	19	16	84
甘肃	Gansu	1	3	215	28	33	127
青海	Qinghai		1	70	11	7	46
宁夏	Ningxia		2	83	10	15	51
新疆	Xinjiang			106	16	16	65
新疆兵团	Xinjiang Production and Construction Corps			12	1	2	8

4-2-3　续表 3　Continued 3

地区	Region	普通高等院校 Regular Higher Education Institutions			
		录取残疾考生 Students Enrolled			
		专科(高职) Students of Vocational College	盲 Students with Visual Disability	聋 Students with Hearing Disability	肢残 Students with Physical Disability
		人 person	人 person	人 person	人 person
全　国	**Nationwide**	**7662**	**870**	**1045**	**4614**
北　京	Beijing	25	5	2	14
天　津	Tianjin	24	2	5	15
河　北	Hebei	256	31	47	143
山　西	Shanxi	266	18	38	176
内蒙古	Inner Mongolia	172	16	24	107
辽　宁	Liaoning	145	14	28	91
吉　林	Jilin	141	13	22	82
黑龙江	Heilongjiang	85	11	21	48
上　海	Shanghai	36	3	5	21
江　苏	Jiangsu	188	15	46	93
浙　江	Zhejiang	252	25	61	146
安　徽	Anhui	315	24	47	182
福　建	Fujian	95	8	15	55
江　西	Jiangxi	350	38	40	220
山　东	Shandong	621	72	103	347
河　南	Henan	510	48	76	322
湖　北	Hubei	275	39	45	155
湖　南	Hunan	418	52	42	266
广　东	Guangdong	502	45	65	321
广　西	Guangxi	211	31	22	126
海　南	Hainan	37	4	6	17
重　庆	Chongqing	191	23	20	123
四　川	Sichuan	378	46	62	212
贵　州	Guizhou	475	62	28	307
云　南	Yunnan	733	91	59	475
西　藏	Tibet	30	7	5	16
陕　西	Shaanxi	59	4	8	37
甘　肃	Gansu	341	46	38	189
青　海	Qinghai	107	18	11	67
宁　夏	Ningxia	111	12	17	54
新　疆	Xinjiang	290	44	33	173
新疆兵团	Xinjiang Production and Construction Corps	23	3	4	14

三、就业
Employment

4-3-1 残疾人就业状况
Employment of Persons with Disabilities

地区	Region	就业合计 Employed PWDs	按比例就业 Employed through Quoto Scheme	集中就业 Employed through PWDs-Oriented Post	个体就业 Self-Employed
		人 person	人 person	人 person	人 person
全　国	**Nationwide**	**8616671**	**784203**	**278160**	**634090**
北　京	Beijing	100722	58474	2599	3197
天　津	Tianjin	67357	44272	472	6213
河　北	Hebei	471172	11544	3999	11024
山　西	Shanxi	265968	5857	6036	11106
内蒙古	Inner Mongolia	185804	10175	5198	19234
辽　宁	Liaoning	240946	33331	12202	16770
吉　林	Jilin	180084	7860	4557	18366
黑龙江	Heilongjiang	234690	17237	5225	25078
上　海	Shanghai	70913	46610	9359	500
江　苏	Jiangsu	337631	80879	44718	26931
浙　江	Zhejiang	307197	85725	36870	37209
安　徽	Anhui	479729	10982	6424	40399
福　建	Fujian	211621	14313	4445	20049
江　西	Jiangxi	371282	12869	19221	43325
山　东	Shandong	504746	68014	16329	29867
河　南	Henan	512538	23249	12088	87121
湖　北	Hubei	408731	31702	18975	24236
湖　南	Hunan	404639	23836	13176	30800
广　东	Guangdong	302334	64699	6351	12421
广　西	Guangxi	321680	11373	1632	12535
海　南	Hainan	38388	4438	435	1058
重　庆	Chongqing	240835	16412	9497	18403
四　川	Sichuan	805183	21745	10592	45720
贵　州	Guizhou	337583	8782	6396	19428
云　南	Yunnan	422375	16175	6913	16569
西　藏	Tibet	16589	573	373	645
陕　西	Shaanxi	236524	10460	4098	14957
甘　肃	Gansu	243720	6468	1886	15391
青　海	Qinghai	44111	1952	1662	2707
宁　夏	Ningxia	56944	5159	1386	4767
新　疆	Xinjiang	173492	20480	4214	15651
新疆兵团	Xinjiang Production and Construction Corps	21143	8558	832	2413

4-3-1 续表 Continued

地 区	Region	公益性岗位就业 Employed through Welfare Post	辅助性就业 Assistive Employment	灵活就业（含社区、居家就业）Flexible Employment	从事农村种养加 Engaged in Agricultural Planting, Husbandry and Processing
		人 person	人 person	人 person	人 person
全 国	**Nationwide**	**146648**	**143442**	**2387697**	**4242431**
北 京	Beijing	1554	1457	22498	10943
天 津	Tianjin	1107	15	1652	13626
河 北	Hebei	1442	2272	74728	366163
山 西	Shanxi	1062	1042	49980	190885
内蒙古	Inner Mongolia	1448	891	55412	93446
辽 宁	Liaoning	6127	6855	40164	125497
吉 林	Jilin	2737	1105	44982	100477
黑龙江	Heilongjiang	5805	1922	78537	100886
上 海	Shanghai	2623	4070	6536	1215
江 苏	Jiangsu	52486	13184	33368	86065
浙 江	Zhejiang	3821	13216	82992	47364
安 徽	Anhui	3050	9401	152582	256891
福 建	Fujian	2401	2405	68534	99474
江 西	Jiangxi	10487	7562	159797	118021
山 东	Shandong	4588	2687	119018	264243
河 南	Henan	4051	16745	107744	261540
湖 北	Hubei	3624	6234	130148	193812
湖 南	Hunan	2385	5898	130395	198149
广 东	Guangdong	5368	7825	72323	133347
广 西	Guangxi	1622	2009	66350	226159
海 南	Hainan	486	156	7747	24068
重 庆	Chongqing	2414	2597	73156	118356
四 川	Sichuan	5909	15239	373545	332433
贵 州	Guizhou	2959	2875	107670	189473
云 南	Yunnan	1662	4120	102044	274892
西 藏	Tibet	165	57	8809	5967
陕 西	Shaanxi	4243	4445	67916	130405
甘 肃	Gansu	2934	3456	64296	149289
青 海	Qinghai	1173	556	15602	20459
宁 夏	Ningxia	1034	1097	19397	24104
新 疆	Xinjiang	5430	1847	44127	81743
新疆兵团	Xinjiang Production and Construction Corps	451	202	5648	3039

四、扶贫
Poverty Alleviation

4-4-1　农村贫困残疾人实用技术培训
Training on Practical Skills and Technologies for PWDs in Rual Areas

地区	Region	残疾人实用技术培训 Training on Practical Skills and Technologies for PWDs		
		本年度培训残疾人 Training on Practical Skills and Technologies for PWDs in 2020	扫盲教育 Anti-Illiteracy Education	本年度培训投入经费 Fund for Training on Practical Skills and Technologies for PWDs in 2020
		万人次 10,000 person-times	人 person	万元 10,000 yuan
全　国	**Nationwide**	**45.7**	**45755**	**20853.6**
北　京	Beijing	0.2		199.0
天　津	Tianjin			
河　北	Hebei	1.9	900	963.7
山　西	Shanxi	1.1	483	506.1
内蒙古	Inner Mongolia	2.7	8214	1145.6
辽　宁	Liaoning	0.9	175	511.2
吉　林	Jilin	0.9	300	317.4
黑龙江	Heilongjiang	0.9	530	216.9
上　海	Shanghai	1.4		85.3
江　苏	Jiangsu	0.7	1521	187.4
浙　江	Zhejiang	0.6	524	214.8
安　徽	Anhui	1.9	1761	818.3
福　建	Fujian	1.2	2191	221.2
江　西	Jiangxi	0.8	513	450.0
山　东	Shandong	1.5	486	564.7
河　南	Henan	3.3	1312	1071.8
湖　北	Hubei	2.3	1745	972.7
湖　南	Hunan	1.9	3161	2705.0
广　东	Guangdong	1.2	1194	481.3
广　西	Guangxi	1.2	314	625.5
海　南	Hainan	0.5	904	529.3
重　庆	Chongqing	1.1	1730	529.5
四　川	Sichuan	6.8	5069	2536.5
贵　州	Guizhou	1.3	1344	470.5
云　南	Yunnan	3.4	4693	1985.4
西　藏	Tibet	0.1	122	79.6
陕　西	Shaanxi	2.1	829	768.1
甘　肃	Gansu	1.7	2518	879.6
青　海	Qinghai	0.4	566	137.4
宁　夏	Ningxia	0.6	1028	218.5
新　疆	Xinjiang	0.8	1157	371.1
新疆兵团	Xinjiang Production and Construction Corps	0.4	471	90.1

4-4-2 扶贫资金与残疾人扶贫贷款
Poverty Alleviation Funds and Loans

地 区	Region	扶贫资金 Poverty Alleviation Funds		残疾人扶贫贷款 Poverty Alleviation Funds and Loans			
				康复扶贫贴息贷款 Interest-subsidized Loans for Rehabilitation			
		省级财政投入 Poverty Alleviation Fund from the Provincial Budget	社会募集 Fund Raised from Society	本年度贷款实际落实 Allocated Loans in 2020	本年度贷款财政贴息资金数额 Amount of Interest Subsidy by Government Finance for Loans in 2020	本年度项目贷款扶持贫困残疾人 Financially Difficult PWDs Supported by Loans for Project in 2020	本年度到户贷款扶持贫困残疾人 Financially Difficult PWDs Supported by Loans for Househould in 2020
		万元 10,000 yuan	万元 10,000 yuan	万元 10,000 yuan	万元 10,000 yuan	人 person	人 person
全 国	**Nationwide**	**52957.1**	**1911.5**	**13900.4**	**717.0**	**2394**	**1764**
北 京	Beijing						
天 津	Tianjin						
河 北	Hebei	1497.1	19.6	61.5	4.3		31
山 西	Shanxi	264.5					
内蒙古	Inner Mongolia						
辽 宁	Liaoning	3500.2	53.0				
吉 林	Jilin	1785.3					
黑龙江	Heilongjiang	139.4	25.0				
上 海	Shanghai						
江 苏	Jiangsu	1763.6	120.0	2094.5	95.9	1	305
浙 江	Zhejiang	21061.1	86.7				
安 徽	Anhui	398.4	232.1	560.0	17.3	10	5
福 建	Fujian	908.1	292.6	1411.6	63.2	318	318
江 西	Jiangxi	970.0	46.9				
山 东	Shandong	72.7					
河 南	Henan	210.0					
湖 北	Hubei	629.0	20.0	908.0	55.3	222	242
湖 南	Hunan	2658.0	302.3	5510.8	325.2	1198	212
广 东	Guangdong	85.3	66.4				
广 西	Guangxi	7913.8	3.8	18.0	0.7		6
海 南	Hainan	71.0					
重 庆	Chongqing	1147.8	66.0				
四 川	Sichuan	4588.0	60.0				
贵 州	Guizhou	332.5	167.5				
云 南	Yunnan	629.4	37.5				
西 藏	Tibet						
陕 西	Shaanxi	785.1					
甘 肃	Gansu	1135.0	267.0				
青 海	Qinghai	7.7					
宁 夏	Ningxia	404.0	45.2	3336.0	155.1	645	645
新 疆	Xinjiang						
新疆兵团	Xinjiang Production and Construction Corps						

4-4-3 社会帮扶与残疾人扶贫基地建设
Social Assistance and Poverty Alleviation Bases

地 区	Region	社会帮扶 Social Assistance for PWDs	残疾人扶贫基地建设 Poverty Alleviation Bases for PWDs		
		结对帮扶受益残疾人 Individuals who Assisted PWDs in One-to-one Way	残疾人扶贫基地 Poverty Alleviation Bases for PWDs	安置残疾人就业 PWDs Provided with Employment Opportunities	扶持带动贫困残疾人 Benefited PWDs
		人 person	个 unit	人 person	户 household
全 国	**Nationwide**	**467081**	**4581**	**56026**	**95602**
北 京	Beijing		34	657	141
天 津	Tianjin		11	122	69
河 北	Hebei	5142	144	2052	3193
山 西	Shanxi	10128	28	918	585
内蒙古	Inner Mongolia	4673	93	777	796
辽 宁	Liaoning	7393	27	368	775
吉 林	Jilin	5904	188	1404	3794
黑龙江	Heilongjiang	3776	55	840	573
上 海	Shanghai		227	3626	2736
江 苏	Jiangsu	13067	146	2331	2356
浙 江	Zhejiang	14718	388	1709	3665
安 徽	Anhui	35166	118	1316	1336
福 建	Fujian	16199	56	599	1007
江 西	Jiangxi	42740	454	2419	2514
山 东	Shandong	25578	184	3174	1842
河 南	Henan	3729	68	4708	4464
湖 北	Hubei	30930	91	1437	2556
湖 南	Hunan	40609	429	6537	8623
广 东	Guangdong	366	55	1470	966
广 西	Guangxi	16662	134	796	15459
海 南	Hainan	773	36	383	255
重 庆	Chongqing	32304	196	1434	1567
四 川	Sichuan	27811	240	4038	4424
贵 州	Guizhou	31494	189	2132	4104
云 南	Yunnan	30191	386	2694	14874
西 藏	Tibet	25	1	9	8
陕 西	Shaanxi	8633	126	2201	3449
甘 肃	Gansu	36682	212	3398	5489
青 海	Qinghai	1107	53	807	517
宁 夏	Ningxia	6144	39	516	1607
新 疆	Xinjiang	13779	136	801	1085
新疆兵团	Xinjiang Production and Construction Corps	1358	37	353	773

4−4−4 农村贫困残疾人危房改造
House Renovation for Financially Difficnlt Persons with Disabilities in Rural Areas

地区	Region	本年度危房改造实际完成 Houses Renovated for PWDs in 2020 户 household	本年度危房改造项目受益贫困残疾人 Financially Difficnlt PWDs Benefited from House Renovation Projects in 2020 人 person	本年度投入资金 Fund Input in Houses Renovation in 2020 万元 10,000 yuan	省级投入资金 Fund from Provincial Budgets 万元 10,000 yuan	地市级投入资金 Fund from the Municipal Budgets 万元 10,000 yuan	县级投入资金 Fund from County-Level Budgets 万元 10,000 yuan
全国	**Nationwide**	**48041**	**55806**	**63014.1**	**37668.0**	**5132.4**	**20213.7**
北京	Beijing	2468	2468	1728.9			1728.9
天津	Tianjin	349	349	1064.3	716.3		348.0
河北	Hebei	448	495	382.2	164.9	7.0	210.2
山西	Shanxi	376	460	636.6	533.3	12.6	90.6
内蒙古	Inner Mongolia	493	536	148.7	95.3	23.5	29.9
辽宁	Liaoning	2577	2954	5437.2	3652.1	340.1	1445.0
吉林	Jilin	418	434	414.2	68.9	1.1	344.2
黑龙江	Heilongjiang	3664	5219	5691.2	4395.1	655.3	640.8
上海	Shanghai	67	67	78.9	6.7	20.8	51.4
江苏	Jiangsu	692	698	911.1	431.2	27.3	452.6
浙江	Zhejiang	3413	3681	5301.9	2156.2	215.0	2930.7
安徽	Anhui	2554	3394	2894.8	1430.9	28.6	1435.4
福建	Fujian	668	740	1069.6	127.9	80.4	861.3
江西	Jiangxi	1447	1716	2585.7	2299.1	22.8	263.9
山东	Shandong	5734	7945	5558.2	2904.5	533.1	2120.5
河南	Henan	2155	2472	2853.0	2586.0	116.0	151.0
湖北	Hubei	1449	1637	1192.2	1019.7	33.7	138.9
湖南	Hunan	5992	6478	9235.1	6309.0	372.1	2554.0
广东	Guangdong	2087	2132	1695.0	31.6	1093.8	569.6
广西	Guangxi	1822	1979	1422.5	1159.0	103.2	160.4
海南	Hainan	72	89	22.6	5.8	13.8	3.1
重庆	Chongqing	1525	1615	2043.0	566.2		1476.8
四川	Sichuan	5432	5587	7194.9	4825.8	1151.8	1217.2
贵州	Guizhou	221	223	40.5	35.3		5.2
云南	Yunnan	925	1421	1394.0	1325.8	37.2	31.0
西藏	Tibet	4	4	12.0		12.0	
陕西	Shaanxi	165	167	151.6	4.6	144.3	2.7
甘肃	Gansu						
青海	Qinghai	18	18	8.0	8.0		
宁夏	Ningxia	578	596	1710.5	777.1	2.0	931.4
新疆	Xinjiang	194	194	50.5	31.5		19.0
新疆兵团	Xinjiang Production and Construction Corps	34	38	85.0		85.0	

五、社会保障
Social Security

4-5-1 残疾人参加社会保险情况
Social Insurance Coverage of Persons with Disabilities

地 区	Region	残疾居民参加城乡社会养老保险 Residents with Disabilities Covered by Pension Insurance	享受养老保金 PWDs Drawing Pension	重度残疾人 Persons with Severe Disability
		万人 10,000 persons	万人 10,000 persons	万人 10,000 persons
全 国	**Nationwide**	**2699.2**	**1140.5**	**472.3**
北 京	Beijing	7.6	2.2	0.9
天 津	Tianjin	7.9	5.2	2.2
河 北	Hebei	153.3	59.6	25.7
山 西	Shanxi	91.2	41.9	13.9
内蒙古	Inner Mongolia	50.1	24.1	9.4
辽 宁	Liaoning	46.1	20.9	8.9
吉 林	Jilin	49.0	19.8	9.1
黑龙江	Heilongjiang	48.9	19.7	6.6
上 海	Shanghai	9.8	4.7	1.1
江 苏	Jiangsu	117.3	52.7	23.9
浙 江	Zhejiang	73.1	36.8	13.5
安 徽	Anhui	155.7	60.6	31.8
福 建	Fujian	70.6	34.3	14.9
江 西	Jiangxi	90.6	30.9	12.4
山 东	Shandong	178.7	82.7	42.8
河 南	Henan	281.5	124.3	41.4
湖 北	Hubei	124.4	49.7	22.0
湖 南	Hunan	157.0	65.5	30.7
广 东	Guangdong	99.5	34.7	20.6
广 西	Guangxi	98.6	46.0	18.5
海 南	Hainan	15.9	6.2	3.6
重 庆	Chongqing	56.6	24.5	9.8
四 川	Sichuan	247.4	107.3	46.2
贵 州	Guizhou	89.4	40.3	10.5
云 南	Yunnan	107.5	41.0	15.9
西 藏	Tibet	10.2	3.3	1.1
陕 西	Shaanxi	97.0	42.5	12.4
甘 肃	Gansu	97.0	36.7	11.7
青 海	Qinghai	12.1	5.3	2.5
宁 夏	Ningxia	15.3	6.1	3.0
新 疆	Xinjiang	37.5	10.9	4.8
新疆兵团	Xinjiang Production and Construction Corps	2.2	0.4	0.3

4-5-1 续表 Continued

地 区	Region	残疾居民参加城乡社会养老保险 Residents with Disabilities Covered by Pension Insurance				
		60周岁以下参保残疾人 PWDs under 60	重度残疾人 Persons with Severe Disability	全部或部分代缴 PWDs Whose Pension Premium Were Fully or Partially Covered by Government	其他残疾人 Other PWDs	全部或部分代缴 PWDs Whose Pension Premium Were Fully or Partially Covered by Government
		万人 10,000 persons	万人 10,000 persons	万人 10,000 persons	万人 10,000 persons	万人 10,000 persons
全 国	**Nationwide**	**1558.8**	**680.1**	**657.9**	**878.6**	**303.7**
北 京	Beijing	5.4	3.5	3.5	1.9	1.9
天 津	Tianjin	2.7	2.3	2.3	0.4	0.4
河 北	Hebei	93.7	35.8	34.9	57.9	12.8
山 西	Shanxi	49.3	19.8	18.9	29.5	8.0
内蒙古	Inner Mongolia	26.0	11.9	11.8	14.1	5.8
辽 宁	Liaoning	25.2	10.8	10.3	14.5	3.5
吉 林	Jilin	29.2	15.8	15.4	13.5	7.0
黑龙江	Heilongjiang	29.2	11.3	10.6	17.9	5.0
上 海	Shanghai	5.2	4.1	4.1	1.1	0.3
江 苏	Jiangsu	64.7	29.6	29.0	35.1	18.2
浙 江	Zhejiang	36.3	13.6	13.6	22.7	21.3
安 徽	Anhui	95.1	44.7	42.4	50.4	6.4
福 建	Fujian	36.4	20.3	20.1	16.0	14.5
江 西	Jiangxi	59.7	24.2	24.0	35.5	16.2
山 东	Shandong	96.1	46.9	45.8	49.2	8.9
河 南	Henan	157.2	49.7	46.8	107.5	4.9
湖 北	Hubei	74.7	36.9	35.6	37.8	8.1
湖 南	Hunan	91.5	47.5	47.2	44.0	25.0
广 东	Guangdong	64.8	44.8	43.7	20.0	12.8
广 西	Guangxi	52.6	26.6	25.6	26.0	11.8
海 南	Hainan	9.7	5.2	5.1	4.6	1.8
重 庆	Chongqing	32.2	13.6	13.0	18.6	6.7
四 川	Sichuan	140.1	54.1	52.2	86.0	26.9
贵 州	Guizhou	49.1	21.1	20.4	28.0	5.6
云 南	Yunnan	66.5	24.7	22.9	41.8	25.1
西 藏	Tibet	6.9	2.3	2.3	4.6	1.2
陕 西	Shaanxi	54.5	18.1	17.5	36.4	20.2
甘 肃	Gansu	60.3	21.9	21.0	38.4	8.6
青 海	Qinghai	6.8	3.4	3.2	3.4	2.7
宁 夏	Ningxia	9.2	4.7	4.6	4.5	1.9
新 疆	Xinjiang	26.6	10.1	9.5	16.6	9.7
新疆兵团	Xinjiang Production and Construction Corps	1.8	0.9	0.8	1.0	0.5

4-5-2 托养服务
Institutional Care Services

地 区	Region	托养服务机构合计 Institutions Providing Care Services	寄宿制托养服务 Boarding Institutions Providing Care Services	日间照料托养服务机构 Institutions Providing Day-Care Service	综合托养服务机构 Institutions Providing Combined Care Services	托养残疾人 PWDs Receiving Care Services	寄宿制机构中托养残疾人 PWDs in Boarding Care Institutions
		个 unit	个 unit	个 unit	个 unit	人 person	人 person
全 国	**Nationwide**	**8370**	**1945**	**3615**	**1369**	**537043**	**42823**
北 京	Beijing	251	251			41005	1445
天 津	Tianjin	67	12	55		59011	83
河 北	Hebei	312	69	21	65	15366	2207
山 西	Shanxi	193	24	17	44	7868	514
内蒙古	Inner Mongolia	153	81	11	34	3691	620
辽 宁	Liaoning	178	72	33	34	18969	2221
吉 林	Jilin	110	55	16	17	8310	525
黑龙江	Heilongjiang	94	6	2	11	4673	199
上 海	Shanghai	222		222		5515	
江 苏	Jiangsu	1850	67	1464	272	27470	1360
浙 江	Zhejiang	1295	150	1023	122	19538	1993
安 徽	Anhui	410	192	74	106	19834	1841
福 建	Fujian	105	46	50	7	18393	1297
江 西	Jiangxi	172	30	24	66	14235	437
山 东	Shandong	353	113	89	61	15205	3421
河 南	Henan	461	267	22	117	19525	7954
湖 北	Hubei	218	40	56	42	10340	1243
湖 南	Hunan	258	39	68	57	23072	1860
广 东	Guangdong	157	28	115	5	4773	1655
广 西	Guangxi	166	27	12	21	32148	2842
海 南	Hainan	51	13	2	1	30927	729
重 庆	Chongqing	147	37	57	21	23673	962
四 川	Sichuan	206	42	34	45	36832	1709
贵 州	Guizhou	122	16	8	53	7518	630
云 南	Yunnan	189	36	20	33	21733	1681
西 藏	Tibet	2	1			34	11
陕 西	Shaanxi	180	61	22	33	10471	1776
甘 肃	Gansu	104	23	22	22	25951	59
青 海	Qinghai	63	18	15	20	2902	253
宁 夏	Ningxia	66	17	19	4	5956	526
新 疆	Xinjiang	152	79	37	31	1118	527
新疆兵团	Xinjiang Production and Construction Corps	63	33	5	25	987	243

4–5–2　续表 1　Continued 1

地　区	Region	托养残疾人 PWDs Receiving Institutional Care Services							
		智力残疾人 Persons with Intellectual Disability	精神残疾人 Persons with Mental Disability	重度肢体残疾人 Persons with Severe Physical Disability	日间照料机构中托养残疾人 PWDs Receiving Day Care	智力残疾人 Persons with Intellectual Disability	精神残疾人 Persons with Mental Disability	重度肢体残疾人 Persons with Severe Physical Disability	综合托养服务机构中托养残疾人 PWDs in Institutions Providing Combined Services
		人 person	人 person	人 person	人 person	人 person	人 person	人 person	人 person
全　国	**Nationwide**	**9751**	**23993**	**6907**	**51004**	**26142**	**12559**	**10566**	**23237**
北　京	Beijing								
天　津	Tianjin				204				
河　北	Hebei	346	1761	98	818	259	131	424	591
山　西	Shanxi	86	268	160	218	68	49	101	285
内蒙古	Inner Mongolia	272	125	194	621	178	184	258	211
辽　宁	Liaoning	482	1558	181	654	541	56	57	1075
吉　林	Jilin	120	296	108	177	75	35	67	337
黑龙江	Heilongjiang	22	170	7	240	21	6	213	10
上　海	Shanghai				5515	5505	5	2	
江　苏	Jiangsu	534	636	167	14339	5988	3232	4438	2699
浙　江	Zhejiang	676	711	535	14891	7975	4947	1467	2654
安　徽	Anhui	372	1137	271	493	191	211	86	1167
福　建	Fujian	317	315	634	600	397	149	33	127
江　西	Jiangxi	56	312	61	1173	528	336	263	808
山　东	Shandong	1036	1876	486	602	367	104	128	658
河　南	Henan	1683	3994	2191	1708	332	475	839	4140
湖　北	Hubei	231	956	48	1235	460	484	283	1071
湖　南	Hunan	792	648	393	3125	1556	967	549	1208
广　东	Guangdong	873	513	230					69
广　西	Guangxi	234	2570	27	464	240	169	55	971
海　南	Hainan	37	691	1	4	2	1	1	
重　庆	Chongqing	187	665	105	1022	352	365	305	257
四　川	Sichuan	281	1098	330	1176	532	237	392	1439
贵　州	Guizhou	59	479	32	128	7	18	65	592
云　南	Yunnan	206	1291	133	135	60	49	26	926
西　藏	Tibet	1		10					
陕　西	Shaanxi	315	1250	178	202	121	43	37	744
甘　肃	Gansu	28	17	14	57	27	11	19	19
青　海	Qinghai	114	31	65	562	205	56	278	743
宁　夏	Ningxia	174	207	122	331	53	138	89	4
新　疆	Xinjiang	179	239	100	175	67	34	62	318
新疆兵团	Xinjiang Production and Construction Corps	38	179	26	135	35	67	29	114

4-5-2 续表 2 Continued 2

地 区	Region	托养残疾人 PWDs in the Institutions								享受居家托养服务残疾人 PWDs Recieving Care Service at Home
		以寄宿制方式托养的残疾人 PWDs in Boarding Institu-tions	智 力 残疾人 Persons with Intellectual Disability	精 神 残疾人 Persons with Mental Disability	重度肢体残疾人 Persons with Severe Physical Disability	以日间照料方式托养的残疾人 PWDs Receiving Day Care	智 力 残疾人 Persons with Intellectual Disability	精 神 残疾人 Persons with Mental Disability	重度肢体残疾人 Persons with Severe Physical Disability	
		人 person	人 person	人 person	人 person	人 person	人 person	人 person	人 person	人 person
全 国	**Nationwide**	**13778**	**3618**	**7550**	**2381**	**9459**	**3148**	**3151**	**2756**	**419979**
北 京	Beijing									39560
天 津	Tianjin									58724
河 北	Hebei	339	40	270	28	252	64	61	73	11750
山 西	Shanxi	240	74	70	96	45	4	13	28	6851
内蒙古	Inner Mongolia	158	62	17	75	53	4	15	34	2239
辽 宁	Liaoning	988	287	568	133	87	50	6	31	15019
吉 林	Jilin	319	52	151	114	18	3	2	13	7271
黑龙江	Heilongjiang	10	3	4	3					4224
上 海	Shanghai									
江 苏	Jiangsu	1277	587	410	250	1422	700	297	389	9072
浙 江	Zhejiang	1185	634	333	195	1469	813	522	98	
安 徽	Anhui	678	165	407	100	489	107	231	151	16333
福 建	Fujian	60	11	35	14	67	30	11	25	16369
江 西	Jiangxi	111	25	58	28	697	156	305	198	11817
山 东	Shandong	484	81	372	31	174	71	48	54	10524
河 南	Henan	2628	486	1638	495	1512	174	582	627	5723
湖 北	Hubei	479	36	430	13	592	141	266	144	6791
湖 南	Hunan	616	249	279	87	592	264	200	124	16879
广 东	Guangdong	41	20	17	3	28	26		2	3049
广 西	Guangxi	913	66	816	27	58	3	2	53	27871
海 南	Hainan									30194
重 庆	Chongqing	113	25	71	17	144	22	108	11	21432
四 川	Sichuan	1038	201	626	154	401	170	75	136	32508
贵 州	Guizhou	507	95	287	56	85	18	23	35	6168
云 南	Yunnan	623	172	337	114	303	34	181	88	18991
西 藏	Tibet									23
陕 西	Shaanxi	332	67	164	100	412	116	130	161	7749
甘 肃	Gansu	18	7	8	3	1		1		25816
青 海	Qinghai	265	111	47	93	478	154	40	264	1344
宁 夏	Ningxia	4	4							5095
新 疆	Xinjiang	296	40	117	132	22	8	5	3	98
新疆兵团	Xinjiang Production and Construction Corps	56	18	18	20	58	16	27	14	495

六、专门协会
Specialized Associations

4-6-1 省(自治区、直辖市)专门协会建立情况
Establishment of Special Associations at Provincial Level

地区	Region	盲人协会 Associations of Persons with Visual Disability	聋人协会 Associations of Persons with Hearing Disability	肢残人协会 Associations of Persons with Physical Disability	智力残疾人及亲友协会 Associations of Persons with Intellectual Disability and Their Relatives and Friends	精神残疾人及亲友协会 Associations of Persons with Psychosocial Disability and Their Relatives and Friends
		个 unit	个 unit	个 unit	个 unit	个 unit
全国	**Nationwide**	**32**	**32**	**32**	**31**	**31**
北京	Beijing	1	1	1	1	1
天津	Tianjin	1	1	1	1	1
河北	Hebei	1	1	1	1	1
山西	Shanxi	1	1	1	1	1
内蒙古	Inner Mongolia	1	1	1	1	1
辽宁	Liaoning	1	1	1	1	1
吉林	Jilin	1	1	1	1	1
黑龙江	Heilongjiang	1	1	1	1	1
上海	Shanghai	1	1	1	1	1
江苏	Jiangsu	1	1	1	1	1
浙江	Zhejiang	1	1	1	1	1
安徽	Anhui	1	1	1	1	1
福建	Fujian	1	1	1	1	1
江西	Jiangxi	1	1	1	1	1
山东	Shandong	1	1	1	1	1
河南	Henan	1	1	1	1	1
湖北	Hubei	1	1	1	1	1
湖南	Hunan	1	1	1	1	1
广东	Guangdong	1	1	1	1	1
广西	Guangxi	1	1	1	1	1
海南	Hainan	1	1	1	1	1
重庆	Chongqing	1	1	1	1	1
四川	Sichuan	1	1	1	1	1
贵州	Guizhou	1	1	1	1	1
云南	Yunnan	1	1	1	1	1
西藏	Tibet	1	1	1		
陕西	Shaanxi	1	1	1	1	1
甘肃	Gansu	1	1	1	1	1
青海	Qinghai	1	1	1	1	1
宁夏	Ningxia	1	1	1	1	1
新疆	Xinjiang	1	1	1	1	1
新疆兵团	Xinjiang Production and Construction Corps	1	1	1	1	1

4-6-2 市(地、州、盟)专门协会建立情况
Establishment of Specialized Associations at Municipal Level

地 区	Region	盲人协会 Associations of Persons with Visual Disability	聋人协会 Associations of Persons with Hearing Disability	肢残人协会 Associations of Persons with Physical Disability	智力残疾人及亲友协会 Associations of Persons with Intellectual Disability and Their Relatives and Friends	精神残疾人及亲友协会 Associations of Persons with Psychosocial Disability and Their Relatives and Friends	智力残疾人及亲友协会和精神残疾人及亲友协会合一的协会 Associations of Persons with Intellectual Disability and Psychosocial Disability and Their Relatives and Friends
		个 unit	个 unit	个 unit	个 unit	个 unit	个 unit
全 国	**Nationwide**	**330**	**330**	**332**	**325**	**325**	**4**
北 京	Beijing						
天 津	Tianjin						
河 北	Hebei	11	11	11	11	11	
山 西	Shanxi	11	11	11	11	11	
内蒙古	Inner Mongolia	12	12	12	12	12	
辽 宁	Liaoning	14	14	14	14	14	
吉 林	Jilin	10	10	10	10	10	
黑龙江	Heilongjiang	13	13	13	13	13	
上 海	Shanghai						
江 苏	Jiangsu	13	13	13	13	13	
浙 江	Zhejiang	11	11	11	11	11	
安 徽	Anhui	16	16	16	16	16	
福 建	Fujian	9	9	9	9	9	
江 西	Jiangxi	11	11	11	11	11	
山 东	Shandong	16	16	16	16	16	
河 南	Henan	18	18	18	18	18	
湖 北	Hubei	13	13	13	13	13	
湖 南	Hunan	14	14	14	14	14	
广 东	Guangdong	21	21	21	21	21	
广 西	Guangxi	14	14	14	14	14	
海 南	Hainan	3	3	3	3	3	
重 庆	Chongqing						
四 川	Sichuan	20	20	20	20	20	
贵 州	Guizhou	9	9	9	9	9	
云 南	Yunnan	16	15	16	15	15	1
西 藏	Tibet	1	2	2			
陕 西	Shaanxi	10	10	11	10	10	
甘 肃	Gansu	15	15	15	15	15	
青 海	Qinghai	8	8	8	8	8	
宁 夏	Ningxia	5	5	5	5	5	
新 疆	Xinjiang	14	14	14	12	12	2
新疆兵团	Xinjiang Production and Construction Corps	2	2	2	1	1	1

4-6-3 县(县级市、市辖区)专门协会建立情况
Establishment of Specialized Associations at County/District Level

地 区	Region	盲人协会 Associations of Persons with Visual Disability	聋人协会 Associations of Persons with Hearing Disability	肢残人协会 Associations of Persons with Physical Disability	智力残疾人及亲友协会 Associations of Persons with Intellectual Disability and Their Relatives and Friends	精神残疾人及亲友协会 Associations of Persons with Psychosocial Disability and Their Relatives and Friends	智力残疾人及亲友协会和精神残疾人及亲友协会合一的协会 Associations of Persons with Intellectual Disability and Psychosocial Disability and Their Relatives and Friends
		个 unit	个 unit	个 unit	个 unit	个 unit	个 unit
全 国	**Nationwide**	**2694**	**2683**	**2712**	**2545**	**2545**	**132**
北 京	Beijing	16	16	16	16	16	
天 津	Tianjin	16	16	16	16	16	
河 北	Hebei	167	167	167	166	165	1
山 西	Shanxi	117	117	117	111	110	10
内蒙古	Inner Mongolia	103	103	103	85	85	18
辽 宁	Liaoning	105	105	105	105	105	
吉 林	Jilin	63	63	63	62	62	
黑龙江	Heilongjiang	123	123	123	122	122	1
上 海	Shanghai	16	16	16	16	16	
江 苏	Jiangsu	99	99	99	92	92	6
浙 江	Zhejiang	91	90	91	72	72	19
安 徽	Anhui	102	103	103	95	93	6
福 建	Fujian	83	81	83	74	74	9
江 西	Jiangxi	84	84	87	83	84	
山 东	Shandong	131	126	129	123	123	2
河 南	Henan	159	158	159	157	157	1
湖 北	Hubei	93	91	94	80	81	10
湖 南	Hunan	123	123	124	113	114	8
广 东	Guangdong	119	119	119	110	111	7
广 西	Guangxi	111	111	111	109	109	2
海 南	Hainan	19	19	19	18	18	1
重 庆	Chongqing	39	39	39	38	38	1
四 川	Sichuan	167	165	172	164	162	2
贵 州	Guizhou	77	77	78	73	74	3
云 南	Yunnan	125	125	127	111	111	14
西 藏	Tibet						
陕 西	Shaanxi	105	104	105	103	105	
甘 肃	Gansu	86	86	86	86	86	
青 海	Qinghai	44	44	45	44	44	
宁 夏	Ningxia	21	21	21	19	20	1
新 疆	Xinjiang	85	87	88	80	77	7
新疆兵团	Xinjiang Production and Construction Corps	5	5	7	2	3	3

七、盲人按摩
Massage by the Blind

4-7-1 盲人按摩
Massage by the Blind

地区	Region	保健按摩人员本年度培训 Blind Health-Care Masseurs Trained in 2020	医疗按摩人员本年度培养 Blind Therapeutical Masseurs Trained in 2020	按摩机构 Institutions of Blind Massage	
				医疗按摩机构 Therapeutical Massage Institrations	保健按摩机构 Health-Care Massage Institrations
		人 person	人 person	人 person	人 person
全　国	**Nationwide**	**12761**	**7820**	**873**	**17313**
北　京	Beijing		202	3	401
天　津	Tianjin	9	93	3	119
河　北	Hebei	463	173	25	380
山　西	Shanxi	384	371	21	231
内蒙古	Inner Mongolia	109	378	146	402
辽　宁	Liaoning	667	70	26	655
吉　林	Jilin	158	297	38	338
黑龙江	Heilongjiang	36	159	43	293
上　海	Shanghai	14	95	1	96
江　苏	Jiangsu	1008	538	53	1315
浙　江	Zhejiang	563	327	89	1130
安　徽	Anhui	279	164	4	267
福　建	Fujian	250	135	39	584
江　西	Jiangxi	118	300	10	1000
山　东	Shandong	870	724	103	1770
河　南	Henan	1340	1129	40	1200
湖　北	Hubei	388	274	45	1213
湖　南	Hunan	568	338	20	732
广　东	Guangdong	269	366	8	1129
广　西	Guangxi	1496	126	4	250
海　南	Hainan	143	22	1	164
重　庆	Chongqing	133	137	17	337
四　川	Sichuan	650	21	6	680
贵　州	Guizhou	447	222	14	345
云　南	Yunnan	902	269	12	948
西　藏	Tibet	25	6		67
陕　西	Shaanxi	455	211	36	454
甘　肃	Gansu	749	266	32	394
青　海	Qinghai	70	120	10	77
宁　夏	Ningxia	97	228	10	207
新　疆	Xinjiang	79	51	13	117
新疆兵团	Xinjiang Production and Construction Corps	22	8	1	18

4-7-1 续表 Continued

地 区	Region	盲人医疗按摩人员专业技术职务任职资格评审 Vocational Qualification Appraisal for Blind Therapeutical Masseurs		盲人保健按摩人员就业 Employed Blind Health-Care Masseurs	盲人医疗按摩人员就业 Employed Blind Therapeutical Masseurs
		中级 Middle-Level Blind Therapeutical Masseurs	初级 Junior-Level Blind Therapeutical Masseurs		
		人 person	人 person	人 person	人 person
全 国	**Nationwide**	**138**	**621**	**7124**	**1683**
北 京	Beijing	5	12		16
天 津	Tianjin	1	8		
河 北	Hebei	37	193	195	167
山 西	Shanxi	10	52	272	111
内蒙古	Inner Mongolia	4	25	97	36
辽 宁	Liaoning	4	4		
吉 林	Jilin	3	7	61	11
黑龙江	Heilongjiang	9		370	113
上 海	Shanghai			20	16
江 苏	Jiangsu	14	79	273	21
浙 江	Zhejiang	1	33	129	22
安 徽	Anhui				37
福 建	Fujian			105	13
江 西	Jiangxi		8	118	
山 东	Shandong	6	62	299	65
河 南	Henan	13	16	1206	225
湖 北	Hubei	10	42	210	11
湖 南	Hunan	4		313	13
广 东	Guangdong				471
广 西	Guangxi	17		168	
海 南	Hainan			574	22
重 庆	Chongqing			675	72
四 川	Sichuan			1300	93
贵 州	Guizhou				
云 南	Yunnan		20	114	6
西 藏	Tibet		8	5	3
陕 西	Shaanxi		39	115	19
甘 肃	Gansu			249	25
青 海	Qinghai			12	7
宁 夏	Ningxia		13	207	86
新 疆	Xinjiang			37	2
新疆兵团	Xinjiang Production and Construction Corps				

八、宣传文化
Publicity and Cultural Activities

4-8-1 宣传文化
Publicity and Cultural Activities

地 区	Region	宣传 Publicity		
		省级 At Provincial Level		
		组织新闻发布会 Press Conferences about Disability	广播电台残疾人专题栏目 Radio Programs on Disability	电视手语栏目 TV Programmes with Sign Language
		次 time	个 unit	个 unit
全 国	**Nationwide**	**35**	**25**	**34**
北 京	Beijing	1	1	3
天 津	Tianjin		1	1
河 北	Hebei	1	1	
山 西	Shanxi		1	1
内蒙古	Inner Mongolia	2		1
辽 宁	Liaoning	1	1	1
吉 林	Jilin	1	1	1
黑龙江	Heilongjiang		1	2
上 海	Shanghai	10	1	2
江 苏	Jiangsu		1	1
浙 江	Zhejiang	2	1	4
安 徽	Anhui		1	1
福 建	Fujian			2
江 西	Jiangxi		2	
山 东	Shandong	1	1	1
河 南	Henan	1	1	1
湖 北	Hubei		1	
湖 南	Hunan	3		
广 东	Guangdong	2	1	1
广 西	Guangxi	1	1	1
海 南	Hainan	1		1
重 庆	Chongqing			1
四 川	Sichuan	2	1	1
贵 州	Guizhou		1	1
云 南	Yunnan		1	1
西 藏	Tibet			
陕 西	Shaanxi		1	1
甘 肃	Gansu	1	1	1
青 海	Qinghai		1	1
宁 夏	Ningxia	5	1	1
新 疆	Xinjiang			1
新疆兵团	Xinjiang Production and Construction Corps			

4-8-1 续表 1 Continued 1

地 区	Region	宣传 Publicity			
		省级 At Provincial Level			
		新促会 Disability Affairs Publicity Commissions	官方微博 Official Blog	官方微信 Official WeChat	入驻政务客户端平台 Government Administrative Platforms Incorporated with Disability Affairs
		个 unit	个 unit	个 unit	个 unit
全 国	**Nationwide**	**15**	**13**	**31**	**20**
北 京	Beijing	1	2	1	2
天 津	Tianjin		1	2	1
河 北	Hebei			1	
山 西	Shanxi				
内蒙古	Inner Mongolia			1	
辽 宁	Liaoning			1	
吉 林	Jilin	1	1	1	3
黑龙江	Heilongjiang			1	2
上 海	Shanghai	1	1	1	1
江 苏	Jiangsu	1		1	
浙 江	Zhejiang	1	1	1	
安 徽	Anhui			1	
福 建	Fujian			1	
江 西	Jiangxi		1	1	1
山 东	Shandong			1	
河 南	Henan	1		1	
湖 北	Hubei			1	1
湖 南	Hunan		1	1	
广 东	Guangdong	1		1	5
广 西	Guangxi	1	1	1	1
海 南	Hainan	1	2	2	1
重 庆	Chongqing	1		1	
四 川	Sichuan	1	1	1	1
贵 州	Guizhou	1		1	
云 南	Yunnan			1	1
西 藏	Tibet		1	1	
陕 西	Shaanxi			1	
甘 肃	Gansu			1	
青 海	Qinghai	1			
宁 夏	Ningxia	1		1	
新 疆	Xinjiang	1		1	
新疆兵团	Xinjiang Production and Construction Corps				

4-8-1 续表 2 Continued 2

地 区	Region	宣传 Publicity 地市级 At Municipal Level 组织新闻发布会 Press Conferences about Disability	广播电台残疾人专题栏目 Radio Programs on Disability	电视手语栏目 TV Programmes with Sign Language	新促会 Societies for Promoting News Relating to PWDs
		次 time	个 unit	个 unit	个 unit
全 国	**Nationwide**	**37**	**209**	**262**	**76**
北 京	Beijing			3	1
天 津	Tianjin		1	3	1
河 北	Hebei	3	9	11	6
山 西	Shanxi		12	9	3
内蒙古	Inner Mongolia	1	4	6	
辽 宁	Liaoning	3	8	15	3
吉 林	Jilin			6	6
黑龙江	Heilongjiang		7	9	3
上 海	Shanghai	6	3	14	3
江 苏	Jiangsu	3	12	16	4
浙 江	Zhejiang	2	13	12	3
安 徽	Anhui	4	17	16	4
福 建	Fujian		3	8	
江 西	Jiangxi	2	6	8	
山 东	Shandong	1	13	8	3
河 南	Henan	3	11	6	12
湖 北	Hubei	1	9	10	1
湖 南	Hunan	1	7	3	2
广 东	Guangdong	4	14	13	8
广 西	Guangxi	3	4	5	
海 南	Hainan			1	
重 庆	Chongqing		10	27	1
四 川	Sichuan		7	9	
贵 州	Guizhou		3	7	1
云 南	Yunnan		4	9	4
西 藏	Tibet		1		
陕 西	Shaanxi		1	2	1
甘 肃	Gansu		27	12	6
青 海	Qinghai			5	
宁 夏	Ningxia		1	5	
新 疆	Xinjiang		1	3	
新疆兵团	Xinjiang Production and Construction Corps		1	1	

4-8-1　续表 3　Continued 3

地　区	Region	文化 Cultural Activities			
		省级 At Provincial Level			
		公共图书馆盲文及盲人有声读物图书室 Reading Rooms with Braille and Audio Reading Materials in Public Library	残疾人文化周 Cultural Week for PWDs	残疾人文化艺术类比赛及展览 Cultural or Artistic Competitions and Exhibitions of PWDs	残疾人艺术团 Arts Groups of PWDs
		个 unit	场次 time	次 time	个 unit
全　国	**Nationwide**	**30**	**190**	**205**	**22**
北　京	Beijing		1	2	1
天　津	Tianjin	1	4	1	4
河　北	Hebei		20	10	
山　西	Shanxi	1	1	1	
内蒙古	Inner Mongolia	1	1	3	
辽　宁	Liaoning	1	3	2	
吉　林	Jilin	2	13	19	
黑龙江	Heilongjiang	1	2	1	1
上　海	Shanghai	1	13	4	1
江　苏	Jiangsu	2	5	6	
浙　江	Zhejiang	1	2	30	1
安　徽	Anhui	1	4	2	
福　建	Fujian	2	3	3	1
江　西	Jiangxi	1	5		
山　东	Shandong	1	1	1	1
河　南	Henan	1	1		
湖　北	Hubei	1	1		1
湖　南	Hunan		1		
广　东	Guangdong	1	3	3	1
广　西	Guangxi	1	3	1	1
海　南	Hainan	1	1	1	2
重　庆	Chongqing	1	64	64	1
四　川	Sichuan	1		36	2
贵　州	Guizhou	1	12	8	
云　南	Yunnan	1	1		
西　藏	Tibet		4		
陕　西	Shaanxi	1	1		1
甘　肃	Gansu	1	18	3	
青　海	Qinghai	1	1	1	1
宁　夏	Ningxia	1	1	2	1
新　疆	Xinjiang	1		1	1
新疆兵团	Xinjiang Production and Construction Corps				

4-8-1 续表 4 Continued 4

地区	Region	文化 Cultural Activities					
		地市级 At Municipal Level				县级 At County Level	
		公共图书馆盲文及盲人有声读物图书室 Reading Rooms with Braille and Audio Reading Materials in Public Library	残疾人文化周 Cultural Week for PWDs	残疾人文化艺术类比赛及展览 Cultural or Artistic Competitions and Exhibitions of PWDs	残疾人艺术团 Arts Groups of PWDs	公共图书馆盲文及盲人有声读物图书室 Reading Rooms with Braille and Audio Reading Materials in Public Library	残疾人文化周 Cultural Week for PWDs
		个 unit	场次 time	次 time	个 unit	个 unit	场次 time
全　国	**Nationwide**	**287**	**882**	**485**	**227**	**941**	**7459**
北　京	Beijing					7	261
天　津	Tianjin					6	103
河　北	Hebei	15	40	28	7	16	366
山　西	Shanxi	7	13	7	11	11	82
内蒙古	Inner Mongolia	10	19	13	1	25	135
辽　宁	Liaoning	16	50	44	15	36	165
吉　林	Jilin	8	15	20	10	41	174
黑龙江	Heilongjiang	12	43	22	11	37	150
上　海	Shanghai					37	353
江　苏	Jiangsu	17	89	47	16	61	959
浙　江	Zhejiang	13	24	34	34	73	837
安　徽	Anhui	14	55	18	8	42	269
福　建	Fujian	6	15	9	1	38	147
江　西	Jiangxi	7	21	6	4	22	144
山　东	Shandong	15	51	74	17	57	256
河　南	Henan	16	39	14	6	58	191
湖　北	Hubei	11	56	18	3	22	143
湖　南	Hunan	9	23	26	28	17	137
广　东	Guangdong	19	81	52	12	43	600
广　西	Guangxi	11	47	2	4	17	192
海　南	Hainan	2	4		1		7
重　庆	Chongqing					40	416
四　川	Sichuan	19	26	6	14	51	330
贵　州	Guizhou	6	56	1	2	20	124
云　南	Yunnan	15	25	5	5	35	214
西　藏	Tibet	2	1			2	
陕　西	Shaanxi	7	13	1	5	46	110
甘　肃	Gansu	14	28	16	6	41	200
青　海	Qinghai	5	8	4	1	10	75
宁　夏	Ningxia	5	12	16	2	23	91
新　疆	Xinjiang	5	9	2	2	6	57
新疆兵团	Xinjiang Production and Construction Corps	1	19		1	1	171

九、体育
Sports

4-9-1 体 育
Sports

地 区	Region	省级 At Provincial Level					
		残疾人群众体育健身活动 Fitness Sports Activities for PWDs	残疾人群众体育健身活动参加人次 Participants of Fitness Sports Activities for PWDs	新增残疾人健身示范点 Exemplary Bases for Fitness Sports of PWDs Established in 2020	新增残疾人社会体育指导员 Coaches for Fitness Sports of PWDs in 2020	残疾人体育比赛 Sports Events for PWDs	参赛残疾人运动员 Disabled Athletes Who Participated in the Sports Events
		次 time	人次 person-time	个 unit	人 person	次 time	人次 person-time
全 国	**Nationwide**	**392**	**79648**	**352**	**1757**	**66**	**6085**
北 京	Beijing	7	3300		83	3	20
天 津	Tianjin	3	1150	99	499		
河 北	Hebei	65	24494	76		6	1200
山 西	Shanxi	2	164	55	603	6	380
内蒙古	Inner Mongolia	3	260		87		
辽 宁	Liaoning	6	800	36		1	141
吉 林	Jilin	3	9600		80	4	336
黑龙江	Heilongjiang	1	583				
上 海	Shanghai	3	8992			2	1887
江 苏	Jiangsu	9	2162	20	151	2	7
浙 江	Zhejiang	4	1800	3	16	4	300
安 徽	Anhui	5	170		20		
福 建	Fujian	30	5000	2	8	1	100
江 西	Jiangxi	1	70	19	18	7	316
山 东	Shandong	2	100	3		1	50
河 南	Henan	3	510			1	10
湖 北	Hubei	3	247				
湖 南	Hunan	2	310	3			
广 东	Guangdong	8	500	10	18	3	300
广 西	Guangxi	1	96		2		
海 南	Hainan					1	70
重 庆	Chongqing	3	8200			1	74
四 川	Sichuan	2	280				
贵 州	Guizhou	2	200	5	50		
云 南	Yunnan	3	200		34	5	80
西 藏	Tibet	3	210			1	17
陕 西	Shaanxi	200	5000	1		7	100
甘 肃	Gansu	5	750	20	5	2	11
青 海	Qinghai	8	3500		78	7	438
宁 夏	Ningxia	5	1000		3	1	248
新 疆	Xinjiang						
新疆兵团	Xinjiang Production and Construction Corps				2		

4-9-1 续表 Continued

地 区	Region	省级 At Provincial Level		地市级 At Municipal Level				残疾人康复体育进家庭服务 Delivery of Rehabilitative Sports to Families with PWDs
		残疾人体育训练基地 Sports Training Bases for PWDs	聘任教练员 Contracted Coaches	残疾人群众体育健身活动 Fitness Sports Activities for PWDs	残疾人群众体育健身活动参加人数 Participants of Fitness Sports Activities for PWDs	新增残疾人体育健身示范点 Exemplary Bases for Fitness Sports of PWDs Established in 2020	新增残疾人社会体育指导员 Coaches for Fitness Sports of PWDs in 2020	
		个 unit	人 person	次 time	人次 person-time	个 unit	人 person	户 household
全 国	**Nationwide**	**258**	**815**	**4206**	**180594**	**367**	**3907**	**109423**
北 京	Beijing	5	53					
天 津	Tianjin	5	15				46	
河 北	Hebei	13	50	3000	76415		709	3997
山 西	Shanxi	5	13	8	511			
内蒙古	Inner Mongolia	2	2	5	223			501
辽 宁	Liaoning	9	40	46	2484	22	13	2468
吉 林	Jilin	16	20	71	16295		30	
黑龙江	Heilongjiang	2	3	6	498			
上 海	Shanghai	5	40					
江 苏	Jiangsu	7	21	417	23214	5		834
浙 江	Zhejiang	9	53	50	12949	7	142	13520
安 徽	Anhui	10	7	41	1821		140	593
福 建	Fujian	18	32	16	1240	11	133	5575
江 西	Jiangxi	13	40	27	1928	7	114	1117
山 东	Shandong	12	60	73	6126	30	270	11162
河 南	Henan	6	55	33	1688	209	1355	
湖 北	Hubei	4	8	34	3560			
湖 南	Hunan	5	13	29	1035	17	5	2498
广 东	Guangdong	8	50	117	10305	40	838	8004
广 西	Guangxi	1	20	9	1112			
海 南	Hainan	12	27	1	5			
重 庆	Chongqing	15	15					
四 川	Sichuan	16	56	47	8246			56982
贵 州	Guizhou	6	11	3	375	1	5	833
云 南	Yunnan	6	20	81	3769	11	71	696
西 藏	Tibet		2					
陕 西	Shaanxi	31	50	14	1647			
甘 肃	Gansu	4	7	42	2419	5	1	
青 海	Qinghai	1	3	7	480			27
宁 夏	Ningxia	6	23	12	1863	2	15	412
新 疆	Xinjiang	6	6	1	100			
新疆兵团	Xinjiang Production and Construction Corps			16	286		20	204

十、维权
Rights Protection

4-10-1　法规体系
Legal System

地　区	Region	制定或修改关于残疾人的专门法规、规章 Disability-specific Laws and Regulations Enacted or Reviewed for PWDs	省级 At Provincial Level	地市级 At Municipal Level	制定或修改保障残疾人权益的规范性文件 Polices Enacted or Reviewed for PWDs	省级 At Provincial Level	地市级 At Municipal Level	县级 At County Level
		个 unit	个 unit	个 unit	个 unit	个 unit	个 unit	个 unit
全　国	**Nationwide**	**9**	**4**	**5**	**249**	**22**	**64**	**163**
北　京	Beijing				1	1		
天　津	Tianjin				2	2		
河　北	Hebei				15		3	12
山　西	Shanxi				6			6
内蒙古	Inner Mongolia				2			2
辽　宁	Liaoning				4		2	2
吉　林	Jilin				9	1	7	1
黑龙江	Heilongjiang				4			4
上　海	Shanghai				6	5		1
江　苏	Jiangsu	2	1	1	12	2	7	3
浙　江	Zhejiang				26		7	19
安　徽	Anhui				5		1	4
福　建	Fujian	1		1	9	1		8
江　西	Jiangxi				14		1	13
山　东	Shandong				23	4	10	9
河　南	Henan	1		1	6		3	3
湖　北	Hubei				5		2	3
湖　南	Hunan				7	1	1	5
广　东	Guangdong	1		1	15		9	6
广　西	Guangxi				1		1	
海　南	Hainan	1	1		3	2		1
重　庆	Chongqing				5	2		3
四　川	Sichuan				16			16
贵　州	Guizhou				5			5
云　南	Yunnan				8		2	6
西　藏	Tibet							
陕　西	Shaanxi				6			6
甘　肃	Gansu	1		1	18		1	17
青　海	Qinghai	1	1		8	1	1	6
宁　夏	Ningxia	1	1		3		3	
新　疆	Xinjiang				5		3	2
新疆兵团	Xinjiang Production and Construction Corps							

4-10-2 执法检查
Law Enforcement Inspection

地区	Region	人大执法检查或专题调研 Inspections and Researches by People's Congresses	省级 At Provincial Level	地市级 At Municipal Level	县级 At County Level
		次 time	次 time	次 time	次 time
全国	**Nationwide**	**318**	**7**	**63**	**248**
北京	Beijing	4			4
天津	Tianjin	1	1		
河北	Hebei	20	1	2	17
山西	Shanxi	24	1	4	19
内蒙古	Inner Mongolia	4		1	3
辽宁	Liaoning	6		5	1
吉林	Jilin	3			3
黑龙江	Heilongjiang	8		1	7
上海	Shanghai	2			2
江苏	Jiangsu	19		4	15
浙江	Zhejiang	52		5	47
安徽	Anhui	14		4	10
福建	Fujian	1			1
江西	Jiangxi	12		2	10
山东	Shandong	15		2	13
河南	Henan	6		3	3
湖北	Hubei	7		2	5
湖南	Hunan	28	2	6	20
广东	Guangdong	23		14	9
广西	Guangxi	6	1	1	4
海南	Hainan	2		1	1
重庆	Chongqing	7			7
四川	Sichuan	24	1	2	21
贵州	Guizhou	1		1	
云南	Yunnan	9		2	7
西藏	Tibet				
陕西	Shaanxi	1			1
甘肃	Gansu	15		1	14
青海	Qinghai	1			1
宁夏	Ningxia	1			1
新疆	Xinjiang	2			2
新疆兵团	Xinjiang Production and Construction Corps				

4-10-2 续表 Continued

地 区	Region	政协视察或专题调研 Inspections and Researches by People's Political Consultative Conferences	省级 At Provincial Level	地市级 At Municipal Level	县级 At County Level
		次 time	次 time	次 time	次 time
全 国	**Nationwide**	**282**	**12**	**53**	**217**
北 京	Beijing	1			1
天 津	Tianjin				
河 北	Hebei	14			14
山 西	Shanxi	11		2	9
内蒙古	Inner Mongolia	4			4
辽 宁	Liaoning	3		2	1
吉 林	Jilin	3			3
黑龙江	Heilongjiang	6		1	5
上 海	Shanghai				
江 苏	Jiangsu	16		4	12
浙 江	Zhejiang	83	6	16	61
安 徽	Anhui	7		1	6
福 建	Fujian	6	2	2	2
江 西	Jiangxi	20	3	3	14
山 东	Shandong	9	1	2	6
河 南	Henan	3			3
湖 北	Hubei	8		2	6
湖 南	Hunan	20		4	16
广 东	Guangdong	13		5	8
广 西	Guangxi	3		1	2
海 南	Hainan	1		1	
重 庆	Chongqing	8			8
四 川	Sichuan	17		4	13
贵 州	Guizhou	2			2
云 南	Yunnan	4			4
西 藏	Tibet				
陕 西	Shaanxi	1			1
甘 肃	Gansu	12			12
青 海	Qinghai	3		1	2
宁 夏	Ningxia	3		2	1
新 疆	Xinjiang	1			1
新疆兵团	Xinjiang Production and Construction Corps				

4-10-3 法制宣传
Publicity on Laws

地 区	Region	省级 At Provincial Level			
		普法宣传教育活动 Activities for Law Publicity and Education	普法宣传教育活动参加人数 Participants of Activities for Law Publicity and Education	残疾人工作者法律培训班 Law Trainings for Staff Working for PWDs	法律培训班参加人数 Trainees of Law Trainings
		次 time	人 person	个 unit	人 person
全 国	**Nationwide**	**526**	**396888**	**44**	**4867**
北 京	Beijing	342	5000	2	150
天 津	Tianjin	2	80	1	50
河 北	Hebei	4	1500	3	200
山 西	Shanxi	4	460	2	112
内蒙古	Inner Mongolia	2	200000	3	145
辽 宁	Liaoning	7	700	3	300
吉 林	Jilin	5	2300	2	260
黑龙江	Heilongjiang	3	5009	1	40
上 海	Shanghai	4	12000		
江 苏	Jiangsu	32	2000	1	100
浙 江	Zhejiang	5	1100	2	760
安 徽	Anhui	1	260	1	60
福 建	Fujian	7	365	2	100
江 西	Jiangxi	9	1321	3	625
山 东	Shandong	5	6000	2	150
河 南	Henan	2	160		
湖 北	Hubei	13	20000	1	120
湖 南	Hunan	1	60		
广 东	Guangdong	1	9586	2	240
广 西	Guangxi	3	500	1	50
海 南	Hainan	32	11000	1	102
重 庆	Chongqing	9	1397	4	833
四 川	Sichuan	2	5270	2	120
贵 州	Guizhou	2	400		
云 南	Yunnan	2	120	1	80
西 藏	Tibet	7	475	2	120
陕 西	Shaanxi	3	2000	1	70
甘 肃	Gansu	8	1200		
青 海	Qinghai	1	106205	1	80
宁 夏	Ningxia	4	240		
新 疆	Xinjiang	4	180		
新疆兵团	Xinjiang Production and Construction Corps				

4-10-4　法律救助
Legal Aid

地区	Region	建立残疾人法律救助协调组织 Legal Assistance and Coordination Organization for PWDs			
		建立残疾人法律救助工作协调机构 Legal Assistance and Coordination Organization for PWDs	省级 At Provincial Level	地市级 At Municipal Level	县级 At County Level
		个 unit	个 unit	个 unit	个 unit
全　国	**Nationwide**	**2881**	**31**	**321**	**2529**
北　京	Beijing	13	1		12
天　津	Tianjin	17	1		16
河　北	Hebei	180	1	11	168
山　西	Shanxi	118	1	11	106
内蒙古	Inner Mongolia	113	1	12	100
辽　宁	Liaoning	115	1	14	100
吉　林	Jilin	70	1	9	60
黑龙江	Heilongjiang	81	1	13	67
上　海	Shanghai	17	1		16
江　苏	Jiangsu	110	1	13	96
浙　江	Zhejiang	101	1	11	89
安　徽	Anhui	112	1	16	95
福　建	Fujian	95	1	9	85
江　西	Jiangxi	112	1	11	100
山　东	Shandong	119	1	14	104
河　南	Henan	176	1	17	158
湖　北	Hubei	94	1	11	82
湖　南	Hunan	134	1	14	119
广　东	Guangdong	109	1	20	88
广　西	Guangxi	121	1	14	106
海　南	Hainan	23	1	3	19
重　庆	Chongqing	13	1		12
四　川	Sichuan	156	1	21	134
贵　州	Guizhou	80	1	8	71
云　南	Yunnan	94	1	13	80
西　藏	Tibet	82	1	7	74
陕　西	Shaanxi	118	1	10	107
甘　肃	Gansu	101	1	14	86
青　海	Qinghai	49	1	6	42
宁　夏	Ningxia	27	1	5	21
新　疆	Xinjiang	119	1	14	104
新疆兵团	Xinjiang Production and Construction Corps	12			12

4-10-4 续表 1 Continued 1

地区	Region	残疾人法律救助工作站 Legal Assistance Stations for PWDs			
		残疾人法律救助工作站 Legal Assistance Stations for PWDs	省级 At Provincial Level	地市级 At Municipal Level	县级 At County Level
		个 unit	个 unit	个 unit	个 unit
全国	**Nationwide**	**2795**	**27**	**322**	**2446**
北京	Beijing	4			4
天津	Tianjin	17	1		16
河北	Hebei	180	1	11	168
山西	Shanxi	115		10	105
内蒙古	Inner Mongolia	112	1	12	99
辽宁	Liaoning	115	1	14	100
吉林	Jilin	70	1	9	60
黑龙江	Heilongjiang	81	1	13	67
上海	Shanghai	17	1		16
江苏	Jiangsu	110	1	13	96
浙江	Zhejiang	101	1	11	89
安徽	Anhui	111		16	95
福建	Fujian	95	1	9	85
江西	Jiangxi	94	1	11	82
山东	Shandong	118	1	14	103
河南	Henan	176	1	17	158
湖北	Hubei	104	1	13	90
湖南	Hunan	134	1	14	119
广东	Guangdong	91	1	20	70
广西	Guangxi	119	1	14	104
海南	Hainan	22		3	19
重庆	Chongqing	13	1		12
四川	Sichuan	156	1	21	134
贵州	Guizhou	73	1	9	63
云南	Yunnan	112	1	12	99
西藏	Tibet	30	1	7	22
陕西	Shaanxi	118	1	10	107
甘肃	Gansu	101	1	14	86
青海	Qinghai	50	1	6	43
宁夏	Ningxia	25	1	5	19
新疆	Xinjiang	119	1	14	104
新疆兵团	Xinjiang Production and Construction Corps	12			12

4-10-5 参政议政
Participation of Persons with Disabilities in Administration and Discussion of State Affairs

地 区	Region	残联协助提出建议、议案和提案 Bills,Suggestions and Proposals Submitted with Assistance of Disabled Persons' Federations		残联办理人大政协建议、提案 Suggestions and Proposals Handled by Disabled Persons' Federations	
		协助人大代表提出议案、建议 Bills and Suggestions Submitted to People's Congresses	协助政协委员提出提案 Proposals Submitted to People's Political Consultative Conferences	办理人大建议 Suggestions of People's Congresses Handled	办理政协提案 Proposals of People's Political Consultative Conferences Handled
		件 case	件 case	件 case	件 case
全 国	**Nationwide**	**260**	**475**	**411**	**698**
北 京	Beijing	2	6	5	16
天 津	Tianjin		2	8	8
河 北	Hebei	9	13	16	16
山 西	Shanxi	5	14	11	11
内蒙古	Inner Mongolia	2	8	6	18
辽 宁	Liaoning	10	12	12	19
吉 林	Jilin	4	2	3	9
黑龙江	Heilongjiang		4	2	3
上 海	Shanghai	3	3	28	15
江 苏	Jiangsu	5	15	32	59
浙 江	Zhejiang	58	87	66	107
安 徽	Anhui	1	16	13	35
福 建	Fujian	13	18	28	30
江 西	Jiangxi	12	31	6	25
山 东	Shandong	31	16	15	28
河 南	Henan	2	16	11	18
湖 北	Hubei	15	24	16	33
湖 南	Hunan	16	22	10	18
广 东	Guangdong	20	26	57	67
广 西	Guangxi	2	12	5	22
海 南	Hainan	3	9	2	13
重 庆	Chongqing	10	20	19	20
四 川	Sichuan	13	23	20	36
贵 州	Guizhou	3	8		10
云 南	Yunnan	5	18	6	11
西 藏	Tibet		1		2
陕 西	Shaanxi		7	4	9
甘 肃	Gansu	8	19	4	15
青 海	Qinghai	6	14	3	4
宁 夏	Ningxia		6	1	11
新 疆	Xinjiang	2	3	2	8
新疆兵团	Xinjiang Production and Construction Corps				2

4-10-6 无障碍环境建设与残疾人机动轮椅车燃油补贴
Promotion of Accessible Environments and Gas Subsidy for Motorized Wheelchairs

地 区	Region	无障碍建设与管理法规、政府令 Regulations and Decrees on Accessible Environments Building and Management	无障碍建设领导协调组织 Leading and Coordinating Bodies for Building Accessible Environments	系统开展无障碍建设市、县 Cities and Counties Carrying Out Systematic Accessibitity Construction	地市级 At Municipal Level	县级 At County Level
		个 unit	个 unit	个 unit	个 unit	个 unit
全 国	**Nationwide**	**674**	**1585**	**1753**	**218**	**1535**
北 京	Beijing	53	164	16		16
天 津	Tianjin	3	17	16		16
河 北	Hebei	48	133	186	11	175
山 西	Shanxi	16	48	77	11	66
内蒙古	Inner Mongolia	17	21	69	9	60
辽 宁	Liaoning	4	52	8	5	3
吉 林	Jilin	18	30	9	4	5
黑龙江	Heilongjiang	3	11	36	2	34
上 海	Shanghai	4	26	15		15
江 苏	Jiangsu	35	82	55	13	42
浙 江	Zhejiang	69	92	102	11	91
安 徽	Anhui	8	33	82	16	66
福 建	Fujian	13	55	51	9	42
江 西	Jiangxi	16	32	127	12	115
山 东	Shandong	49	102	94	13	81
河 南	Henan	98	48	62	5	57
湖 北	Hubei	13	27	84	13	71
湖 南	Hunan	19	51	13		13
广 东	Guangdong	34	41	145	21	124
广 西	Guangxi		126	125	14	111
海 南	Hainan	6	8	6	2	4
重 庆	Chongqing	10	34	38		38
四 川	Sichuan	30	61	61	10	51
贵 州	Guizhou	2	23	26	3	23
云 南	Yunnan	19	64	45	4	41
西 藏	Tibet		1			
陕 西	Shaanxi	28	29	55	4	51
甘 肃	Gansu	46	73	101	15	86
青 海	Qinghai	5	41	14	3	11
宁 夏	Ningxia	5	22	25	5	20
新 疆	Xinjiang	3	36	9	2	7
新疆兵团	Xinjiang Production and Construction Corps		2	1	1	

4-10-6　续表　Continued

地　区	Region	残疾人家庭无障碍改造 Accessibility Renovation for Homes of PWDs	无障碍建设检查 Inspections on Accessibility	无障碍培训 Trainings on Accessibility	残疾人机动轮椅车燃油补贴 Subsidy for Gas Used by Motorized Wheelchairs of PWDs
		人 person	次 time	人次 person-time	人 person
全　国	**Nationwide**	**1673390**	**8576**	**56173**	**341357**
北　京	Beijing	28705	3456	18883	23656
天　津	Tianjin	11394	68	302	12391
河　北	Hebei	56157	114	719	7120
山　西	Shanxi	21749	43	255	8703
内蒙古	Inner Mongolia	17478	52	93	3756
辽　宁	Liaoning	29144	100	2884	11879
吉　林	Jilin	25068	12	108	6132
黑龙江	Heilongjiang	17404	6	91	6177
上　海	Shanghai	26459	646	875	26011
江　苏	Jiangsu	38588	259	4257	14194
浙　江	Zhejiang	137436	816	8967	12528
安　徽	Anhui	88746	77	571	12351
福　建	Fujian	17880	69	1751	2252
江　西	Jiangxi	59186	60	839	18469
山　东	Shandong	269214	249	2494	1843
河　南	Henan	248844	59	575	19185
湖　北	Hubei	61078	61	294	9402
湖　南	Hunan	132493	79	733	48376
广　东	Guangdong	31539	511	862	14787
广　西	Guangxi	34429	89	981	5236
海　南	Hainan	21781	55	1732	5108
重　庆	Chongqing	34917	58	1746	2855
四　川	Sichuan	13174	1349	3419	8113
贵　州	Guizhou	56787	9	58	3993
云　南	Yunnan	57143	61	780	17410
西　藏	Tibet	3734	2	1	2224
陕　西	Shaanxi	52426	56	870	8118
甘　肃	Gansu	23818	56	704	12010
青　海	Qinghai	7721	34	10	12342
宁　夏	Ningxia	12172	36	156	4287
新　疆	Xinjiang	35426	33	131	447
新疆兵团	Xinjiang Production and Construction Corps	1300	1	32	2

4-10-7 残疾人信访
Petitions from Persons with Disabilities

地 区	Region	来信 Petition Letters					
		总计 Subtotal	涉法涉诉类 Regarding Legal Lawsuits	医疗康复类 Medical Rehabilitation	教育类 Education	就业扶贫类 Employment and Poverty Alleviation	社会保障类 Social Security
		件 case	件 case	件 case	件 case	件 case	件 case
全 国	**Nationwide**	**24579**	**821**	**5191**	**1779**	**3023**	**5768**
北 京	Beijing	343	26	29	5	49	39
天 津	Tianjin	131	7	7	2	2	21
河 北	Hebei	282	21	19	8	70	48
山 西	Shanxi	1293	49	651	36	99	105
内蒙古	Inner Mongolia	108	3	41	14	34	7
辽 宁	Liaoning	288	29	36	13	32	48
吉 林	Jilin	352	19	37	2	46	81
黑龙江	Heilongjiang	53	4	4		12	7
上 海	Shanghai	1087	56	171	17	56	180
江 苏	Jiangsu	1008	33	105	57	119	186
浙 江	Zhejiang	1018	29	102	40	134	236
安 徽	Anhui	359	6	130	6	69	41
福 建	Fujian	577	39	50	5	61	175
江 西	Jiangxi	775	2	374	17	105	164
山 东	Shandong	557	13	70	18	75	119
河 南	Henan	534	21	90	38	79	98
湖 北	Hubei	1099	96	85	32	271	407
湖 南	Hunan	1095	70	118	66	168	378
广 东	Guangdong	2433	82	165	320	195	249
广 西	Guangxi	214	15	36	7	38	56
海 南	Hainan	91	6	2		4	28
重 庆	Chongqing	293	4	62	6	40	67
四 川	Sichuan	2096	35	307	135	384	641
贵 州	Guizhou	4729	11	1495	657	239	1687
云 南	Yunnan	1730	17	538	132	278	265
西 藏	Tibet	13	2	5		5	
陕 西	Shaanxi	828	108	162	61	138	216
甘 肃	Gansu	463	6	141	57	19	98
青 海	Qinghai	66		10	4	5	8
宁 夏	Ningxia	441	12	102	6	136	89
新 疆	Xinjiang	218		47	18	60	23
新疆兵团	Xinjiang Production and Construction Corps	5				1	1

4-10-7　续表 1　Continued 1

地　区	Region	来信 Petition Letters				
		权益保障类 Rights and Interest Protection	控告检举类 Accusation and Disclosure	意见建议类 Opinions and Suggestions	非残类 Unrelated with Disability	其他类 Others
		件 case	件 case	件 case	件 case	件 case
全　国	**Nationwide**	**2823**	**373**	**1158**	**762**	**2881**
北　京	Beijing	96	13	21	10	55
天　津	Tianjin	30	8	10		44
河　北	Hebei	29	7	26	3	51
山　西	Shanxi	91	2	36	97	127
内蒙古	Inner Mongolia	7			1	1
辽　宁	Liaoning	32	4	9		85
吉　林	Jilin	37	3	8		119
黑龙江	Heilongjiang	17	3	3		3
上　海	Shanghai	206	36	75	22	268
江　苏	Jiangsu	168	68	100	11	161
浙　江	Zhejiang	135	43	102	14	183
安　徽	Anhui	20	7	9		71
福　建	Fujian	91	38	13		105
江　西	Jiangxi	36	6	34		37
山　东	Shandong	107	25	5	8	117
河　南	Henan	97		88		23
湖　北	Hubei	68	5	88		47
湖　南	Hunan	126	17	70	19	63
广　东	Guangdong	202	25	74	526	595
广　西	Guangxi	23	4	8	1	26
海　南	Hainan	36	10	2	3	
重　庆	Chongqing	31	4	55		24
四　川	Sichuan	316	15	97	24	142
贵　州	Guizhou	457	1	128	6	48
云　南	Yunnan	140	7	18	5	330
西　藏	Tibet	1				
陕　西	Shaanxi	44	6	12	9	72
甘　肃	Gansu	76		62		4
青　海	Qinghai	33	2	1		3
宁　夏	Ningxia	57	4	1	3	31
新　疆	Xinjiang	12	10	3		45
新疆兵团	Xinjiang Production and Construction Corps	2				1

4-10-7 续表 2 Continued 2

地区	Region	来访 Petition Visits					
		总计 Subtotal	涉法涉诉类 Regarding Legal Lawsuits	医疗康复类 Medical Rehabilitation	教育类 Education	就业扶贫类 Employment and Poverty Alleviation	社会保障类 Social Security
		人次 person-time	人次 person-time	人次 person-time	人次 person-time	人次 person-time	人次 person-time
全国	**Nationwide**	**104016**	**4713**	**22704**	**5611**	**16542**	**24582**
北京	Beijing	1543	464	208	14	121	214
天津	Tianjin	1393	303	130	20	134	334
河北	Hebei	3435	178	825	227	684	945
山西	Shanxi	5803	111	2007	309	1041	1425
内蒙古	Inner Mongolia	1614	27	364	77	293	309
辽宁	Liaoning	3819	447	247	108	840	1327
吉林	Jilin	1649	94	167	47	193	442
黑龙江	Heilongjiang	1021	66	117	67	175	230
上海	Shanghai	2189	130	246	60	332	554
江苏	Jiangsu	2974	72	483	99	438	574
浙江	Zhejiang	2647	408	244	92	360	628
安徽	Anhui	3662	44	919	274	710	562
福建	Fujian	1829	87	298	62	313	439
江西	Jiangxi	4064	25	1426	223	721	932
山东	Shandong	3193	139	224	71	245	629
河南	Henan	873	63	120	62	159	202
湖北	Hubei	5790	406	659	110	900	2348
湖南	Hunan	10326	560	1513	841	1738	2688
广东	Guangdong	5403	151	1718	511	784	685
广西	Guangxi	3097	48	1214	305	505	538
海南	Hainan	456	17	17	4	5	18
重庆	Chongqing	3205	347	254	141	652	819
四川	Sichuan	13553	177	2880	612	2106	2774
贵州	Guizhou	675	102	150	41	98	162
云南	Yunnan	7189	65	1868	421	976	2255
西藏	Tibet	29	3	19		5	1
陕西	Shaanxi	5153	113	1990	292	678	916
甘肃	Gansu	1497	13	415	145	197	389
青海	Qinghai	156	4	30	8	18	25
宁夏	Ningxia	2736	47	1240	137	540	427
新疆	Xinjiang	1244	2	423	72	163	286
新疆兵团	Xinjiang Production and Construction Corps	1799		289	159	418	505

4-10-7 续表 3 Continued 3

地 区	Region	来访 Petition Visits				
		权益保障类 Rights and Interest Protection	控告检举类 Accusation and Disclosure	意见建议类 Opinions and Suggestions	非残类 Unrelated with Disability	其他类 Others
		人次 person-time	人次 person-time	人次 person-time	人次 person-time	人次 person-time
全 国	**Nationwide**	**10111**	**941**	**2807**	**1371**	**14634**
北 京	Beijing	301	16	51	3	151
天 津	Tianjin	139	88	41	63	141
河 北	Hebei	317	23	137	11	88
山 西	Shanxi	147	5	12	34	712
内蒙古	Inner Mongolia	100	13	13	142	276
辽 宁	Liaoning	198	33	88	21	510
吉 林	Jilin	312	19	3	26	346
黑龙江	Heilongjiang	272	16	43	10	25
上 海	Shanghai	390	28	197	65	187
江 苏	Jiangsu	346	92	121	45	704
浙 江	Zhejiang	339	37	109	58	372
安 徽	Anhui	146	10	84	28	885
福 建	Fujian	210	18	30	24	348
江 西	Jiangxi	369	4	113	37	214
山 东	Shandong	492	17	146	23	1207
河 南	Henan	147	8	50	5	57
湖 北	Hubei	821	100	121	17	308
湖 南	Hunan	904	247	491	117	1227
广 东	Guangdong	513	9	99	62	871
广 西	Guangxi	203	8	43	17	216
海 南	Hainan	8	20	1		366
重 庆	Chongqing	531	5	102	15	339
四 川	Sichuan	973	41	530	322	3138
贵 州	Guizhou	49	3	11		59
云 南	Yunnan	660	10	29	24	881
西 藏	Tibet	1				
陕 西	Shaanxi	215	40	46	143	720
甘 肃	Gansu	207	2	37	21	71
青 海	Qinghai	63		1		7
宁 夏	Ningxia	190	6	52	17	80
新 疆	Xinjiang	122	23	4	21	128
新疆兵团	Xinjiang Production and Construction Corps	426		2		

十一、组织建设
Disabled Persons' Organizations

4-11-1 省(自治区、直辖市)级残联
Disabled Persons' Federations at Provincial Level

地 区	Region	省市县乡残联实有人员 Staff of Disabled Persons' Federations at Provincial,Municipal, County and Township Level	省级残联机关 Disabled Persons' Federations at Provincial Level		省级残联事业单位 Affiliated Institutions at Provincial Level		
			实有人员 Staff	残疾人干部 Staff with Disability	单位 Affiliated Institu-tions	实有人员 Total Staff	残疾人 Staff with Disability
		人 person	人 person	人 person	个 unit	人 person	人 person
全 国	**Nationwide**	**108156**	**1571**	**147**	**138**	**7229**	**282**
北 京	Beijing	1318	73	11	11	277	21
天 津	Tianjin	965	47	4	4	152	23
河 北	Hebei	5455	49	3	4	158	9
山 西	Shanxi	4243	60	6	4	247	19
内蒙古	Inner Mongolia	2894	31	2	4	169	11
辽 宁	Liaoning	2915	41	4	1	239	6
吉 林	Jilin	2562	39	8	4	101	8
黑龙江	Heilongjiang	2343	42	5	1	50	2
上 海	Shanghai	1148	44	4	6	311	11
江 苏	Jiangsu	4652	66	7	5	123	7
浙 江	Zhejiang	5068	47	6	5	560	13
安 徽	Anhui	3604	50	6	4	185	11
福 建	Fujian	2744	38	2	4	182	26
江 西	Jiangxi	4008	43	2	6	146	
山 东	Shandong	5958	45	7	4	348	8
河 南	Henan	8030	49	7	3	133	5
湖 北	Hubei	3299	55	2	6	64	4
湖 南	Hunan	4814	48	4	6	184	7
广 东	Guangdong	7490	55	4	4	112	5
广 西	Guangxi	3370	34	4	5	218	8
海 南	Hainan	742	69	3	2	86	9
重 庆	Chongqing	1968	40	3	3	152	6
四 川	Sichuan	7815	49	4	3	640	
贵 州	Guizhou	3353	55	7	4	254	12
云 南	Yunnan	3806	65	7	7	159	14
西 藏	Tibet	336	21	1	2	76	
陕 西	Shaanxi	4747	77	3	6	1175	8
甘 肃	Gansu	4253	84	7	9	473	11
青 海	Qinghai	1201	41	4	2	63	3
宁 夏	Ningxia	629	55	4	2	39	2
新 疆	Xinjiang	2349	48	5	5	143	13
新疆兵团	Xinjiang Production and Construction Corps	77	11	1	2	10	

4-11-1 续表 Continued

地区	Region	干部队伍综合培训情况 Training of Staff						志愿者助残情况 Volunteers	
		省级举办综合培训班 Provincial-level General Trainings	参加省级综合培训人次 Trainees on Provincial-level Trainings	省级举办残疾人干部培训班 Provincial-level Trainings for Staff with Disability	参加省级残疾人干部培训人次 Trainees on Provincial-level Trainings for Staff with Disability	参加全国培训人次 Trainees on State-level Trainings	参加全国残疾人干部培训人次 Trainees on State-level Trainings for Staff with Disability	志愿者登记在册 Registered Volunteers	受助残疾人 PWDs Helped by Volunteers
		期 session	人次 person-time	期 session	人次 person-time	人次 person-time	人次 person-time	人 person	人次 person-time
全国	**Nationwide**	**100**	**6973**	**7**	**453**	**50**	**3**	**6922**	**82875**
北京	Beijing	2	260	1	73			54	1980
天津	Tianjin	8	329						
河北	Hebei	1	800			1	1	616	4816
山西	Shanxi							55	550
内蒙古	Inner Mongolia	3	150					84	5840
辽宁	Liaoning	17	1160						
吉林	Jilin	1	69	1	69			316	2592
黑龙江	Heilongjiang	1	110					1	10
上海	Shanghai	1	23					277	26821
江苏	Jiangsu	2	380						
浙江	Zhejiang	1	119			34			
安徽	Anhui	2	210						
福建	Fujian	1	80	1	120				
江西	Jiangxi	7	360	1	11	15	2		
山东	Shandong	1	47					15	315
河南	Henan	1	420					97	7651
湖北	Hubei							5300	31000
湖南	Hunan								
广东	Guangdong	1	60					100	1000
广西	Guangxi	1	260	1	70				
海南	Hainan								
重庆	Chongqing	6	540	1	50				
四川	Sichuan	2	150						
贵州	Guizhou	1	148						
云南	Yunnan	2	180					2	150
西藏	Tibet								
陕西	Shaanxi	1	84					5	150
甘肃	Gansu	1	130						
青海	Qinghai	1	38						
宁夏	Ningxia	30	366						
新疆	Xinjiang	5	500	1	60				
新疆兵团	Xinjiang Production and Construction Corps								

4-11-2 地市级残联
Disabled Persons' Federations at Municipal Level

地 区	Region	残联 Disabled Persons' Federations	配备了残疾人领导干部的残联 Disabled Persons' Federations Whose Leadership Include PWDs	残联机关 Disabled Persons' Federations 实有人员 Staff	残疾人领导干部 Leaders with Disability	残疾人干部 Ordinary Staff with Disability
		个 unit	个 unit	人 person	人 person	人 person
全 国	**Nationwide**	**339**	**223**	**4971**	**244**	**491**
北 京	Beijing					
天 津	Tianjin					
河 北	Hebei	11	8	229	9	16
山 西	Shanxi	11	6	161	6	10
内蒙古	Inner Mongolia	12	10	176	11	22
辽 宁	Liaoning	15	12	315	14	36
吉 林	Jilin	10	6	147	8	14
黑龙江	Heilongjiang	13	6	163	6	15
上 海	Shanghai					
江 苏	Jiangsu	13	9	293	11	19
浙 江	Zhejiang	11	10	180	10	23
安 徽	Anhui	16	8	187	8	14
福 建	Fujian	9	8	127	9	15
江 西	Jiangxi	11	10	128	10	15
山 东	Shandong	16	11	279	12	23
河 南	Henan	18	6	267	7	18
湖 北	Hubei	13	5	136	6	11
湖 南	Hunan	14	6	191	6	11
广 东	Guangdong	21	16	345	16	33
广 西	Guangxi	15	11	161	11	20
海 南	Hainan	3	2	47	3	5
重 庆	Chongqing					
四 川	Sichuan	21	11	285	13	32
贵 州	Guizhou	10	8	146	8	20
云 南	Yunnan	16	13	224	13	27
西 藏	Tibet	7	2	81	2	5
陕 西	Shaanxi	11	9	154	10	15
甘 肃	Gansu	15	11	223	15	38
青 海	Qinghai	8	5	106	6	6
宁 夏	Ningxia	5	3	49	3	6
新 疆	Xinjiang	14	11	171	11	22
新疆兵团	Xinjiang Production and Construction Corps					

4-11-2 续表 Continued

地 区	Region	事业单位 Affiliated Institutions			干部队伍综合培训情况 Training of Staff				志愿者助残情况 Volunteers	
		单位 Institutions	实有人员 Total Staff	残疾人 Staff with Disability	地市级举办综合培训班 City-level General Trainings	参加地市级培训人次 Trainees on City-level General Trainings	地市级举办残疾人干部培训班 City-level Trainings for Staff with Disability	参加地市级残疾人干部培训人次 Trainees on City-level Trainings for Staff with Disability	志愿者登记在册 Registered Volunteers	受助残疾人 PWDs Helped by Volunteers
		个 unit	人 person	人 person	期 session	人次 person-time	期 session	人次 person-time	人 person	人次 person-time
全 国	**Nationwide**	**674**	**9849**	**410**	**1144**	**16872**	**108**	**4729**	**40381**	**706651**
北 京	Beijing									
天 津	Tianjin									
河 北	Hebei	23	327	9	14	266	4	226	357	2252
山 西	Shanxi	32	505	38	10	514	2	36	79	4985
内蒙古	Inner Mongolia	25	194	7	11	596	2	150	125	11332
辽 宁	Liaoning	7	163	8	22	1440	7	404	5213	19292
吉 林	Jilin	22	231	16	803	606	1	6	423	15010
黑龙江	Heilongjiang	20	147	6	11	88	3	5	64	294
上 海	Shanghai									
江 苏	Jiangsu	31	443	16	16	944	3	183	3574	40385
浙 江	Zhejiang	24	708	23	15	1063	10	163	2507	72576
安 徽	Anhui	29	238	8	20	788	2	40	338	8812
福 建	Fujian	24	280	15	5	241	3	60	1756	19699
江 西	Jiangxi	19	117	5	16	223	3	104	106	6430
山 东	Shandong	39	779	47	12	748	9	367	1811	39851
河 南	Henan	46	901	13	28	578	2	65	15447	97231
湖 北	Hubei	29	231	16	1	90			1984	52800
湖 南	Hunan	30	153	8	19	894	3	198	287	8661
广 东	Guangdong	73	2545	83	29	1460	15	644	1100	74826
广 西	Guangxi	35	415	23	12	422	3	47	149	1310
海 南	Hainan	4	39	2	4	126			400	7072
重 庆	Chongqing									
四 川	Sichuan	33	334	19	34	1106	7	250	483	21473
贵 州	Guizhou	17	90	3	2	150	1	4	48	2430
云 南	Yunnan	27	130	13	16	798	5	339	99	4465
西 藏	Tibet	10	35		6	95	2	30		
陕 西	Shaanxi	17	142	4	6	165	6	120	148	3285
甘 肃	Gansu	23	506	16	13	2668	5	922	3316	177998
青 海	Qinghai	6	54	1	10	444	5	150	42	515
宁 夏	Ningxia	6	39	2	4	139	4	176	118	3490
新 疆	Xinjiang	17	87	7	5	220	1	40	14	29
新疆兵团	Xinjiang Production and Construction Corps	6	16	2					393	10148

4-11-3 县(县级市、市辖区)级残联
Disabled Persons' Federations at County/District Level

地区	Region	残联 Disabled Persons' Federations	配备了残疾人干部的残联 Disabled Persons' Federations with Disabled Staff	残联机关 Disabled Persons' Federations 实有人员 Staff	残疾人干部 Staff with Disability
		个 unit	个 unit	人 person	人 person
全国	**Nationwide**	**2997**	**1456**	**26539**	**2313**
北京	Beijing	16	15	177	29
天津	Tianjin	16	10	184	23
河北	Hebei	173	103	1469	133
山西	Shanxi	118	65	1130	99
内蒙古	Inner Mongolia	103	58	859	104
辽宁	Liaoning	105	42	585	51
吉林	Jilin	70	22	669	44
黑龙江	Heilongjiang	126	33	511	38
上海	Shanghai	16	2	143	3
江苏	Jiangsu	104	48	1280	54
浙江	Zhejiang	95	65	1135	83
安徽	Anhui	117	49	852	71
福建	Fujian	91	28	562	36
江西	Jiangxi	111	60	915	102
山东	Shandong	159	80	1711	130
河南	Henan	173	92	2220	168
湖北	Hubei	108	31	916	46
湖南	Hunan	127	63	1373	99
广东	Guangdong	132	38	1181	50
广西	Guangxi	111	39	770	50
海南	Hainan	20	7	190	7
重庆	Chongqing	41	20	339	27
四川	Sichuan	188	88	1622	139
贵州	Guizhou	91	62	826	97
云南	Yunnan	132	101	1298	181
西藏	Tibet	74	8	121	8
陕西	Shaanxi	117	72	1159	136
甘肃	Gansu	86	78	1078	195
青海	Qinghai	45	14	310	21
宁夏	Ningxia	21	14	172	22
新疆	Xinjiang	97	47	745	65
新疆兵团	Xinjiang Production and Construction Corps	14	2	37	2

4-11-3 续表 Continued

地 区	Region	事业单位 Affiliated Institutions			干部队伍综合培训情况 Training of Staff		志愿者助残情况 Volunteers	
		单位 Institutions	实有人员 Total Staff	残疾人 Staff with Disability	县级举办综合培训班 County-level General Trainings	参加县级培训 Trainees on County-level General Trainings	志愿者登记在册 Registered Volunteers	受助残疾人 PWDs Helped by Volunteers
		个 unit	人 person	人 person	期 session	人次 person-time	人 person	万人次 10,000 person-times
全 国	**Nationwide**	**2612**	**14960**	**810**	**3842**	**152509**	**560303**	**749.1**
北 京	Beijing	41	401	29	42	4779	599	2.1
天 津	Tianjin	24	199	24	31	1463	4143	2.6
河 北	Hebei	90	765	30	176	8409	46901	38.6
山 西	Shanxi	135	663	27	107	4287	2525	7.1
内蒙古	Inner Mongolia	61	276	26	79	3040	2969	3.4
辽 宁	Liaoning	27	124	9	117	5351	5410	7.8
吉 林	Jilin	60	398	21	71	3047	69619	45.7
黑龙江	Heilongjiang	72	265	15	91	1219	86469	58.9
上 海	Shanghai	23	213	24	57	1610	1080	8.5
江 苏	Jiangsu	139	847	36	179	7217	20538	30.5
浙 江	Zhejiang	133	806	59	285	9855	21127	57.7
安 徽	Anhui	68	395	13	165	10209	5500	16.3
福 建	Fujian	137	407	26	122	9357	26325	29.4
江 西	Jiangxi	93	396	26	94	4278	3705	7.6
山 东	Shandong	115	818	33	170	6011	13034	17.4
河 南	Henan	203	1574	37	177	4673	80875	111.6
湖 北	Hubei	125	615	36	77	2390	2227	6.9
湖 南	Hunan	139	846	22	131	5506	2430	6.7
广 东	Guangdong	180	1111	42	251	7876	6071	25.0
广 西	Guangxi	103	417	43	159	4467	3982	6.8
海 南	Hainan	11	75	5	10	711	719	3.2
重 庆	Chongqing	39	212	13	120	4787	20857	62.1
四 川	Sichuan	137	760	36	319	10173	11641	43.3
贵 州	Guizhou	86	418	34	75	3722	1677	8.3
云 南	Yunnan	112	403	46	176	6491	2945	7.6
西 藏	Tibet	1	2	1	7	91		
陕 西	Shaanxi	94	619	20	181	7620	5567	14.3
甘 肃	Gansu	63	378	21	145	6740	102655	92.4
青 海	Qinghai	27	193	23	69	1689	467	3.7
宁 夏	Ningxia	7	64	4	32	1490	1633	3.1
新 疆	Xinjiang	65	297	29	109	3157	5956	8.1
新疆兵团	Xinjiang Production and Construction Corps	2	3		18	794	657	12.4

4-11-4 乡(镇、街道)残联
Disabled Persons' Federations at Township Level

地区	Region	乡(镇、街道)已建残联 Disabled Persons' Federations Established in Townships (Towns, Sub-districts)	残联机关 Disabled Persons' Federation			
			实有人员 Total Staff	专职残联理事长 Full-time Presidents	兼职残联理事长 Part-time Presidents	专职委员 Full-time Commissioners on Disability Issues
		个 unit	人 person	人 person	人 person	人 person
全国	**Nationwide**	**37140**	**43037**	**9100**	**9773**	**59728**
北京	Beijing	327	390	198	49	1719
天津	Tianjin	241	383	186	20	289
河北	Hebei	2288	2458	472	687	3369
山西	Shanxi	1470	1477	113	581	2708
内蒙古	Inner Mongolia	1043	1189	84	273	1425
辽宁	Liaoning	1377	1448	318	954	2340
吉林	Jilin	881	977	150	327	1155
黑龙江	Heilongjiang	1194	1165	117	331	1297
上海	Shanghai	220	437	50	128	1001
江苏	Jiangsu	1272	1600	615	224	1793
浙江	Zhejiang	1366	1632	1071	76	1521
安徽	Anhui	1523	1697	510	315	2846
福建	Fujian	1111	1148	271	381	1540
江西	Jiangxi	1654	2263	317	479	2974
山东	Shandong	1733	1978	497	349	2562
河南	Henan	2407	2886	855	716	5493
湖北	Hubei	1177	1282	275	237	1196
湖南	Hunan	1913	2019	462	418	4214
广东	Guangdong	1645	2141	419	273	2350
广西	Guangxi	1250	1355	143	595	1975
海南	Hainan	225	236	17	131	245
重庆	Chongqing	1031	1225	297	270	1491
四川	Sichuan	2856	4125	318	898	5390
贵州	Guizhou	1414	1564	437	154	1651
云南	Yunnan	1409	1527	426	444	1379
西藏	Tibet					
陕西	Shaanxi	1270	1421	117	102	2804
甘肃	Gansu	1365	1511	306	201	1530
青海	Qinghai	380	434	1	40	432
宁夏	Ningxia	235	211	14	10	246
新疆	Xinjiang	863	858	44	110	709
新疆兵团	Xinjiang Production and Construction Corps					84

4-11-4　续表　Continued

地　区	Region	干部队伍综合培训情况 Training of Staff		志愿者助残情况 Volunteers	
		乡镇级举办综合培训班 Township-level General Trainings	参加乡镇级培训人次 Trainees on Township-level Trainings	志愿者登记在册 Registered Volunteers	受助残疾人 PWDs Helped by Volunteers
		期 session	人次 person-time	万人 10,000 persons	万人次 10,000 person-times
全　国	**Nationwide**	**23939**	**332813**	**105.2**	**1006.4**
北　京	Beijing	576	11763	0.6	54.4
天　津	Tianjin	142	1234	3.1	11.0
河　北	Hebei	1536	16530	10.8	47.3
山　西	Shanxi	606	5214	0.1	2.1
内蒙古	Inner Mongolia	355	4526	0.1	1.0
辽　宁	Liaoning	397	5971	1.2	8.6
吉　林	Jilin	322	4779	5.5	26.4
黑龙江	Heilongjiang	462	4752	13.3	103.1
上　海	Shanghai	340	4082	0.2	56.4
江　苏	Jiangsu	1224	16822	3.6	105.2
浙　江	Zhejiang	1094	20944	1.3	39.1
安　徽	Anhui	1241	12117	0.5	10.4
福　建	Fujian	514	9211	1.7	12.7
江　西	Jiangxi	592	9632	0.3	4.2
山　东	Shandong	908	15272	1.4	34.1
河　南	Henan	1626	10411	15.5	258.2
湖　北	Hubei	415	4278	0.3	6.0
湖　南	Hunan	1044	28098	0.9	13.0
广　东	Guangdong	1231	9147	21.8	11.1
广　西	Guangxi	528	6835	0.2	4.3
海　南	Hainan	42	270	0.0	2.4
重　庆	Chongqing	1145	21542	2.3	26.0
四　川	Sichuan	2396	41430	1.7	36.2
贵　州	Guizhou	691	15721	0.1	8.9
云　南	Yunnan	912	17342	0.5	8.0
西　藏	Tibet				
陕　西	Shaanxi	1255	11794	0.8	3.9
甘　肃	Gansu	1408	15108	16.7	99.5
青　海	Qinghai	342	2448	0.0	2.9
宁　夏	Ningxia	97	993	0.1	4.3
新　疆	Xinjiang	498	4547	0.3	4.4
新疆兵团	Xinjiang Production and Construction Corps			0.0	1.3

4-11-5 村(社区)残疾人组织
Disabled Persons' Federations at Village /Community Level

地 区	Region	已建残协 Associations of PWDs		残协情况 Associations		
		村 In Villages	社区 In Communities	已建残疾人活动室 Recreational Rooms for PWDs	村 In Villages	社区 In Communities
		个 unit	个 unit	个 unit	个 unit	个 unit
全 国	**Nationwide**	**469442**	**69103**	**215950**	**181233**	**34717**
北 京	Beijing	3824	2285	3314	2132	1182
天 津	Tianjin	3065	1163	4147	3023	1124
河 北	Hebei	48080	3332	34308	31759	2549
山 西	Shanxi	21871	2017	6199	5530	669
内蒙古	Inner Mongolia	11289	2029	2225	1655	570
辽 宁	Liaoning	11572	4206	12468	9068	3400
吉 林	Jilin	8909	1612	2417	1911	506
黑龙江	Heilongjiang	6368	1943	2720	1698	1022
上 海	Shanghai	1608	3491	2767	859	1908
江 苏	Jiangsu	14976	4581	14226	10766	3460
浙 江	Zhejiang	17940	2789	14676	12577	2099
安 徽	Anhui	13887	2107	6518	5460	1058
福 建	Fujian	14001	1951	4642	4029	613
江 西	Jiangxi	15502	2293	7796	6694	1102
山 东	Shandong	45784	3840	11354	10162	1192
河 南	Henan	42927	3312	27409	24708	2701
湖 北	Hubei	19223	2425	5370	4730	640
湖 南	Hunan	23829	3118	8865	7663	1202
广 东	Guangdong	18388	4884	6492	4374	2118
广 西	Guangxi	14234	1471	2818	2475	343
海 南	Hainan	2140	218	349	257	92
重 庆	Chongqing	8962	2090	4901	3624	1277
四 川	Sichuan	30159	3678	8759	7405	1354
贵 州	Guizhou	13306	1226	1592	1350	242
云 南	Yunnan	12574	1640	4389	3748	641
西 藏	Tibet	1051	9	556	556	
陕 西	Shaanxi	18458	1953	4751	4152	599
甘 肃	Gansu	15955	1096	7885	7292	593
青 海	Qinghai	4003	405	430	383	47
宁 夏	Ningxia	1582	407	241	75	166
新 疆	Xinjiang	3975	1531	1366	1118	248
新疆兵团	Xinjiang Production and Construction Corps		1			

4-11-5　续表　Continued

地　区	Region	残协专职委员选聘情况 Full-time Commissioners on Disability Issues			志愿者助残情况 Volunteers	
		残协专职委员 Full-time Commissioners on Disability Issues	村 In Villages	社区 In Communties	志愿者登记在册 Registered Volunteers	受助残疾人 PWDs Assisted by Volunteers
		人 person	人 person	人 person	万人 10,000 persons	万人次 10,000 person-times
全　国	**Nationwide**	**492949**	**431398**	**61551**	**91.2**	**870.1**
北　京	Beijing	4539	3224	1315	0.6	34.7
天　津	Tianjin	4135	3044	1091	2.9	11.4
河　北	Hebei	48583	45459	3124	9.4	57.6
山　西	Shanxi	18307	16670	1637	0.2	5.1
内蒙古	Inner Mongolia	12469	10714	1755	0.3	1.8
辽　宁	Liaoning	14350	10624	3726	2.5	54.0
吉　林	Jilin	9771	8209	1562	7.5	53.6
黑龙江	Heilongjiang	3408	1492	1916	10.2	55.8
上　海	Shanghai	2947	1059	1888	0.1	10.2
江　苏	Jiangsu	17083	13155	3928	4.4	91.0
浙　江	Zhejiang	18624	15370	3254	0.9	24.6
安　徽	Anhui	14452	12529	1923	0.7	11.0
福　建	Fujian	14112	12099	2013	0.7	11.8
江　西	Jiangxi	12054	10199	1855	0.5	2.9
山　东	Shandong	73579	67006	6573	1.5	48.4
河　南	Henan	42033	38497	3536	18.7	198.7
湖　北	Hubei	11908	10532	1376	0.6	12.1
湖　南	Hunan	19737	17048	2689	0.8	7.8
广　东	Guangdong	21156	17737	3419	12.8	6.6
广　西	Guangxi	14943	13535	1408	0.2	2.5
海　南	Hainan	2662	2320	342	0.1	2.1
重　庆	Chongqing	9566	7564	2002	2.3	34.5
四　川	Sichuan	37024	34969	2055	2.1	33.3
贵　州	Guizhou	12660	11037	1623	0.2	10.8
云　南	Yunnan	12481	11122	1359	0.3	9.0
西　藏	Tibet	33	33			
陕　西	Shaanxi	20717	18590	2127	0.9	6.2
甘　肃	Gansu	15498	14477	1021	8.6	61.2
青　海	Qinghai	1821	1519	302	0.1	3.3
宁　夏	Ningxia	560	376	184	0.2	2.7
新　疆	Xinjiang	1670	1181	489	1.0	5.1
新疆兵团	Xinjiang Production and Construction Corps	67	8	59	0.0	0.3

十二、残疾人服务设施建设
Service Facilities for Persons with Disabilities

4-12-1 残疾人综合服务设施
Comprehensive Service Facilities for Persons with Disabilities

地区	Region	已竣工 Completed Projects		
		本年度新竣工 Projects Completed in 2020		
		项目个数 Projects	建设规模 Construction Area	总投资 Total Investment
		个 unit	平方米 square meter	万元 10,000 yuan
全国	**Nationwide**	**45**	**298640**	**115109.4**
北京	Beijing			
天津	Tianjin			
河北	Hebei			
山西	Shanxi	4	5950	2589.0
内蒙古	Inner Mongolia	1	3000	1200.0
辽宁	Liaoning			
吉林	Jilin	1	460	138.0
黑龙江	Heilongjiang	1	600	98.0
上海	Shanghai			
江苏	Jiangsu	3	29335	26320.0
浙江	Zhejiang	4	55184	24625.0
安徽	Anhui	2	13603	5000.0
福建	Fujian			
江西	Jiangxi	3	11125	2442.0
山东	Shandong			
河南	Henan			
湖北	Hubei	3	16252	6510.0
湖南	Hunan	1	8000	1600.0
广东	Guangdong	3	19386	7183.0
广西	Guangxi	1	2000	543.6
海南	Hainan			
重庆	Chongqing			
四川	Sichuan	5	24870	9355.0
贵州	Guizhou	1	7002	1799.0
云南	Yunnan			
西藏	Tibet	1	1292	460.0
陕西	Shaanxi	1	3398	6516.8
甘肃	Gansu			
青海	Qinghai	3	31965	10120.0
宁夏	Ningxia			
新疆	Xinjiang	6	60219	7110.0
新疆兵团	Xinjiang Production and Construction Corps	1	5000	1500.0

4-12-1 续表 1 Continued 1

地 区	Region	已竣工 Completed Projects 累计已竣工 Completed Projects in Total 项目个数 Projects	建设规模 Construction Area	总投资 Total Investment
		个 unit	平方米 square meter	万元 10,000 yuan
全 国	**Nationwide**	**2318**	**6123446**	**1962452.9**
北 京	Beijing	8	95721	63880.2
天 津	Tianjin	24	116429	63859.9
河 北	Hebei	137	139645	28629.1
山 西	Shanxi	49	134183	37944.4
内蒙古	Inner Mongolia	61	97144	26837.7
辽 宁	Liaoning	110	285188	104341.3
吉 林	Jilin	48	87413	25499.8
黑龙江	Heilongjiang	98	114412	36460.0
上 海	Shanghai	17	23992	11782.1
江 苏	Jiangsu	79	474627	200611.2
浙 江	Zhejiang	89	641944	279438.7
安 徽	Anhui	89	250996	61912.8
福 建	Fujian	84	273025	92614.6
江 西	Jiangxi	76	98407	22314.5
山 东	Shandong	115	336369	89344.2
河 南	Henan	106	269330	67776.2
湖 北	Hubei	89	203214	49747.5
湖 南	Hunan	94	120556	23676.2
广 东	Guangdong	107	663778	229222.0
广 西	Guangxi	98	148740	26718.2
海 南	Hainan	10	13643	4190.0
重 庆	Chongqing	28	88259	29163.1
四 川	Sichuan	170	491206	140747.7
贵 州	Guizhou	56	65156	13525.6
云 南	Yunnan	125	164139	31855.6
西 藏	Tibet	48	60900	19875.0
陕 西	Shaanxi	80	176588	46966.0
甘 肃	Gansu	93	97804	30246.2
青 海	Qinghai	23	94204	30033.3
宁 夏	Ningxia	15	30450	7685.2
新 疆	Xinjiang	83	255598	63239.7
新疆兵团	Xinjiang Production and Construction Corps	9	10384	2315.0

4-12-1 续表 2 Continued 2

地 区	Region	在建项目 Projects under Construction		
		项目个数 Projects	建设规模 Construction Area	总投资 Total Investment
		个 unit	平方米 square meter	万元 10,000 yuan
全 国	**Nationwide**	**61**	**558804**	**239089.2**
北 京	Beijing			
天 津	Tianjin			
河 北	Hebei	1	500	200.0
山 西	Shanxi	3	12116	5724.3
内蒙古	Inner Mongolia	7	64098	26416.6
辽 宁	Liaoning	1	6500	1130.0
吉 林	Jilin			
黑龙江	Heilongjiang	1	1500	200.0
上 海	Shanghai			
江 苏	Jiangsu	2	19500	5920.0
浙 江	Zhejiang	1	6920	7900.0
安 徽	Anhui	2	8818	2950.0
福 建	Fujian	1	3342	885.0
江 西	Jiangxi			
山 东	Shandong	3	141200	52680.0
河 南	Henan	6	30525	7734.0
湖 北	Hubei	3	34122	6062.0
湖 南	Hunan	2	12397	7056.0
广 东	Guangdong	7	109581	81757.0
广 西	Guangxi	3	2461	373.0
海 南	Hainan			
重 庆	Chongqing	1	5864	2640.0
四 川	Sichuan	4	15953	4732.0
贵 州	Guizhou	2	9700	2308.0
云 南	Yunnan	3	21302	5813.7
西 藏	Tibet	1	1002	460.0
陕 西	Shaanxi	3	20269	7510.0
甘 肃	Gansu			
青 海	Qinghai			
宁 夏	Ningxia			
新 疆	Xinjiang	4	31136	8637.7
新疆兵团	Xinjiang Production and Construction Corps			

4-12-1 续表 3 Continued 3

地 区	Region	筹建项目 Projects under Discussion and Preparation		
		项目个数 Projects	建设规模 Construction Area	总投资 Total Investment
		个 unit	平方米 square meter	万元 10,000 yuan
全 国	**Nationwide**	**8**	**56691**	**41043.3**
北 京	Beijing			
天 津	Tianjin			
河 北	Hebei			
山 西	Shanxi			
内蒙古	Inner Mongolia			
辽 宁	Liaoning	1	640	300.0
吉 林	Jilin			
黑龙江	Heilongjiang			
上 海	Shanghai			
江 苏	Jiangsu	1	3000	1500.0
浙 江	Zhejiang			
安 徽	Anhui			
福 建	Fujian			
江 西	Jiangxi			
山 东	Shandong	1	5812	1950.0
河 南	Henan			
湖 北	Hubei			
湖 南	Hunan	1	1200	420.0
广 东	Guangdong	3	40339	35097.3
广 西	Guangxi	1	5700	1776.0
海 南	Hainan			
重 庆	Chongqing			
四 川	Sichuan			
贵 州	Guizhou			
云 南	Yunnan			
西 藏	Tibet			
陕 西	Shaanxi			
甘 肃	Gansu			
青 海	Qinghai			
宁 夏	Ningxia			
新 疆	Xinjiang			
新疆兵团	Xinjiang Production and Construction Corps			

4-12-2 残疾人康复设施
Rehabilitation Service Facilities for Persons with Disabilities

地 区	Region	已竣工 Completed Projects		
		本年度新竣工 Projects Completed in 2020		
		项目个数 Projects	建设规模 Construction Area	总投资 Total Investment
		个 unit	平方米 square meter	万元 10,000 yuan
全 国	**Nationwide**	**84**	**498201**	**128108.8**
北 京	Beijing			
天 津	Tianjin			
河 北	Hebei	1	2020	1035.0
山 西	Shanxi	1	8000	1680.0
内蒙古	Inner Mongolia	5	22301	5680.0
辽 宁	Liaoning			
吉 林	Jilin	2	17809	8098.3
黑龙江	Heilongjiang			
上 海	Shanghai			
江 苏	Jiangsu	2	1700	350.0
浙 江	Zhejiang			
安 徽	Anhui			
福 建	Fujian	3	12173	3308.0
江 西	Jiangxi	13	84746	16597.0
山 东	Shandong	2	20204	5757.2
河 南	Henan			
湖 北	Hubei	5	24279	7007.6
湖 南	Hunan	8	47906	8878.0
广 东	Guangdong	4	7900	2851.7
广 西	Guangxi			
海 南	Hainan			
重 庆	Chongqing	3	27373	9819.0
四 川	Sichuan	1	3500	1000.0
贵 州	Guizhou	3	16895	5924.0
云 南	Yunnan	3	20322	5528.0
西 藏	Tibet			
陕 西	Shaanxi	4	25840	4343.0
甘 肃	Gansu	7	36493	12718.8
青 海	Qinghai	1	4000	1220.0
宁 夏	Ningxia	5	31866	9981.4
新 疆	Xinjiang	11	82875	16331.7
新疆兵团	Xinjiang Production and Construction Corps			

4-12-2 续表 1 Continued 1

地 区	Region	已竣工 Completed Projects		
		累计已竣工 Completed Projects in Total		
		项目个数 Projects	建设规模 Construction Area	总投资 Total Investment
		个 unit	平方米 square meter	万元 10,000 yuan
全 国	**Nationwide**	**1063**	**4627150**	**1463676.3**
北 京	Beijing	3	13221	8273.7
天 津	Tianjin	10	18720	10886.0
河 北	Hebei	12	75228	24284.1
山 西	Shanxi	47	156994	44224.0
内蒙古	Inner Mongolia	29	139330	45678.6
辽 宁	Liaoning	19	96320	23279.5
吉 林	Jilin	13	94311	51856.3
黑龙江	Heilongjiang	9	61546	14567.0
上 海	Shanghai	5	100462	45136.9
江 苏	Jiangsu	63	247652	100418.1
浙 江	Zhejiang	45	321800	129758.7
安 徽	Anhui	24	151344	52531.4
福 建	Fujian	217	74838	20402.1
江 西	Jiangxi	30	210407	41248.4
山 东	Shandong	110	701703	202975.5
河 南	Henan	29	198412	44499.5
湖 北	Hubei	21	109781	32992.0
湖 南	Hunan	47	185287	43943.5
广 东	Guangdong	53	227794	74954.2
广 西	Guangxi	14	95363	22561.7
海 南	Hainan	3	12894	4590.0
重 庆	Chongqing	19	153650	55356.5
四 川	Sichuan	45	210554	92075.9
贵 州	Guizhou	19	163771	43058.0
云 南	Yunnan	12	76381	22022.9
西 藏	Tibet	14	31850	11721.0
陕 西	Shaanxi	41	115317	30257.2
甘 肃	Gansu	30	163537	43475.5
青 海	Qinghai	7	37858	14810.0
宁 夏	Ningxia	21	139044	48432.7
新 疆	Xinjiang	39	163642	34150.7
新疆兵团	Xinjiang Production and Construction Corps	13	78136	29254.8

4−12−2 续表 2 Continued 2

地 区	Region	在建项目 Projects under Construction		
		项目个数 Projects	建设规模 Construction Area	总投资 Total Investment
		个 unit	平方米 square meter	万元 10,000 yuan
全 国	**Nationwide**	**303**	**2394075**	**797704.0**
北 京	Beijing			
天 津	Tianjin			
河 北	Hebei	6	89336	44723.0
山 西	Shanxi	11	75953	28913.7
内蒙古	Inner Mongolia	8	43385	13434.0
辽 宁	Liaoning	3	22480	5305.0
吉 林	Jilin	2	13200	3371.0
黑龙江	Heilongjiang			
上 海	Shanghai			
江 苏	Jiangsu	2	68487	51748.0
浙 江	Zhejiang	6	93277	61334.5
安 徽	Anhui	6	45218	10590.0
福 建	Fujian	2	11150	3679.5
江 西	Jiangxi	22	159616	50893.3
山 东	Shandong	4	18457	5540.0
河 南	Henan	25	203086	65667.6
湖 北	Hubei	24	200114	62821.0
湖 南	Hunan	21	164802	39805.0
广 东	Guangdong	1	2600	500.0
广 西	Guangxi	24	214123	81056.1
海 南	Hainan	4	18337	7667.8
重 庆	Chongqing	6	69482	30739.0
四 川	Sichuan	9	59040	17423.2
贵 州	Guizhou	47	352379	83396.3
云 南	Yunnan	14	124207	36264.7
西 藏	Tibet	5	20085	7912.8
陕 西	Shaanxi	11	89017	26690.0
甘 肃	Gansu	15	100541	25335.7
青 海	Qinghai	2	9740	2941.0
宁 夏	Ningxia	4	23761	8012.0
新 疆	Xinjiang	18	97904	20440.0
新疆兵团	Xinjiang Production and Construction Corps	1	4300	1500.0

4-12-2　续表 3　Continued 3

地　区	Region	筹建项目 Projects under Discussion and Preparation		
		项目个数 Projects	建设规模 Construction Area	总投资 Total Investment
		个 unit	平方米 square meter	万元 10,000 yuan
全　国	**Nationwide**	**27**	**212223**	**55449.6**
北　京	Beijing			
天　津	Tianjin			
河　北	Hebei	1	2000	360.0
山　西	Shanxi	1	5470	1871.0
内蒙古	Inner Mongolia	1	4800	800.0
辽　宁	Liaoning			
吉　林	Jilin			
黑龙江	Heilongjiang			
上　海	Shanghai			
江　苏	Jiangsu	1	3000	300.0
浙　江	Zhejiang			
安　徽	Anhui	2	21100	5805.0
福　建	Fujian	1	15693	6810.0
江　西	Jiangxi	2	11500	2210.0
山　东	Shandong	2	25450	3364.6
河　南	Henan	1	5868	1650.0
湖　北	Hubei	4	28144	8965.0
湖　南	Hunan	2	5851	2330.0
广　东	Guangdong	1	3000	400.0
广　西	Guangxi	1	19618	6210.0
海　南	Hainan	1	16145	5717.9
重　庆	Chongqing			
四　川	Sichuan			
贵　州	Guizhou	4	33128	5247.0
云　南	Yunnan			
西　藏	Tibet			
陕　西	Shaanxi			
甘　肃	Gansu	2	11457	3409.1
青　海	Qinghai			
宁　夏	Ningxia			
新　疆	Xinjiang			
新疆兵团	Xinjiang Production and Construction Corps			

4-12-3 残疾人托养设施
Institutional Care Service Facilities for Persons with Disabilities

地 区	Region	已竣工 Completed Projects		
		本年度新竣工 Projects Completed in 2020		
		项目个数 Projects	建设规模 Construction Area	总投资 Total Investment
		个 unit	平方米 square meter	万元 10,000 yuan
全 国	**Nationwide**		**325803**	**94322.4**
北 京	Beijing			
天 津	Tianjin			
河 北	Hebei	2	4999	903.6
山 西	Shanxi	2	7144	2272.0
内蒙古	Inner Mongolia	1	2875	1174.0
辽 宁	Liaoning	3	5461	1191.0
吉 林	Jilin			
黑龙江	Heilongjiang	2	4012	980.0
上 海	Shanghai			
江 苏	Jiangsu	2	2885	1620.0
浙 江	Zhejiang	3	26383	17455.0
安 徽	Anhui			
福 建	Fujian	1	5000	1196.0
江 西	Jiangxi	4	9473	1915.0
山 东	Shandong	1	3500	669.0
河 南	Henan	3	12016	2450.0
湖 北	Hubei	4	9753	1313.6
湖 南	Hunan	3	8745	3300.0
广 东	Guangdong	1	1957	420.0
广 西	Guangxi	2	5046	1352.6
海 南	Hainan	1	3000	1715.6
重 庆	Chongqing	5	27231	5999.0
四 川	Sichuan	3	15407	3396.0
贵 州	Guizhou	6	41329	11896.0
云 南	Yunnan	10	28661	7009.0
西 藏	Tibet			
陕 西	Shaanxi	1	6391	5250.0
甘 肃	Gansu	6	21172	6175.9
青 海	Qinghai			
宁 夏	Ningxia	4	13100	4772.0
新 疆	Xinjiang	13	44393	6242.2
新疆兵团	Xinjiang Production and Construction Corps	6	15872	3655.0

4-12-3 续表 1 Continued 1

地 区	Region	已竣工 Completed Projects		
		累计已竣工 Completed Projects in Total		
		项目个数 Projects	建设规模 Construction Area	总投资 Total Investment
		个 unit	平方米 square meter	万元 10,000 yuan
全 国	**Nationwide**	**1024**	**2854248**	**773420.2**
北 京	Beijing			
天 津	Tianjin	13	7963	3586.0
河 北	Hebei	31	97204	20213.3
山 西	Shanxi	15	41921	10414.7
内蒙古	Inner Mongolia	34	72367	22558.4
辽 宁	Liaoning	22	81975	36036.7
吉 林	Jilin	12	34261	10401.0
黑龙江	Heilongjiang	27	62239	14353.9
上 海	Shanghai	12	7260	1593.0
江 苏	Jiangsu	113	335072	98725.4
浙 江	Zhejiang	51	356052	145420.3
安 徽	Anhui	16	49467	13415.0
福 建	Fujian	47	74826	16223.5
江 西	Jiangxi	35	93282	20430.7
山 东	Shandong	36	112656	29338.9
河 南	Henan	37	119865	22602.0
湖 北	Hubei	30	67954	13014.2
湖 南	Hunan	51	104122	22254.5
广 东	Guangdong	16	71411	15284.8
广 西	Guangxi	25	61670	16098.1
海 南	Hainan	4	9885	3381.2
重 庆	Chongqing	12	52189	15168.3
四 川	Sichuan	34	86066	23322.0
贵 州	Guizhou	61	220430	51453.3
云 南	Yunnan	39	101312	27749.4
西 藏	Tibet	4	15294	4865.8
陕 西	Shaanxi	56	141368	27441.0
甘 肃	Gansu	32	80874	20251.6
青 海	Qinghai	32	61667	18364.2
宁 夏	Ningxia	13	31990	10242.0
新 疆	Xinjiang	60	108086	19158.8
新疆兵团	Xinjiang Production and Construction Corps	54	93523	20058.5

4-12-3 续表 2 Continued 2

地 区	Region	在建项目 Projects under Construction 项目个数 Projects	建设规模 Construction Area	总投资 Total Investment
		个 unit	平方米 square meter	万元 10,000 yuan
全 国	**Nationwide**	**163**	**622447**	**207352.2**
北 京	Beijing			
天 津	Tianjin			
河 北	Hebei	1	6000	1000.0
山 西	Shanxi	5	10291	2519.5
内蒙古	Inner Mongolia	9	24557	5445.0
辽 宁	Liaoning	5	17626	3605.0
吉 林	Jilin	3	9248	2870.0
黑龙江	Heilongjiang	5	18968	4633.7
上 海	Shanghai			
江 苏	Jiangsu			
浙 江	Zhejiang	13	105898	53875.7
安 徽	Anhui	2	7298	1620.0
福 建	Fujian	2	6026	1990.0
江 西	Jiangxi	2	3000	460.0
山 东	Shandong	1	3500	680.0
河 南	Henan	6	32009	8927.5
湖 北	Hubei	8	36212	15050.4
湖 南	Hunan	12	43511	17654.9
广 东	Guangdong	1	4000	3990.0
广 西	Guangxi	12	37691	9745.8
海 南	Hainan	1	4139	1440.0
重 庆	Chongqing	2	15537	5133.0
四 川	Sichuan	5	16202	4600.0
贵 州	Guizhou	26	94664	25711.0
云 南	Yunnan	18	53151	16350.0
西 藏	Tibet	1	5748	2095.0
陕 西	Shaanxi	3	5188	1388.0
甘 肃	Gansu	11	39660	10590.2
青 海	Qinghai	1	2430	730.0
宁 夏	Ningxia	2	4934	2009.0
新 疆	Xinjiang	3	10459	2060.0
新疆兵团	Xinjiang Production and Construction Corps	3	4500	1178.7

4-12-3 续表 3 Continued 3

地 区	Region	筹建项目 Projects under Discussion and Preparation		
		项目个数 Projects	建设规模 Construction Area	总投资 Total Investment
		个 unit	平方米 square meter	万元 10,000 yuan
全 国	**Nationwide**	**18**	**54924**	**19349.2**
北 京	Beijing			
天 津	Tianjin			
河 北	Hebei	1	8000	1600.0
山 西	Shanxi	2	5320	1976.0
内蒙古	Inner Mongolia			
辽 宁	Liaoning	2	3200	1100.0
吉 林	Jilin			
黑龙江	Heilongjiang			
上 海	Shanghai			
江 苏	Jiangsu			
浙 江	Zhejiang	1	2200	700.0
安 徽	Anhui			
福 建	Fujian			
江 西	Jiangxi			
山 东	Shandong	1	2000	460.0
河 南	Henan			
湖 北	Hubei	1	4980	2000.0
湖 南	Hunan	2	3964	998.0
广 东	Guangdong	1	3000	2875.0
广 西	Guangxi	1	2549	930.2
海 南	Hainan			
重 庆	Chongqing	1	4606	1381.0
四 川	Sichuan	1	5000	1500.0
贵 州	Guizhou			
云 南	Yunnan	2	3948	1429.0
西 藏	Tibet	1	4158	1700.0
陕 西	Shaanxi	1	2000	700.0
甘 肃	Gansu			
青 海	Qinghai			
宁 夏	Ningxia			
新 疆	Xinjiang			
新疆兵团	Xinjiang Production and Construction Corps			

十三、信息化建设
Application of IT

4-13-1 残疾人事业信息化建设
Application of IT in the Work for Persons with Disabilities

地区	Region	门户网站 Websites	省级 At Provincial Level	地市级 At Municipal Level	县级 At County Level	本年度省级统计工作培训情况 Training for Statistics and Management at Provincial Level in 2020 举办统计工作培训班 Trainings for Statistics and Management	参加统计工作培训班 Participants of Trainings
		个 unit	个 unit	个 unit	个 unit	期 session	人次 person-time
全　国	**Nationwide**	**1047**	**31**	**256**	**760**	**35**	**2207**
北　京	Beijing	13	1		12	2	210
天　津	Tianjin	4	1		3	2	80
河　北	Hebei	56	1	10	45	1	24
山　西	Shanxi	27	1	8	18	1	25
内蒙古	Inner Mongolia	40	1	9	30	1	60
辽　宁	Liaoning	18	1	13	4	1	30
吉　林	Jilin	22	1	8	13	1	25
黑龙江	Heilongjiang	12	1	4	7	1	95
上　海	Shanghai	14	1		13	1	85
江　苏	Jiangsu	71	1	13	57	1	80
浙　江	Zhejiang	43	1	10	32	1	110
安　徽	Anhui	66	1	16	49	1	35
福　建	Fujian	104	1	10	93	1	30
江　西	Jiangxi	34	1	6	27	2	50
山　东	Shandong	62	1	16	45	1	30
河　南	Henan	57	1	18	38	1	45
湖　北	Hubei	43	1	12	30	1	125
湖　南	Hunan	28	1	14	13	1	156
广　东	Guangdong	62	1	20	41	1	50
广　西	Guangxi	57	1	11	45	1	69
海　南	Hainan	6	1	1	4	1	60
重　庆	Chongqing	11	1		10	1	50
四　川	Sichuan	66	1	18	47	1	60
贵　州	Guizhou	14	1	4	9	1	100
云　南	Yunnan	21	1	8	12	1	50
西　藏	Tibet	1	1			1	80
陕　西	Shaanxi	35	1	9	25	1	70
甘　肃	Gansu	33	1	10	22	1	120
青　海	Qinghai	13	1	4	8	1	65
宁　夏	Ningxia	6	1	3	2	2	78
新　疆	Xinjiang	7	1	1	5	1	60
新疆兵团	Xinjiang Production and Construction Corps	1			1		

分省统计报告

Provincial Statistical Reports

2020 年北京市残疾人事业发展统计公报

2020 年是全面建成小康社会和“十三五”规划收官之年，也是攻坚克难的一年。市委、市政府始终格外关心关注残疾人群体，统筹推进疫情防控和残疾人事业发展。市残联系统强化民生残联、智慧残联、法治残联、廉洁残联建设，切实发挥党和政府的桥梁纽带作用，在严峻考验和巨大压力中展现新担当、新作为，推动首都残疾人事业高质量发展。

一、康复

康复服务保持“全覆盖”态势，残疾预防联防联控的工作机制基本形成，18 项指标达到《残疾预防行动计划》要求。0-15 岁持证和非持证残疾儿童一体化保障落地落实，33344 人享受居家康复培训，5.6 万人享受专项康复保障，27.6 万人接受普及型康复项目，对残疾人购买的 10 万件辅具给予补贴，有康复需求的残疾人接受康复服务覆盖率 99.9%。

二、教育

全面落实《北京市特殊教育提升计划（2017-2020 年）》，残疾儿童少年义务教育入学率达 99%,融合教育比例达到近 70%，实现了零拒绝、全覆盖。义务教育阶段办学体系基本完善，教育投入持续加大，教育专业支持服务网络逐步建立，融合教育质量明显提升。与教育部门共同搭建特殊教育支持服务平台，为 2100 名残疾学生建立助学服务档案，推动“一人一案”电子化进程。

三、就业

“稳就业”成效明显。2020 年，党政机关定向招录 11 名残疾人公务员，发挥示范引领作用。实施残保金分档减缴免缴，为 9500 余家用人单位落实用人单位招用残疾人岗位补贴和社会保险补贴，最大限度支持用人单位稳定残疾人就业岗位。大力扶持残疾人自主创业就业，为 2.1 万自主创业就业残疾人落实社会保险补贴。实施“一生一策”就业帮扶，有就业意愿应届残疾人大学生就业率 95.3%。432 家职业康复站为 8825 名智力、精神和重度肢体残疾人就近就便提供职业康复服务。菜单式免费职业技能培训惠及 8012 人次。

残疾人就业局势保持总体稳定。截至 2020 年底，全市劳动年龄内持证残疾人数 180186 人，城乡就业残疾人数 119799 人。

培训盲人医疗按摩人员 302 名；现有保健按摩机构 401 个，医疗按摩机构 2 个；12 人通过盲人医疗按摩人员初级职称评审，5 人通过中级职称评审。

四、社会保障

城乡一体、特性突出、普惠共享的保障体系更加完善，残疾人基本公共服务均等化水平明显提升。兜底保障应享尽享，率先建立了普惠型重度残疾人托养服务补贴制度，重度残疾人与失能失智、重度残疾、高龄父母共同入住机构享受专门倾斜；未享受低保、低收入的重度残疾人家庭申请支出型临时救助上浮 10%；优化残疾人参加城乡居民基本医疗保险工作机制，做到应保尽保；采取灵活精细、流量管理的服务模式统筹开展喘息托养；试点区居民医保参保残疾人长期护理保险获全额资助；低保、两项补贴、走访慰问等政策补贴惠及残疾人 46 万人次。

五、扶贫

共完成 2468 户农村残疾人家庭危房改造，投入资金 17289000 元，2468 名残疾人受益。

六、宣传文化

残疾人自立自强故事在新华社海外版刊发，无障碍环境建设专项行动成为中国无障碍史上的一次创举，疫情防控新闻发布会在全国率先配备手语翻译，原创话剧入选“戏剧中国”上佳话剧剧本，北京市“抗击新冠肺炎疫情表彰”“人民满意的公务员集体”“北京青年五四奖章”榜上有名，残疾人工作日益成为推动包容发展、展现首都文明进步的一道亮丽风景。

注重残健融合宣传普及，中央、市属媒体报道近7000篇，北京新闻“以首善标准推动残疾人事业融合发展”为题综合展示“十三五”期间成就，近万人次参与首届“健康杯”残疾人体育大会，24万人次参与投票、13万人在线收看、2008人现场参与第十届社区（村）文艺汇演，更多残疾人走出家门、融入社会、展现风采。

加强宣传推广，积极推动残疾人手工艺品、残疾人非物质文化遗产传承项目纳入北京2022年冬奥会冬残奥会宣传推广大局，将残疾人元素嵌入整体设计，努力挖掘残疾人特殊优势、体现好“京味儿”，展示中国社会的开放与包容，讲好“中国故事”。

截至2020年底，全市共有残疾人专题广播节目1个、电视手语栏目3个，电视手语栏目3个。

截至2020年底，市、区两级公共图书馆共设立盲文及盲文有声读物阅览室7个，共开展残疾人文化周活动262场次，市级残疾人艺术团1个。

七、体育

扎实推进冬残奥会主办城市备战任务。实施冬季残奥项目振兴计划，组建专班，倒排工期，全力以赴推进《北京冬奥会冬残奥会筹办工作任务书》14项主责任务、《市残联冬残奥行动计划》60项任务落地。充分认识主办城市成绩的重要意义，6个大项15名运动员进入国家集训队，承担国家轮椅冰壶队、国家残疾人高山滑雪队集训任务。经市政府同意，筹备建设气膜式冰壶冰球运动馆，建成后可保障残疾人冬季冰上项目运动队全年无间断训练，也可组织举办小型残疾人冰上运动赛事及承接群众性冰上活动项目。开发适合残疾人广泛参与、具有首都特色的模拟冰雪项目，每年过万人上冰雪。

八、维权

2020年，制定或修改保障残疾人权益的市级规范性文件1个。区级以上人大开展《中华人民共和国残疾人保障法》执法检查和专题调研4次；政协开展视察和专题调研1次。开展省级普法宣传教育活动342次，5000人参加；举办省级法律培训班2个，150人参加。

残疾人参政议政工作稳步开展，市、区两级残联协助人大代表、政协委员提出议案、建议、提案8件，办理议案、建议、提案21件。

无障碍建设法规、标准进一步完善。共出台了53个市、区级无障碍环境建设与管理法规、政府令和规范性文件；16个地市、县系统开展无障碍环境建设；开展无障碍环境建设检查3456次，无障碍培训18883人次。

九、组织建设

推进志愿服务，编写残疾人志愿服务手册，举办迎冬奥助残志愿服务知识竞赛，强化冬奥常识、助残知识技能、礼仪接待、语言文化、竞赛服务、专业康复训练等专项培训，已有1675名残疾人成功报名冬奥冬残奥志愿者。

2020年，市、区、乡镇（街道）共有残联343个，区残联16个，乡镇（街道）残联338个；社区（村）残协6060个。

市、区、乡镇（街道）残联工作人员1318人，乡镇（街道）残联、村（社区）残协专职委员总计7031名。区级配备了残疾人干部的残联16个。

共建立各类残疾人专门协会85个，其中市级专门协会5个，区级专门协会80个。助残社会组织219个。

十、服务设施

加快市残疾人职业康复和托养服务中心项目建设，落实康复中心、辅具中心、文体中心、冬奥展示温馨家园等“窗口接待单位”任务，力争成为2022年冬奥会冬残奥会期间向国际社会展示人文形象的重要窗口。

截至2020年底，已竣工的各级残疾人综合服务设施8个，总建设规模95721.1平方米，总投资63880.2万元；已竣工的各级残疾人康复设施3个，总建设规模13221.4平方米，总投资8273.7万元。

十一、信息化

深入落实“放管服”改革要求，配合相关业务部门完善残疾人网上服务，支撑业务流程优化，深化与 14 个部门 33 类数据共享，主责办理事项办事材料、办理时限分别压缩至 81%、70%，残疾人服务“应上必上”互联网。北京市残疾人网上服务作为全国三个经典案例之一写入《2020 年联合国电子政务调查报告》。

2020 年天津市残疾人事业发展统计公报

2020 年，天津市残联坚持以习近平新时代中国特色社会主义思想为指导，深入贯彻落实习近平总书记关于残疾人事业的重要论述和习近平总书记对天津工作“三个着力”重要要求，认真落实市委、市政府和中国残联安排部署，统筹做好疫情防控和残疾人事业发展，突出解决残疾人急难愁盼问题，不断增强残疾人获得感、幸福感、安全感。

一、康复

积极推进残疾人社区康复工作。截至 2020 年底，在 16 个市辖区开展了社区康复工作，全市共有社区康复协调员 4141 人，康复服务设施 328 个。

2020 全年共有 46309 名残疾儿童及持证残疾人得到了基本康复服务，并实现了不同程度的康复。其中包括 0-6 岁残疾儿童 1869 人，得到基本康复服务的持证残疾人中，各类别残疾人数及占比如下：

1．视力残疾人共 3215 人，约占 6.9%。其中接受康复医疗服务的 126 人，接受康复训练服务的 510 人，接受辅助器具服务的 1076 人，接受支持性服务的 1798 人。

2．听力残疾人为 2946 人、言语残疾人为 141 人，两个类别共约占 6.7%。其中接受康复医疗服务的 185 人，接受康复训练服务的 142 人，接受辅助器具服务的 1171 人，接受支持性服务的 1995 人。

3．肢体残疾人共 26934 人，约占 58.2%。其中接受康复医疗服务的 2211 人，接受康复训练服务的 743 人，接受辅助器具服务的 13902 人，接受支持性服务的 11823 人。

4．智力残疾人共 3169 人，约占 6.8%。其中接受康复医疗服务的 189 人，接受康复训练服务的 410 人，接受支持性服务的 2821 人，其他 61 人。

5．精神残疾人共 6589 人，约占 14.2%。其中接受康复医疗服务的 5355 人，接受康复训练服务的 1487 人，接受支持性服务的 1653 人，其他 1 人。

6．多重残疾人共 1525 人，约占 3.3%。

7.0-17 岁未持证残疾儿童 1790 人，约占 3.9%。

以上接受基本康复服务的各类别残疾人中，部分残疾人接受了两种及两种以上康复服务。

截至 2020 年底，全市共建立残疾人康复服务机构 95 个，其中残联系统所属康复机构 19 个。按机构属性划分：卫生部门所属机构最多，共计 27 个；按康复类别划分，精神康复机构最多，共计 43 个。康复机构在岗人员达 2441 人，其中，管理人员 248 人，业务人员 1627 人，其他人员 566 人。

二、教育

2020 年，继续认真落实《天津市第二期特殊教育提升计划（2017-2020）实施方案》，全面精准掌握本市适龄入学残疾儿童少年接受各类教育情况。为接受各阶段教育的残疾学生和贫困残疾人在校健全子女发放助学金，残疾人整体素质有所提高。全市各特教学校义务教育阶段对残疾学生继续实施“三免一补”（免交杂费、教科书费、住宿费，补贴生活费）政策，实现义务教育阶段免费教育。实施残疾人事业专项彩票公益金助学项目，带动各地对 162 名残疾儿童给予学前教育资助。全面落实残疾考生参加普通高考工作，为残疾考生提供便利。残疾人特殊教育事业发展稳定。开办特殊教育普通高中 2 所，在校生 183 人。其中聋生 74 人，盲生 109 人。有 69 名残疾人被普通高等院校录取，130 名残疾人进入高等特殊教育学院学习。

三、就业

2020 年，加强残疾人就业服务，多种方式促进残疾人就业，多渠道促进残疾人高校毕业生就业创业。

城乡持证残疾人就业人数为 67357 人。就业形式主要集中在按比例就业、个体就业和农村种植、养殖、加工业，其中：按比例就业为 44272 人，个体就业为 6213 人，农村种植、养殖、加工业为 13626 人。

本年度继续加大对盲人按摩人员培训及培养力度，培训盲人保健按摩人员 9 人，培养盲人医疗按摩人员 93 人；保健按摩机构数 119 个，医疗按摩机构 3 个。

四、社会保障

2020 年，全面落实残疾人医疗参保、医疗救助、大病救助政策，推进残疾人积极纳入全民参保计划，提高残疾人参加城乡居民基本养老保险参保率。全市实际参保的残疾居民为 78728 人，较 2019 年增加了 1710 人。其中领取待遇的有 51636 人【注[1]】，较 2019 年增加了 289 人。60 周岁以下参保残疾居民 27092 人。22950 名 60 岁以下参保重度残疾人中，22917 名享受了参保个人缴费资助政策，占比 99.9%。4142 名非重度残疾人享受了个人缴费资助政策。

残疾人托养服务工作稳步推进，有需求且符合条件的托养服务对象基本实现了全覆盖。残疾人托养服务机构达到 67 个，其中寄宿制托养服务机构 12 个，日间照料机构 55 个。托养残疾人总数 59011 人，其中享受居家托养服务残疾人 58724 人,较 2019 年增加了 13980 人。

五、扶贫

2020 年，积极动员机关、企事业单位、志愿者组织及党员、干部、学生、街坊邻里等社会各界，采取多种形式，进行“帮、包、带、扶”，并充分发挥工会、共青团、妇联等团体和组织在残疾人帮扶工作中的作用。困难残疾人生产生活状况得到进一步改善，11 个残疾人扶贫基地安置 122 名残疾人就业，辐射带动 69 户残疾人家庭增收。加大农村困难残疾人危房改造力度，本年度完成 349 户农村困难残疾人危房改造，投入危房改造资金 1064.3 万元，349 名残疾人受益。

六、维权

2020 年，制定或修改保障残疾人权益的规范性文件 2 个；各级人大、政协的检查或专题调研 1 次，开展省级普法宣传教育活动 2 次，举办省级法律培训班 1 次，对残疾人保障法的贯彻实施起到了重要的推动作用。

残疾人参政议政工作稳步开展，各级残联协助人大代表、政协委员提出议案、建议、提案 2 件，办理议案、建议、提案 16 件。

全市无障碍环境建设法规基础得到进一步夯实。截至 2020 年底，建立无障碍环境建设领导协调组织 17 个；全市 16 个区全部系统开展无障碍建设。大力实施各类无障碍建设项目，全市大多数新建主要城市道路、公共建筑物、居住建筑都建设了相应的无障碍设施，同时加强了无障碍改造和对已建无障碍设施的管理，我市城市无障碍设施建设得到进一步加强，大大方便了广大残疾人、老年人、妇女、儿童、伤病人和全体社会成员参与社会生活。

2020 年，全市各级残联信访部门共处理来信 131 件，接待来访 1393 人次。完善天津市“助残一键通”和法规政策信息平台建设，残疾人 12385 维权热线运转良好，拓宽残疾人诉求表达渠道，为残疾人维护自身合法权益提供便捷途径，接听和解答残疾人来电 7056 通。

七、宣传文化体育

2020 年,全市公共图书馆共设立盲文及盲人有声读物阅览室 7 个。开展丰富多彩的群众性残疾人文化活动，举办残疾人文化周活动 107 场次，残疾人参加文化活动 27716 人次。新增设立社区残疾人健身示范点 99 个，培养残疾人社会体育指导员 715 名。

八、组织建设

天津市共有各类残疾人 57 万，其中持证残疾人 36.9 万，占残疾人总数的 64.7%。截至 2020 年底，全市共建立残联 257 个，其中：已建区残联 16 个，乡镇（街道）残联 241 个；已建村（社区）残协 4228 个，已建残疾人活动室 4147 个。全市残联系统实有工作人员共 965 人，乡镇（街道）、村（社区）选聘残疾人专职委员总计 4424 名。全市共建立各类残疾人专门协会 85 个，助残社会组织共有 6 个。各专门协会认真履行职责，各级残联组织全面开展干部职工和专职委员培训工作，基层组织队伍建设得到进一步加强，越来越多的残疾人得到不同程度的

注[1] 领取待遇的人员为 60 周岁以上的参加养老保险的人员，60 周岁以下人员未领取。

帮助。

九、信息化建设

残疾人信息化建设队伍不断壮大，全市各级残联均配备统计工作人员。各级残联独立建立网站 2 个，搭载上级残联、同级政府网站 2 个。重点加大信息化基础设施建设、技术保障和安全投入，提高了残疾人工作信息化水平。

2020年河北省残疾人事业发展统计公报

2020年，在省委、省政府的坚强领导下，省残联紧紧围绕省委省政府工作大局，以落实省委“3689”“六稳”“六保”为重点，聚焦残疾人中心工作、聚焦残疾人需求，坚定信心，主动作为，确保党中央、国务院和省委、省政府决策部署落地见效，带动残疾人工作整体提档升级。

一、康复

2020年，266186名持证残疾人及残疾儿童得到基本康复服务，其中0-6岁残疾儿童7722人。得到康复服务的持证残疾人中，有视力残疾人17809名、听力残疾人15095名、言语残疾人1807名、肢体残疾人157963名、智力残疾人15251名、精神残疾人37636名、多重残疾人15925名。全年共为74374名残疾人提供各类辅助器具。

截至2020年底，共有残疾人康复机构444个，其中残联系统康复机构58个。康复机构在岗人员达12364人，其中，管理人员1307人，业务人员9217人，其他人员1840人。

二、教育

实施残疾人事业专项彩票公益金助学项目，为818名家庭经济困难残疾儿童享受普惠性学前教育提供资助。

2020年，共有特殊教育普通高中（部、班）10个，在校生1175人，其中聋生694人，盲生187人，其他294人。残疾人中等职业学校（班）4个，在校生289人，毕业生189人，毕业生中186人获得职业资格证书。有414名残疾人被普通高等院校录取。

900名残疾青壮年文盲接受了扫盲教育。

三、就业

城乡持证残疾人就业人数为471172人，其中按比例就业11544人，集中就业3999人，个体就业11024人，公益性岗位就业1442人，辅助性就业2272人，灵活就业（含社区、居家就业）74728人，从事农业种养加366163人。

培训盲人保健按摩人员463名、盲人医疗按摩人员173名；现有保健按摩机构380个，医疗按摩机构25个；193人获得盲人医疗按摩人员初级职务任职资格，37人获得中级职务任职资格。

四、社会保障

截至2020年底，残疾居民参加城乡社会养老保险人数1533043名，357934名60岁以下参保重度残疾人中，34866人享受了参保个人缴费资助政策，占比97.4%。127768名非重度残疾人享受了个人缴费资助政策。595898人领取养老金。

残疾人托养服务机构312个，其中寄宿制托养服务机构69个，日间照料机构21个，综合性托养服务机构65个，为3616名残疾人提供了托养服务。11750名残疾人接受居家服务。1286名托养服务管理和服务人员接受了各级各类专业培训。

五、扶贫开发

共有18903人次农村残疾人接受了实用技术培训，31名贫困残疾人获得康复扶贫贴息贷款扶持，144个残疾人扶贫基地安置2052名残疾人就业，辐射带动3193户残疾人家庭增收。

共完成448户农村贫困残疾人家庭危房改造，投入资金3821777.7元，495名残疾人受益。

六、宣传文化

截至2020年底，共有省级残疾人专题广播节目1个；市级残疾人专题广播节目9个、电视手语栏目11个。

截至2020年底，省市县三级公共图书馆共设立盲文及盲文有声读物阅览室31个，共开展残疾人文化周活动426场次；市级残疾人艺术团7个。

七、体育

新增设立社区残疾人健身示范点76个，为3997户重度残疾人提供康复体育进家庭服务，培养残疾人社会体育指导员761名。

八、维权

2020年，制定或修改保障残疾人权益的市级规范性文件3个、县级12个。县级以上人大开展《中华人民共和国残疾人保障法》执法检查和专题调研20次；政协开展视察和专题调研14次。开展省级普法宣传教育活动4次，1500人参加；举办省级法律培训班3个，200人参加。

残疾人参政议政工作稳步开展，各地残联协助人大代表、政协委员提出议案、建议、提案22件，办理议案、建议、提案32件。

无障碍建设法规、标准进一步完善。共出台了48个省、市、县级无障碍环境建设与管理法规、政府令和规范性文件；186个市、县系统开展无障碍环境建设；开展无障碍环境建设检查114次，无障碍培训719人次。

九、组织建设

2020年，市县乡共有残联2472个，各市已建残联11个，县（市、区）残联已建173个，乡镇（街道）残联已建2288个；社区（村）已建残协51412个。

省市县乡残联工作人员5455人，乡镇（街道）残联、村（社区）残协专职委员总计51953名。市级配备了残疾人领导干部的残联8个，县级配备了残疾人干部的残联103个。

共建立各类残疾人专门协会893个，其中省级专门协会已建5个，市级专门协会已建55个，县级专门协会已建833个。助残社会组织27个。

十、服务设施

截至2020年底，已竣工的各级残疾人综合服务设施137个，总建设规模139645.0平方米，总投资28629.1万元；已竣工的各级残疾人康复设施12个，总建设规模75228.3平方米，总投资24284.1万元；已竣工的各级残疾人托养服务设施31个，总建设规模97204.4平方米，总投资20213.3万元。

十一、信息化建设

截至2020年底，10个市级、45个县级残联开通网站。

2020年山西省残疾人事业发展统计公报

2020年，各级残联坚持以习近平新时代中国特色社会主义思想为指导，深入学习贯彻习近平总书记关于残疾人事业的重要论述和指示批示精神，全面贯彻党的十九大和十九届二中、三中、四中、五中全会精神，按照省委、省政府和中国残联的决策部署，残疾人脱贫攻坚、全面小康和疫情防控等重点工作成绩显著，残疾人工作上了一个新台阶。

一、康复

2020年，13.9万名持证残疾人及残疾儿童得到基本康复服务，其中0-6岁残疾儿童5175人。得到康复服务的持证残疾人中，有视力残疾人9092名、听力残疾人9337名、言语残疾人110名、肢体残疾人8.2万名、智力残疾人9701名、精神残疾人2万名、多重残疾人6536名。全年共为6.4万名残疾人提供各类辅助器具。

截至2020年底，共有残疾人康复机构317个，其中残联系统康复机构60个。康复机构在岗人员达1.1万人，其中，管理人员954人，业务人员8483人，其他人员1572人。

二、教育

实施残疾人事业专项彩票公益金助学项目，为509名家庭经济困难残疾儿童享受普惠性学前教育提供资助。

2020年，共有特殊教育普通高中（部、班）9个，在校生1215人，其中聋生476人，盲生50人，其他689人。残疾人中等职业学校（班）2个，在校生68人，毕业生8人，毕业生中7人获得职业资格证书。有459名残疾人被普通高等院校录取。

三、就业

城乡持证残疾人就业人数为26.6万人，其中按比例就业5857人，集中就业6036人，个体就业1.1万人，公益性岗位就业1062人，辅助性就业1042人，灵活就业（含社区、居家就业）5万人，从事农业种养加19.1万人。

培训盲人保健按摩人员384名、盲人医疗按摩人员371名；现有保健按摩机构231个，医疗按摩机构21个；52人获得盲人医疗按摩人员初级职务任职资格，10人获得中级职务任职资格。

四、社会保障

截至2020年底，残疾居民参加城乡社会养老保险人数91.2万名，19.8万名60岁以下参保重度残疾人中，18.9万名享受了参保个人缴费资助政策，占比95.3%。8万名非重度残疾人享受了个人缴费资助政策。41.9万人领取养老金。

残疾人托养服务机构193个，其中寄宿制托养服务机构24个，日间照料机构17个，综合性托养服务机构44个，为1017名残疾人提供了托养服务。6851名残疾人接受居家服务。728名托养服务管理和服务人员接受了各级各类专业培训。

五、扶贫

共有1.1万人次农村残疾人接受了实用技术培训，28个残疾人扶贫基地安置918名残疾人就业，辐射带动585户残疾人家庭增收。

共完成376户农村贫困残疾人家庭危房改造，投入资金636.6万元，460名残疾人受益。

六、宣传文化

截至2020年底，共有省级残疾人专题广播节目1个、电视手语栏目1个；地级残疾人专题广播节目12个、电视手语栏目9个。

截至2020年底，省地县三级公共图书馆共设立盲文及盲文有声读物阅览室19个，共开展残疾人文化周活动96场次；省地两级残联艺术团11个。

七、体育

新增设立社区残疾人健身示范点55个，培养残疾人社会体育指导员 603 名。

八、维权

2020 年，制定或修改保障残疾人权益的县级规范性文件 6 个。县级以上人大开展《中华人民共和国残疾人保障法》执法检查和专题调研 24 次；政协开展视察和专题调研 11 次。开展省级普法宣传教育活动 4 次，460 人参加；举办省级法律培训班 2 个，112 人参加。

残疾人参政议政工作稳步开展，各地残联协助人大代表、政协委员提出议案、建议、提案 19 件，办理议案、建议、提案 22 件。

无障碍建设法规、标准进一步完善。共出台了 16 个省、地、县级无障碍环境建设与管理法规、政府令和规范性文件；77 个地市、县系统开展无障碍环境建设；开展无障碍环境建设检查 43 次，无障碍培训 255 人次。

九、组织建设

2020 年，市县乡共有残联 1599 个，各地市已建残联 11 个，县（市、区）残联已建 118 个，乡镇（街道）残联已建 1470 个；社区（村）已建残协 2.4 万个。

省市县乡残联工作人员 4243 人，乡镇（街道）残联、村（社区）残协专职委员总计 2.1 万名。地市级配备了残疾人领导干部的残联 6 个，县级配备了残疾人干部的残联 65 个。

共建立各类残疾人专门协会 642 个，其中省级专门协会已建 5 个，市级专门协会已建 55 个，县级专门协会已建 582 个。助残社会组织 18 个。

十、服务设施

截至 2020 年底，已竣工的各级残疾人综合服务设施 49 个，总建设规模 13.4 万平方米，总投资 37944.4 万元；已竣工的各级残疾人康复设施 47 个，总建设规模 15.7 万平方米，总投资 44224 万元；已竣工的各级残疾人托养服务设施 15 个，总建设规模 4.2 万平方米，总投资 10414.7 万元。

十一、信息化

截至 2020 年底，8 个地级、18 个县级残联开通网站。

2020 年内蒙古自治区残疾人事业发展统计公报

2020 年，全区残疾人工作以习近平新时代中国特色社会主义思想为指导，全面贯彻党的十九大和十九届二中、三中、四中、五中全会精神和自治区党委十届十二次全会精神，以落实自治区残联七代会各项任务为抓手，凝心聚力、主动作为，“十三五”各项任务指标和年度工作任务全部完成，建档立卡残疾人全部脱贫，各项工作取得了显著成绩。

一、康复

2020 年，全面贯彻落实《自治区政府关于建立残疾儿童康复救助制度的实施意见》，持续开展残疾人精准康复和康复服务行动，全区 69701 名持证残疾人及残疾儿童得到基本康复服务，其中 0-6 岁残疾儿童 2748 人。在得到康复服务的持证残疾人中，有视力残疾人 4954 名、听力残疾人 5664 名、言语残疾人 263 名、肢体残疾人 38802 名、智力残疾人 2870 名、精神残疾人 11664 名、多重残疾人 3781 名。全年共为 37893 名残疾人提供各类辅助器具。

截至 2020 年底，共有残疾人康复机构 272 个，其中残联系统康复机构 63 个。康复机构在岗人员达 6104 人，其中，管理人员 620 人，业务人员 4127 人，其他人员 1357 人。

二、教育

实施残疾人事业专项彩票公益金助学项目，为 46 名家庭经济困难残疾儿童享受普惠性学前教育提供资助，带动各地对 681 名残疾儿童给予学前教育资助。

2020 年，共有特殊教育普通高中（部、班）4 个，在校生 374 人，其中聋生 362 人，其他 12 人。残疾人中等职业学校（班）4 个，在校生 237 人，毕业生 29 人，均未获得职业资格证书。有 331 名残疾人被普通高等院校录取，8214 名残疾青壮年文盲接受了扫盲教育。

三、就业

2020 年，城乡持证残疾人就业人数为 185804 人，其中按比例就业 10175 人，集中就业 5198 人，个体就业 19234 人，公益性岗位就业 1448 人，辅助性就业 891 人，灵活就业（含社区、居家就业）55412 人，从事农业种养加 93446 人。

2020 年，培训盲人保健按摩人员 109 名、盲人医疗按摩人员 378 名；截至 2020 年底，现有保健按摩机构 402 个，医疗按摩机构 146 个；25 人获得盲人医疗按摩人员初级职务任职资格，4 人获得中级职务任职资格。

四、社会保障

截至 2020 年底，残疾居民参加城乡社会养老保险人数 500942 名，118944 名 60 岁以下参保重度残疾人中，117796 名享受了参保个人缴费资助政策，占比 99.0%。57825 名非重度残疾人享受了个人缴费资助政策。240857 人领取养老金。

残疾人托养服务工作稳步推进，残疾人托养服务机构 153 个，其中寄宿制托养服务机构 81 个，日间照料机构 11 个，综合性托养服务机构 34 个，为 1452 名残疾人提供了托养服务。2239 名残疾人接受居家服务。34 名托养服务管理和服务人员接受了各级各类专业培训。

五、扶贫

圆满完成贫困残疾人脱贫攻坚任务。全区共有 27444 人次农村残疾人接受了实用技术培训，93 个残疾人扶贫基地安置 777 名残疾人就业，辐射带动 796 户残疾人家庭增收。

全区共完成 493 户农村贫困残疾人家庭危房改造，投入资金 148.72 万元，536 名残疾人受益。

六、宣传文化

截至 2020 年底，全区共有自治区级残疾人电视手语栏目 1 个；盟市残疾人专题广播节目 4 个、电视手语栏目 6 个。

截至 2020 年底，全区公共图书馆共设立盲文及盲文有声读物阅览室 36 个，共开展残疾人文化周活动 155 场次；盟市级残疾人艺术团 1 个。

七、体育

2020 年，为 501 户重度残疾人提供康复体育进家庭服务，培养残疾人社会体育指导员 106 名。

八、维权

2020 年，自治区和盟市均未制定或修改关于残疾人的专门法规、规章；2 个旗县制定或修改保障残疾人权益的规范性文。县级以上人大开展《中华人民共和国残疾人保障法》执法检查和专题调研 4 次；政协开展视察和专题调研 4 次。开展省级普法宣传教育活动 2 次，20 万人参加；举办省级法律培训班 3 个，145 人参加。

残疾人参政议政工作稳步开展，各地残联协助人大代表、政协委员提出议案、建议、提案 10 件，办理议案、建议、提案 24 件。

无障碍建设法规、标准进一步完善。全区共出台了 17 个无障碍环境建设与管理法规、政府令和规范性文件；有 69 个盟市、旗县系统开展无障碍环境建设；全区开展无障碍环境建设检查 52 次，无障碍培训 93 人次。

九、组织建设

2020 年，全区盟市、旗县（市、区）、乡镇三级共有残联 1158 个，其中：盟市残联 12 个，旗县（市、区）残联 103 个，乡镇（街道）残联 1043 个；社区（村）已建残协 13318 个。

全区残联工作人员 2894 人，乡镇（街道）残联、村（社区）残协专职委员总计 13897 名。盟市级配备了残疾人领导干部的残联 10 个，旗县（市、区）级配备了残疾人干部的残联 58 个。

全区共建立各类残疾人专门协会 562 个，其中:自治区级专门协会 5 个，盟市级专门协会 60 个，旗县（市、区）级专门协会 497 个。助残社会组织 36 个。

十、服务设施

截至 2020 年底，已竣工的各级残疾人综合服务设施 61 个，总建设规模 97144.4 平方米，总投资 26837.7 万元；已竣工的各级残疾人康复设施 29 个，总建设规模 139330.2 平方米，总投资 45678.6 万元；已竣工的各级残疾人托养服务设施 34 个，总建设规模 72366.5 平方米，总投资 22558.3 万元。

十一、信息化

截至 2020 年底，9 个地级、30 个县级残联开通网站。全区共有持证残疾人 78.3 万人。与自治区民政厅、教育厅、人社厅、扶贫办等部门进行数据共享。

2020 年辽宁省残疾人事业发展统计公报

2020 年，省残联坚决贯彻党中央、国务院和省委省政府决策部署，积极应对新冠肺炎疫情影响，紧扣全面建成小康社会目标和辽宁全面振兴、全方位振兴任务，统筹做好常态化疫情防控和残疾人各项工作，聚焦“两不愁三保障”突出问题，落实“六稳”“六保”任务，加紧补齐残疾人民生领域短板，健全完善残疾人帮扶制度，推进残联改革和残联组织治理体系和治理能力现代化，推动残疾人事业高质量发展。

一、康复

2020 年，177239 名持证残疾人及残疾儿童得到基本康复服务，其中 0-6 岁残疾儿童 4550 人。得到康复服务的持证残疾人中，有视力残疾人 17929 名、听力残疾人 10744 名、言语残疾人 573 名、肢体残疾人 86582 名、智力残疾人 14484 名、精神残疾人 32220 名、多重残疾人 11357 名。全年共为 39848 残疾人提供各类辅助器具。

截至 2020 年底，全省共有残疾人康复机构 416 个，其中，残联系统康复机构 75 个。康复机构在岗人员达 11623 人，其中，管理人员 1304 人，业务人员 8294 人，其他人员 2025 人。

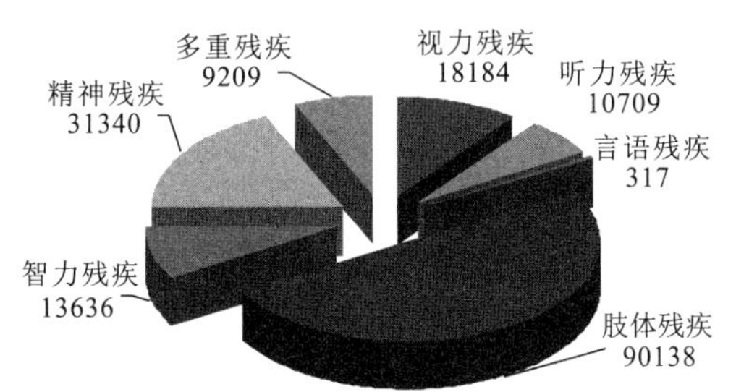

图 1　2020 年残疾人接受康复服务情况（单位：人）

二、教育

2020 年，实施残疾人事业专项彩票公益金助学项目，为全省 1472 名家庭经济困难残疾儿童享受普惠性学前教育提供资助，带动各地对 142 名残疾儿童给予学前教育资助。

2020 年，全省共有特殊教育普通高中（部、班）6 个，在校生 278 人，其中聋生 238 人，盲生 4 人，其他 36 人。残疾人中等职业学校（班）15 个，在校生 955 人，毕业生 229 人，毕业生中 92 人获得职业资格证书。全省有 296 名残疾人被普通高等院校录取，75 名残疾人进入高等特殊教育学院学习。

175 名残疾青壮年文盲接受了扫盲教育。

三、就业

2020 年全省城乡持证残疾人就业人数为 240946 人，其中按比例就业 33331 人，集中就业 12202 人，个体就业 16770 人，公益性岗位就业 6127 人，辅助性就业 6855 人，灵活就业（含社区、居家就业）40164 人，从事农业种养加 125497 人。

培训盲人保健按摩人员 667 人次、盲人医疗按摩人员 70 人次；现有保健按摩机构 655 个，医疗按摩机构 26 个；4 人获得盲人医疗按摩人员初级职务任职资格，4 人获得中级职务任职资格。

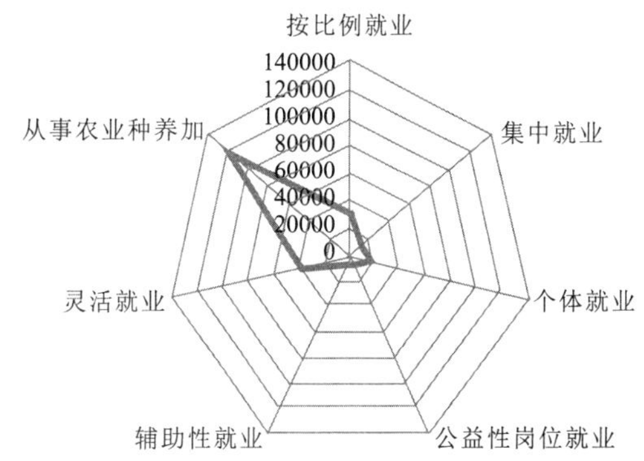

图 2　2020 年城乡持证残疾人就业形式（单位：人）

四、社会保障

截至 2020 年底，残疾居民参加城乡社会养老保险人数达到 46.1 万，10.8 万名 60 岁以下参保重度残疾人中，10.3 万名享受了参保个人缴费资助政策，占比 95.9%。3.5 万名非重度残疾人享受了个人缴费资助政策。领取养老金待遇的人数达到 20.9 万。

全省共有残疾人托养服务机构 178 个，全年共为 18969 名残疾人提供服务。524 名托养服务管理和服务人员接受了各级各类专业培训。

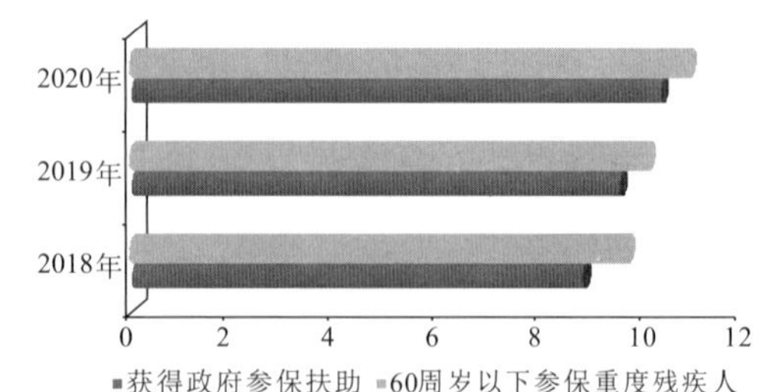

图3　2018-2020年60周岁以下参保重度残疾人获得政府参保扶助情况（单位：万人）

五、扶贫

2020年，全省共有9098人次农村残疾人接受了实用技术培训，27个残疾人扶贫基地安置368名残疾人就业，辐射带动775户残疾人家庭增收。

共完成2577户农村贫困残疾人家庭危房改造，投入资金5437.2万元，2954名残疾人受益。

六、宣传文化

截至2020年底，全省共有省级残疾人专题广播节目1个、电视手语栏目1个；市级残疾人专题广播节目8个、电视手语栏目15个。

截至2020年底，省市县三级公共图书馆共设立盲文及盲文有声读物阅览室53个，共开展残疾人文化周活动218场次；市级残联艺术团15个。

七、体育

2020年，我省以推进残疾人竞技体育、群众体育和特奥体育均衡协同发展为重点，积极承接中国残联残奥、冬残奥训练项目，夯实残奥、群体、特奥发展基础，充分发挥残运会大型体育融入全民健身，促进特奥体育融合活动。根据疫情防控常态化要求，广泛开展“残疾人健身周”“特奥日”“残疾人冰雪运动季”系列品牌活动。全省基层残疾人健身体育工作网格化管理精细化程度不断提升。

八、维权

2020年，制定或修改保障残疾人权益的市级规范性文件2个、县级2个。县级以上人大开展《中华人民共和国残疾人保障法》执法检查和专题调研6次；政协开展视察和专题调研3次。开展省级普法宣传教育活动7次，700人参加；举办省级法律培训班3个，300人参加。

残疾人参政议政工作稳步开展，各地残联协助人大代表、政协委员提出议案、建议、提案22件，办理议案、建议、提案31件。

无障碍建设法规、标准进一步完善。共出台了4个省、市级无障碍环境建设与管理法规、政府令和规范性文件；8个市、县系统开展无障碍环境建设；全省开展无障碍环境建设检查100次，无障碍培训2884人次。

表1　2020年度全省残疾人参政议政情况

级　别	人大			政协		
	人大代表（人）	协助人大代表提出议案、建议（件）	办理人大建议（件）	政协委员（人）	协助政协委员提出提案（件）	办理政协提案（件）
省　级	0	3	2	1	3	4
地市级	11	5	10	32	5	14
县　级	113	2	0	84	4	1
总　计	124	10	12	117	12	19

九、组织建设

2020年，全省市县乡共有残联1497个，其中各市残联15个，县（市、区）残联105个，乡镇（街道）残联1377个；社区（村）残协15778个。

省市县乡残联工作人员2915人，乡镇（街道）残联、村（社区）残协专职委员总计16698名。12个市级残联配备了残疾人领导干部，42个县级残联配备了残疾人干部。

全省共建立各类残疾人专门协会600个，其中省级专门协会5个，市级专门协会70个，县级专门协会525个。全省助残社会组织共有46个。

十、服务设施

截至2020年底，全省已竣工的各级残疾人综合服务设施110个，总建设规模28.5万平方米，总投资10.4亿元；已竣工的各级残疾人康复设施19个，总建设规模9.6万平方米，总投资2.3亿元；已竣工

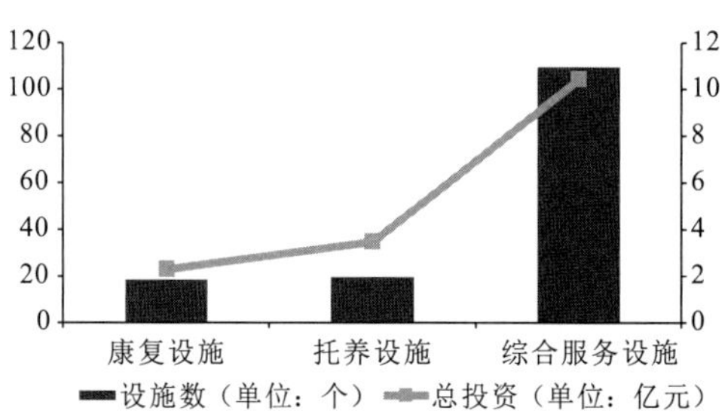

图4　2020年度全省残疾人服务设施建设情况

的各级残疾人托养服务设施 22 个，总建设规模 8.2 万平方米，总投资 3.6 亿元。

十一、信息化

截至 2020 年底，全省 13 个市级、4 个县级残联开通网站。

2020年吉林省残疾人事业发展统计公报

2020年，吉林省残联认真贯彻落实习近平新时代中国特色社会主义思想和党的十九大、十九届二中、三中、四中、五中全会精神，按照省委、省政府确定的重点任务，围绕大局、主动作为，推动残疾人事业再上新台阶，取得新成效。

一、康复

2020年，147041名持证残疾人及残疾儿童得到基本康复服务，其中，得到康复服务的持证残疾人中，有视力残疾人12616名、听力残疾人9461名、言语残疾人317名、肢体残疾人83992名、智力残疾人10586名、精神残疾人21998名、多重残疾人6348名。全年共为44804残疾人提供各类辅助器具。

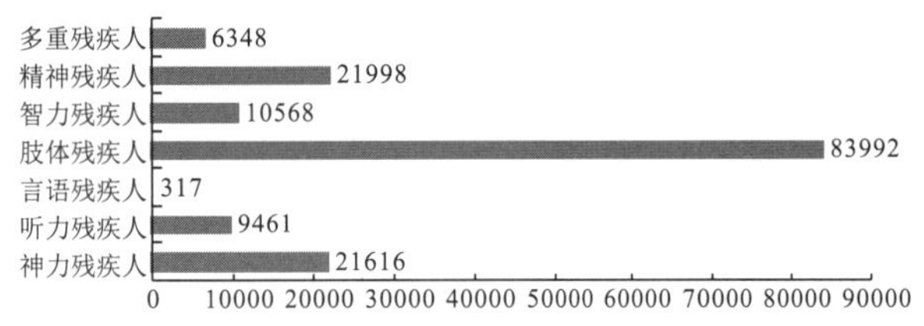

图1　得到康复服务的持证残疾人（单位：人）

截至2020年底，共有残疾人康复机构286个，其中残联系统康复机构55个。康复机构在岗人员达9145人，其中，管理人员1246人，业务人员6221人，其他人员1678人。

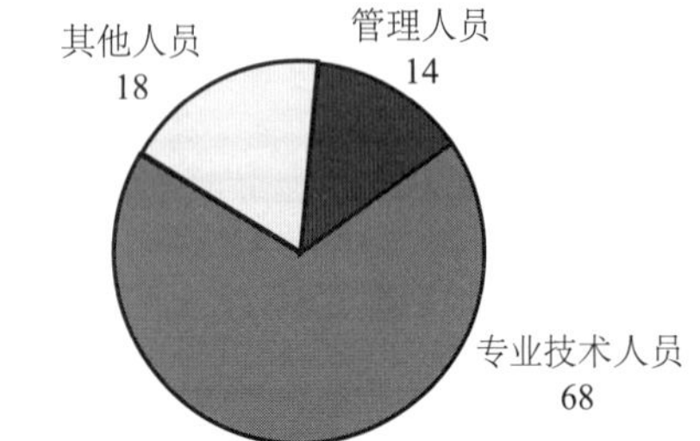

图2　2020年残疾人康复机构在岗人员情况（单位：%）

二、教育

实施残疾人事业专项彩票公益金助学项目，为221名家庭经济困难残疾儿童享受普惠性学前教育提供资助，带动各地对16名残疾儿童给予学前教育资助。

2020年，共有特殊教育普通高中（部、班）5个，在校生234人。残疾人中等职业学校（班）2个，在校432人，毕业生86人。有360名残疾人被普通高等院校录取，204名残疾人进入高等特殊教育学院学习。为参加2020年普通高考的67名残疾学生提供了合理便利服务。为1032名残疾学生和938名贫困残疾人家庭子女发放扶残助学金。

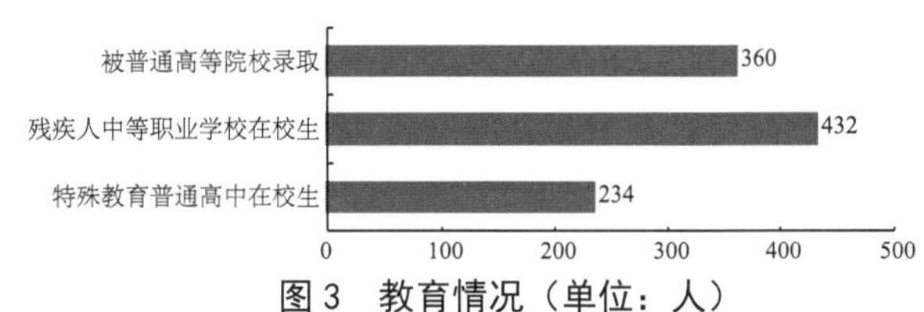

图3　教育情况（单位：人）

300名残疾青壮年文盲接受了扫盲教育。

三、就业

城乡持证残疾人就业人数为180084人，其中按比例就业7860人，集中就业4557人，个体就业18366人，公益性岗位就业2737人，辅助性就业1105人，灵活就业（含社区、居家就业）44982人，从事农业种养加100477人。

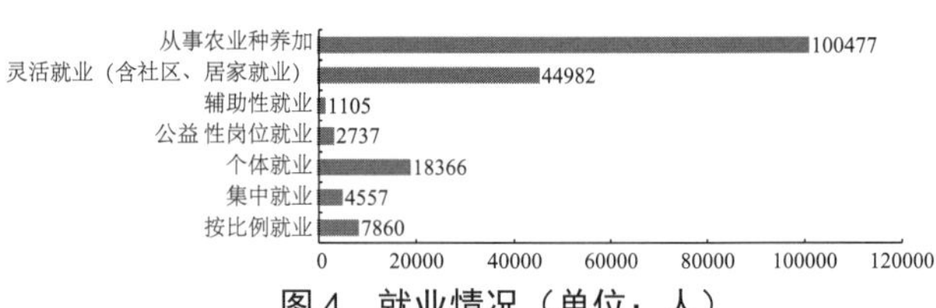

图4　就业情况（单位：人）

现有保健按摩机构338个，医疗按摩机构38个；7人获得盲人医疗按摩人员初级职务任职资格，3人获得中级职务任职资格。

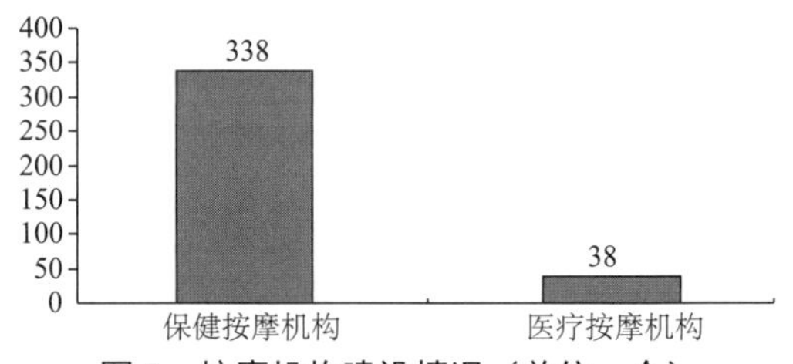

图5　按摩机构建设情况（单位：个）

四、社会保障

截至2020年底，残疾居民参加城乡社会养老保险人数490117名，157609名60岁以下参保重度残疾人中，153654享受了参保个人缴费资助政策，占比97.5%。69875名非重度残疾人享受了个人缴费资助政策。197907人领取养老金。

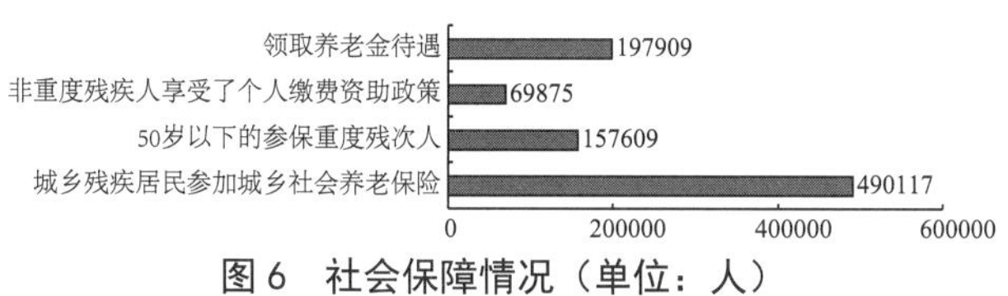

图6 社会保障情况（单位：人）

残疾人托养服务机构110个，其中寄宿制托养服务机构55个，日间照料机构16个，综合性托养服务机构17个，为1039名残疾人提供了托养服务。7271名残疾人接受居家服务。360名托养服务管理和服务人员接受了各级各类专业培训。

29.4万名残疾人享受困难残疾人生活补贴，32.6万名残疾人享受重度残疾人护理补贴。

五、扶贫

共有8981人次农村残疾人接受了实用技术培训，帮助13097个农村贫困残疾人家庭通过发展生产实现增收，188个残疾人扶贫基地安置1404名残疾人就业，辐射带动3794户残疾人家庭增收。

共完成418户农村贫困残疾人家庭危房改造，投入资金4142145元，434名残疾人受益。

六、宣传文化

截至2020年底，省级残疾人专题广播节目1个、电视手语栏目1个；地级残疾人电视手语栏目6个。

截至2020年底，省地县三级公共图书馆共设立盲文及盲文有声读物阅览室51个，共开展残疾人文化周活动202场次；省地两级残联艺术团10个。

七、体育

新增设立社区残疾人健身示范点200个，培养残疾人社会体育指导员500名。

八、维权

2020年，制定或修改保障残疾人权益的省级规范性文件1个、地级7个、县级1个。县级以上人大开展《中华人民共和国残疾人保障法》执法检查和专题调研3次；政协开展视察和专题调研3次。开展省级普法宣传教育活动5次，2300人参加；举办省级法律培训班2个，260人参加。

残疾人参政议政工作稳步开展，各地残联协助人大代表、政协委员提出议案、建议、提案6件，办理议案、建议、提案12件。

无障碍建设法规、标准进一步完善。9个地市、县系统开展无障碍环境建设；开展无障碍环境建设检查12次，无障碍培训108人次。

九、组织建设

2020年，市县乡共有残联961个，各地市已建残联10个，县（市、区）残联已建70个，乡镇（街道）残联已建881个。

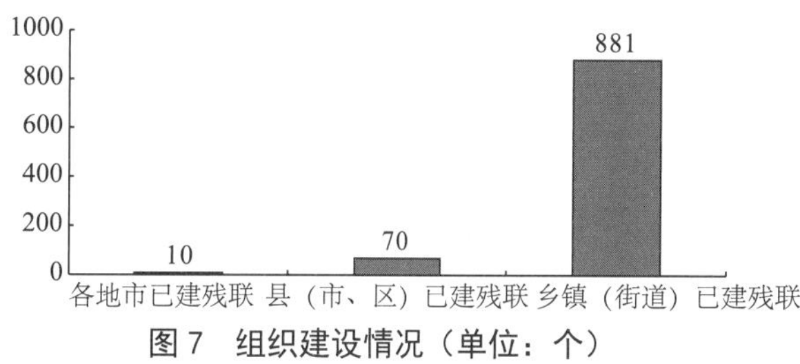

图7 组织建设情况（单位：个）

省市县乡残联工作人员2562人，乡镇（街道）残联、村（社区）残协专职委员总计10926名。地市级配备了残疾人领导干部的残联6个，县级配备了残疾人干部的残联22个。

共建立各类残疾人专门协会368个，其中省级专门协会已建5个，市级专门协会已建50个，县级专门协会已建313个。助残社会组织61个。

十、服务设施

截至2020年底，已竣工的各级残疾人综合服务设施48个，总建设规模87413.2平方米，总投资25499.8万元；已竣工的各级残疾人康复设施13个，总建设规模94310.7平方米，总投资51856.3万元；已竣工的各级残疾人托养服务设施12个，总建设规模34260.8平方米，总投资10401.0万元。

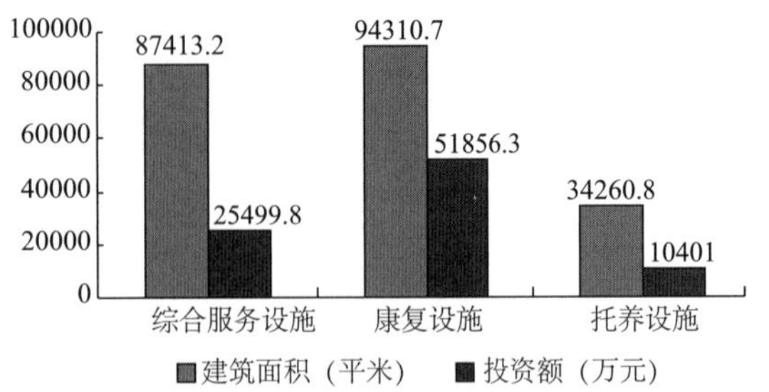

图 8　吉林省残疾人综合服务设施建设情况

十一、信息化

截至 2020 年底，8 个地级、13 个县级残联开通网站。

实施“同梦、同行、同心”4G 卡信息扶贫助残项目，全省累计办理“三同”卡 16 万多张，为广大残疾人朋友节约通讯费超过 2000 万元。

继续发挥互联网宣传阵地作用，省残联网站全年发布信息 4525 条；微信平台发布信息 1127 条；省残联网站全年点击率 3800 万次以上;吉林残联快手政务号粉丝超过 130 万，举办直播活动 40 余场，引领带动全省残疾人网络创业者走入新经济，通过网络创业增收，进一步讲好吉林残疾人故事。

2020 年黑龙江省残疾人事业发展统计公报

2020 年，黑龙江省各级残联坚持以习近平新时代中国特色社会主义思想为指导，深入学习贯彻习近平总书记关于残疾人事业的重要论述和指示批示精神，全面贯彻党的十九大和十九届二中、三中、四中、五中全会精神，按照党中央、国务院决策部署，残疾人脱贫攻坚、全面小康和疫情防控等重点工作成绩显著，残疾人工作上了一个新台阶。

一、康复

2020 年，全面落实《黑龙江省人民政府关于建立残疾儿童康复救助制度的实施意见》，全省普遍建立残疾儿童康复救助工作体系和服务网络。以贫困残疾人为重点，持续组织实施“因人施策式”残疾人精准康复服务行动，105950 名持证残疾人及残疾儿童得到基本康复服务，其中 0-6 岁残疾儿童 2496 人。得到康复服务的持证残疾人中，有视力残疾人 9526 名、听力残疾人 5068 名、言语残疾人 72 名、肢体残疾人 63861 名、智力残疾人 9104 名、精神残疾人 12575 名、多重残疾人 3831 名、0-17 岁非持证残疾儿童 1913 名。全年共为 35284 名残疾人提供各类辅助器具。积极维护残疾人健康，保障贫困残疾人基本医疗。协调省卫健委共同印发《关于进一步做好我省建档立卡贫困残疾人家庭医生签约服务工作的通知》，推进贫困残疾人家庭医生签约服务。

加强残疾人康复机构规范化建设，持续深化社区康复工作。组织参加全国残联系统康复人才实名制培训。截至 2020 年底，共有残疾人康复机构 279 个，其中残联系统康复机构 14 个。康复机构在岗人员达 5913 人，其中，管理人员 668 人，业务人员 4355 人，其他人员 890 人。贯彻落实《关于印发<黑龙江省残疾儿童定点康复服务机构准入标准和服务规范（试行）>的通知》，截至 2020 年底，全省共确定残疾儿童定点康复服务机构 90 家，其中人工耳蜗植入手术定点医院 3 家、听力定点康复训练机构 11 家、语言定点康复训练机构 3 家、儿童助听器验配机构 4 家、肢体残疾儿童定点康复服务机构 29 家、肢体矫治定点机构 2 家、智力残疾儿童定点康复服务机构 44 家；孤独症儿童定点康复服务机构 45 家。贯彻落实《国家残疾预防行动计划（2016-2020 年）》，组织开展以“残疾预防，从儿童早期干预做起”为主题的第四次残疾预防日宣传教育活动。

二、教育

以普及适龄残疾儿童少年义务教育、推广国家通用手语和国家通用盲文为重点，进一步改善残疾人教育支持保障条件。配合教育部实现 2020 年底适龄残疾儿童少年义务教育入学率达到 95%的目标。会同教育部修订《残疾人中等职业学校设置标准》，推动修订《普通高等学校招生体检工作指导意见》。《〈中华人民共和国国歌〉国家通用手语方案》作为语言文字规范发布实施。组织研制国家通用手语和国家通用盲文水平等级标准、手语翻译资格（水平）标准，研建国家通用盲文测试大纲和题库。

2020 年，共有残疾人中等职业学校（班）5 个，在校生 131 人，毕业生 33 人。有 181 名残疾人被普通高等院校录取，100 名残疾人进入高等特殊教育学院学习。

530 名残疾青壮年文盲接受了扫盲教育。

三、就业

2020 年，全面落实《黑龙江省残疾人自主创业就业扶持办法》，多地相继出台有关扶持政策，加大残疾人就业工作机制和制度建设力度。推动联合出台《黑龙江省落实<关于完善残疾人就业保障金制度更好促进残疾人就业的总体方案>的意见》，在优化征收、规范使用、强化监督、健全服务、低保渐退等方面予以明确。

加强“就业援助月”“全国助残日”等重要节点宣传效能，开展多种形式专项就业服务。加强与五八公益基金会等社会组织合作，实施“创翼计划”就业项目，探索互联网+残疾人就业多种实现模式。加强残疾人就业创业孵化基地建设，带动残疾人自主创业就业。加强残疾人职业培训（示范）基地标准化建设，截至 2020 年，我省现有国家级残疾人职业培训示范基地 3 家，国家级残疾人职业培训基地 15 家。加强“龙在云端”省级示范培训品牌创建，通过省级引领示范，逐步形成全省规模化培训。加强“龙在云端”筑梦商城电商平台运营监督，助力残疾人在新业态领域云端筑梦。加强残疾人就业和职业培训实名制信息大数据分析，准确把握残疾人就业状况和培训需求趋势，健全残疾人就业和职业培训状况季通报制度和高校残疾人毕业生周通报制度，促进有需求有意愿残疾人有效培训、稳定就业。全年城乡新增残疾人就业 12157 人，其中，城镇新增就业 7204 人，农村新增就业 4953 人；城乡新增残疾人实名培训 9377 人。

加强盲人医疗按摩专业人才队伍建设，全年取得中级职务任职资格 6 人，培训医疗按摩人员 199 人，新增盲人医疗按摩就业人员 46 人，现有医疗按摩机构 37 家；加强盲人保健按摩培训工作，全年培训保健按摩人员 213 人，新增盲人保健按摩就业人员 46 人，现有保健按摩机构 269 家。2020 年全国盲人医疗按摩人员考试中，我省考生考试通过率 42.22%。

举办 2020 年黑龙江省残疾人岗位精英职业技能竞赛暨首届盲人按摩大师赛。举办 2020 年黑龙江省残疾人就业服务机构工作人员职业指导竞赛。组织参加 2020 年全国残疾人岗位精英职业技能竞赛暨残疾人就业服务机构工作人员职业指导竞赛。

四、社会保障

紧紧围绕省政府关于《黑龙江省“十三五”加快残疾人小康进程规划》和省残联第七次代表大会部署要求，结合新型冠状病毒疫情防控，扎实做好“六稳”工作、全面落实“六保”任务，着力保障和改善残疾人生活，在发展中补齐残疾人民生短板，残疾人社会保障工作成效显著。

为全面落实《黑龙江省人民政府关于印发黑龙江省全面建立困难残疾人生活补贴和重度残疾人护理补贴制度实施办法》，做好残疾人两项补贴发放工作，省民政厅、省财政厅、省残联又联合下发了《关于进一步做好残疾人两项补贴发放工作的通知》《关于印发<黑龙江省困难残疾人生活补贴和重度残疾人护理补贴发放工作排查整改方案>的通知》《关于进一步明确困难残疾人生活补贴和重度残疾人护理补贴发放工作各级职能分工的通知》，促进了全省残疾人两项补贴发放工作优质高效开展。在各级党委、政府高度重视下，经过各有关部门通力协作，截至到 2020 年 10 月，残疾人两项补贴发放 671625 人，发放资金 60658.12 元，做到了应发尽发。

认真贯彻落实省政府关于《黑龙江省“十三五”加快残疾人小康进程规划》，省民政厅　省扶贫开发领导小组办公室　省人力资源和社会保障厅　省卫生和计划生育委员会　省残疾人联合会下发了《关于贯彻落实<黑龙江省加强农村最低生活保障制度与扶贫开发政策有效衔接工作实施方案>的通知》,切实将生活困难和重度残疾人纳入适用的政策保障范围，残疾人救助、救济等保障政策得到有效落实。截至到 2020 年 10 月，全省共有 35.8 万生活困难较大的残疾人纳入低保范围；有 33884 残疾人纳入供养；有 50 万残疾人享受医疗、教育、住房、就业和水电气暖等优惠政策或救助。

按照《黑龙江省“十三五”加快残疾人小康进程规划》“贫困和重度残疾人参加城乡居民基本养老保险，由当地政府为其代缴部分或全部最低缴费档次的养老保险费”规定，省人社厅、财政厅下发了《关于建立城乡居民基本养老保险待遇确定和基础养老金正常调整机制的指导意见》，各地积极做好残疾人参加保险工作。截至到 2020 年 10 月底，全省有 224284 人参加职工养老保险，有 414031 人参加城乡社会养老保险，占应参加人数的 92%；有 185399 人参加职工医疗保险，有 740460 人参加社会医疗保险，占应参加人数的 95%。其中有 79961 享受城乡养老保险缴费补贴，有 394927 享受医疗保险缴费补贴。

五、扶贫开发

省残联认真落实党中央决策部署，学习贯彻习近平总书记在脱贫攻坚座谈会上的讲话精神，落实省委省政府和中国残联具体要求，紧紧围绕“全面建成小康社会，残疾人一个也不能少”的目标，按照“问需响应、精准施策、政策联动、持续帮扶、激发动能、社会动员、长效巩固”七措并举的脱贫工作思路，统筹推进新冠肺炎疫情防控和贫困残疾人脱贫攻坚，把打赢“两个战役”作为重要政治任务和必须完成的硬任务，扎实推进贫困残疾人脱贫攻坚取得决定性成效，纳入建档立卡贫困残疾人全部实现稳定脱贫，脱贫不稳定户中残疾人全部消除返贫风险、边缘户中残疾人全部消除致贫风险，圆满完成贫困残疾人脱贫攻坚任务。

全省共有 8792 人次农村残疾人接受了实用技术培训；3271 名贫困残疾人获得康复扶贫贴息贷款扶持；55 个残疾人扶贫基地安置 840 名残疾人就业，辐射带动 573 户残疾人家庭增收；对 3664 户农村贫困残疾人家庭实施危房改造，投入资金 56911539.3 元，有 5219 名残疾人受益。

六、宣传文化

2020 年，省残联以打赢疫情防控的人民战争为核心，坚决做好残疾人常态化疫情防控工作，迅速普及疫情防控知识，积极宣传我省各级残联疫情防控工作，省残联微信公众号上连续推出《特殊艺术，龙江残疾人战“疫”作品展播》7 期。在全国助残日之际，省残联紧扣“助残脱贫决胜小康”主题，精心策划了“关心你的残疾人邻居志愿者征集”“助残日扶贫带货直播”“法律援助惠民生•助力残疾人脱贫攻坚”“创翼计划，互联网助残就业”“防疫不松，脱贫不误”等十项特色主题活动。我省推荐的候选人在中国残联评选中荣获十大“2020 年度助残新闻人物”。全省各地残联分级分层分类以助力残疾人脱贫攻坚为抓手，线上线下形式相结合，持续开展“学听跟”和“百团千场”巡讲活动，参与人数达 10 万人次。组织新闻媒体走基层，采写、刊发全省自强和助残典型百余名。涌现出全国劳模刘洪霞、脱贫攻坚奋进奖获得者乔福军、全省最美脱贫攻坚奋斗者辛敏等贫困残疾人自强典型。中央电视台新闻联播节目 2 次报道了我省残疾人脱贫攻坚典型事迹。《黑龙江省残联：多举措扎实推进贫困残疾人脱贫攻坚工作》被 36 家媒体全网推送宣传。开展“决战脱贫攻坚共创美好生活”文化交流展示活动，在极光新闻平台上进行的朗诵和征文投票中，总投票达到 258 万票。

截至 2020 年底，有省级残疾人专题广播节目 1 个、电视手语栏目 2 个；市级残疾人专题广播节目 7 个、电视手语栏目 9 个。

截至 2020 年底，省市县三级公共图书馆共设立盲文及盲文有声读物阅览室 50 个，共开展残疾人文化周活动 195 场次；省市两级残联艺术团 12 个。

七、体育

备战北京冬残奥会和东京残奥会，组织冬残奥 6 个项目 5 支队伍、夏残奥 14 个项目 17 支队伍开展训练，举办残奥单板滑雪、越野滑雪、亚洲杯比赛，参赛获得 30 枚金牌，参加 2020 年自行车、羽毛球国际赛事获得 17 枚金牌，经过努力，残疾人体育领域实现疫情“零感染”。

八、维权

各级残联维权组织建设进一步加强，残疾人事业法律法规体系进一步完善，无障碍环境建设取得新突破，残疾人维权工作全面开展。

2020 年，制定或修改保障残疾人权益的规范性文件级 4 个。县级以上人大开展《中华人民共和国残疾人保障法》执法检查和专题调研 8 次；政协开展视察和专题调研 6 次。开展省级普法宣传教育活动 3 次，5009 人参加。

残疾人参政议政工作稳步开展，各地残联协助人大代表、政协委员提出议案、建议、提案 4 件，办理议案、建议、提案 5 件。

无障碍建设法规、标准进一步完善。共出台了 3 个省、地、县级无障碍环境建设与管理法规、政府令和规范性文件；36 个地市、县系统开展无障碍环境建设；开展无障碍环境建设检查 6 次，无障碍培训 91 人次。

九、组织建设

2020 年，市县乡共有残联 1333 个，各地市已建残联 13 个，县（市、区）残联已建 126 个，乡镇（街道）残联已建 1194 个；社区（村）已建残协 8311 个。

省市县乡残联工作人员 2343 人，乡镇（街道）残联、村（社区）残协专职委员总计 4705 名。地市级配备了残疾人领导干部的残联 6 个，县级配备了残疾人干部的残联 33 个。

共建立各类残疾人专门协会 684 个，其中省级专门协会已建 5 个，市级专门协会已建 65 个，县级专门协会已建 614 个。助残社会组织 16 个。

十、服务设施

残疾人服务设施建设得到全面发展。截至 2020 年底，已竣工的各级残疾人综合服务设施 1 个，总建设规模 600 平方米，总投资 98 万元；已竣工的各级残疾人托养服务设施 2 个，总建设规模 4012 平方米，总投资 980 万元。

十一、信息化建设

截至 2020 年底，4 个市级、7 个县级残联开通网站。与公安厅、民政厅、教育厅、人力资源社会保障厅、省医保局、省税务局等部门建立共享机制，基于残疾人人口基础数据库，落实残联重点业务应用建设，推动“一网通办”。

2020年上海市残疾人事业发展统计公报

2020年，上海市残联以习近平新时代中国特色社会主义思想为指导，深入贯彻落实党的十九大、十九届二中、三中、四中、五中全会文件精神，坚持建制度、练内功、优服务、强供给，持续加强疫情下残疾人民生保障，圆满完成了“十三五”规划提出的各项任务和指标。

一、康复

全市有16.7万残疾儿童及持证残疾人得到基本康复服务,其中0-17岁儿童0.4万。得到康复服务的持证残疾人中，有视力残疾人2.9万、听力残疾人1.9万、言语残疾人0.1万、肢体残疾人8.4万、智力残疾人1.2万、精神残疾人1.5万、多重残疾人0.5万。得到康复服务的未持证残疾人0.2万。全年共为7.1万残疾人提供各类辅助器具适配服务。

截至2020年底，全市提供残疾康复服务的机构有1083个，其中，100个提供视力残疾康复服务，66个提供听力言语残疾康复服务，326个提供肢体残疾康复服务，334个提供智力残疾康复服务，355个提供精神残疾康复服务，262个提供辅助器具服务（部分机构提供多种形式的康复服务）。开展残疾康复在岗人员达8808人，其中，管理人员1369人，专业技术人员4609人，其他人员2830人。

二、教育

进一步完善特殊教育体系，加快特殊职业教育发展。全市设立了18个特殊职业教育办学点，其中1个特殊教育普通高中（班），在校盲人学生33人。残疾人中职教育（班）17个，在校生812人，已毕业65人，其中有7人获得职业资格证书。

完善残疾人考试辅助服务举措，全年为48名残疾人考生参加中考、高中学业水平考，春、秋两季高考等考试提供盲文试卷、单独设置考场等便利，共有75名残疾考生被普通高校录取，另有10名残疾考生被高等特殊教育机构录取。

三、就业与扶贫

2020年，全市持证残疾人就业年龄段内（男：16岁-59岁，女：16岁-54岁）的就业人数为7.1万人，其中分散按比例就业4.7万人，集中就业0.9万人，务农0.1万人，辅助性就业、公益性岗位就业0.7万人，灵活就业、自主创业等0.7万人。

继续推动农村困难残疾人劳动增收，积极扶持涉残涉农经济组织，全市有227个残疾人扶贫基地，1.4万人次残疾人得到实用技术培训，安置3626名残疾人就业，辐射带动残疾人2736户。67户农村困难残疾人家庭得到无障碍改造。

2020年，全市残联系统开展东西部扶贫协作和对口支援工作，重点帮扶云南和贵州遵义等地区残疾人脱贫。

四、社会保障

截至2020年底，残疾居民参加城乡社会养老保险9.8万名，60周岁以下的参保残疾人中有4.1万名重度残疾人。

落实“困难残疾人生活补贴”和“重度残疾人护理补贴”（简称“两项补贴”）制度，享受“两项补贴”的残疾人总数为31.3万，其中享受困难残疾人生活补贴9.1万，享受重度残疾人护理补贴22.2万。

五、宣传文化

举办第30次“全国助残日”第21个“上海助残周”“同心抗疫决胜小康”——庆祝第29个国际残疾人日暨上海市残疾人艺术团汇报演出等大型活动。截至2020年底，全年组织新闻发布会10次。市级残疾人电视手语栏目2个，区级残疾人专题广播节目3个、电视手语栏目14个。全年通过市残联官网、微信、微博及抖音发布各类信息1915篇，视频330条。市残联微信公众号阅读量过万的有67篇，最高转发数量2201次。

继续推进公共图书馆盲人阅览室建设、无障碍电影放映和残疾人文化活动。截至 2020 年底，全市共设立 38 个盲文及盲人有声读物图书馆，制作社区无障碍电影剧本 50 部。市区两级开展残疾人文化周活动 366 场次，全年有 16.3 万人次残疾人参加各级各类文化活动，其中，2020 年残疾人读书系列活动累计吸引残疾人 1.4 万人次参与，共收到 16 个区残疾人“最美瞬间”征文、摄影、书画、视频投稿作品 250 余件。

六、体育

全年累计开展市级各类残疾人群众体育健身活动 3 次，举办残疾人体育比赛 2 次，残疾人群众体育健身活动参与人数 8992 人次，参赛残疾人运动员 1887 人次，聘任教练员 40 名，全市共设 5 个残疾人体育训练基地。

全年因疫情原因，所有国际、全国赛事停办。上海作为残疾人体育国家集训基地，抓好 3 支国家队在国家集训基地的训练工作，共计 78 人参与了国家队集训。上海队共计 220 人参加了上海运动队集训。举办“爱在上海”残健融合比赛，采用线上联赛加线下冠亚军决赛的方式进行。本次比赛总共有 32 支队伍参加，参赛残疾人运动员达到 150 余人。

七、维权

全市加快推进法治残联建设，制定或修改保障残疾人权益的规范性文件 5 个。市区两级人大开展《中华人民共和国残疾人保障法》执法检查和专题调研 2 次，开展市级普法宣传教育活动 4 次，线上线下累计 1.2 万人次参加。

全市成立残疾人法律救助工作协调机构 18 个，建立残疾人法律救助工作站 17 个。全年共受理残疾人群众来信 1087 件，来电 8711 次，来访 2189 人次，相关信访件均得到妥善处理。

截至 2020 年底，本市残联系统人大代表市级 42 人，其中市级 4 人，区、街道（乡镇）代表 39 人，其中 1 人同时兼任市、区级人大代表；本市残联系统政协委员 16 人，其中市级 3 人，区级 13 人。残疾人参政议政工作得到加强，全市残联系统协助人大代表、政协委员提出议案、建议、提案 3 件，办理议案、建议、提案 27 件。

截至 2020 年底，全市累计出台了 2 个区级无障碍环境建设与管理规范性文件；全市开展无障碍环境建设检查 646 次，无障碍工作培训 875 人次。开通 12345 市民热线手语视频服务。在金融、航空、社区公共服务场所推广“在线手语视频服务”。持续推进本市政府网站全网无障碍改造工作。

八、组织建设

全市市、区、街道（乡镇）共有残联组织 237 个，其中市级 1 个、区级 16 个、街道（乡镇）级 220 个。全市已建居（村）残疾人协会 5099 个，已建比例为 99.5%，其中：有固定办公场所 5000 个，占 97.6%；有办公经费 3614 个，占 70.5%；配备办公设备 4578 个，占 89.3%。

全市残联系统实有人员 1148 人。市、区、街道（乡镇）残联领导班子已配备 154 名兼职副理事长，其中:市残联 2 名、区残联 25 名、街道（乡镇）128 名。街道（乡镇）、居（村）选聘残疾人专职委员 3948 名。

全市共建立市区两级残疾人专门协会 85 个，其中:市级 5 个、区级 80 个，有办公场所 73 个，占 85.9%。

全市助残社会组织 172 个。发布《2020 上海市助残服务机构汇编》《2021 上海市助残服务项目汇编》。组织开展上海优秀志愿助残服务组织及项目展示交流活动。公开征集服务标识，提升助残志愿服务影响力。开发“云助残服务平台”，助力志愿服务供需精准对接。

九、服务设施建设

截至 2020 年底，全市累计投入使用的各级残疾人综合服务设施 17 个，总建设规模为 2.4 万平方米，总投资额 1.2 亿元。累计已投入使用的各级残疾人托养设施 12 个，总建设规模为 7260 平方米，总投资额为 1593 万元。累计已投入使用的各级残疾人康复设施 5 个，总建设规模为 10.1 万平方米，总投资额 4.5 亿元。

十、信息化建设

截至 2020 年底，全市残疾人人口基础数据库持证残疾人 59.5 万人，比上年增加 1.7 万人。2020 年为深入推进“一网通办”，进一步加大残疾人相关政务服务事项整合力度，提升协同服务能力，市残联会同市民政局、市教委和市大数据中心等部门和单位，有序推进高效办成助残“一件事”。对照“一次告知、一表申请、一口受理、一网办理、统一发证、一体管理”业务流程再造的总体要求，助残“一件事”按照“部门之间业务串联、残疾人证业务并联”管理架构重塑业务流程，通过搭建助残“一件事”主题办理模块，将多部门、跨层级的 12 个业务事项整合，以“数据跑路”代替“群众跑路”，大幅精简办事材料、时间和跑动次数，全面提升残疾人群众办事的满意度和获得感。

2020年江苏省残疾人事业发展统计公报

2020年是“十三五”规划和全面建成小康的收官之年，也是应对疫情等重大考验之年。这一年，江苏省残联全面贯彻党的十九大、十九届二中、三中、四中、五中全会、中央经济工作会议、省委十三届九次全会和第三十五次全国残联工作会议精神，深入落实习近平总书记关于残疾人事业的重要论述和视察江苏重要讲话指示精神，在严抓疫情防控与复工复训的基础上，推动残疾人工作法规政策更加健全，残疾人脱贫攻坚取得决定性成就，以市县残疾人康复和托养中心为重点的服务机构建设基本完成，各项基本服务逐步普及，进一步提亮了江苏高水平全面小康的成色。

一、康复

按照省政府规章年度立法计划，《江苏省残疾预防和残疾人康复实施办法》于2020年12月20日经省人民政府第73次常务会议讨论通过，自2021年2月1日起施行。与省教育厅等六部门联合出台《江苏省残疾儿童基本康复服务管理暂行办法》(苏残发〔2020〕23号)、制定《江苏省残疾儿童基本康复服务实施规范》(苏残发〔2020〕33号)和《省残联办公室关于推进开展全类别残疾儿童基本康复服务工作的通知》(苏残办函〔2020〕15号)，进一步规范我省残疾儿童康复救助服务。

全年27.7万名持证残疾人及残疾儿童得到基本康复服务，其中0-6岁残疾儿童2.1万人。得到康复服务的持证残疾人中，有视力残疾人2.3万名、听力残疾人1.0万名、言语残疾人123名、肢体残疾人11.4万名、智力残疾人2.5万名、精神残疾人7.8万名、多重残疾人0.8万名。全年共为7.3万残疾人提供各类辅助器具。

截至2020年底，共有残疾人康复机构473个，其中残联系统康复机构92个。康复机构在岗人员达1.4万人，其中，管理人员1363人，业务人员1.1万人，其他人员2038人。

二、教育

与省教育厅等七部门联合出台《关于做好义务教育阶段重度残疾儿童少年送教服务工作的指导意见》，制定《江苏省学前融合教育试点资金管理规定（试行）》和支出绩效目标表，保障残疾儿童接受教育权利。

实施残疾人事业专项彩票公益金助学项目，为217名家庭经济困难残疾儿童享受普惠性学前教育提供资助，带动各地对578残疾儿童给予学前教育资助。

2020年，共有特殊教育普通高中（部、班）4个，在校生534人，其中聋生465人，盲生27人，其他42人。残疾人中等职业学校（班）10个，在校生1694人，毕业生333人，毕业生中98人获得职业资格证书。有428名残疾人被普通高等院校录取，94名残疾人进入高等特殊教育学院学习。

1521名残疾青壮年文盲接受了扫盲教育。

三、就业

召开2020年全省高校残疾人毕业生就业创业服务工作网络视频会议，建立“一生一册”档案，开展“一人一策”帮扶。2020届全省高校残疾人毕业生就业服务率为99.89%、就业率为92.51%。

城乡持证残疾人就业人数为33.8万人，其中按比例就业8.1万人，集中就业4.5万人，个体就业2.7万人，公益性岗位就业5.2万人，辅助性就业1.3万人，灵活就业（含社区、居家就业）3.3万人，从事农业种养加8.6万人。

培训盲人保健按摩人员1008名、盲人医疗按摩人员538名；现有保健按摩机构1315个，医疗按摩机构53个。

四、社会保障

贯彻落实国家六部委《关于完善残疾人就业保障金制度更好促进残疾人就业的总体方案》，于4

月30日正式出台《关于进一步完善残疾人就业保障金更好促进残疾人就业的通知》。和民政部门共同推动“两项补贴”提标扩面，有条件的地区已将困难残疾人生活补贴对象扩面至低保外的三、四级智力、精神残疾人，圆满完成了托养和“残疾人之家”建设任务。

截至2020年底，残疾居民参加城乡社会养老保险人数117.3万名，29.6万名60岁以下参保重度残疾人中，29.0万享受了参保个人缴费资助政策，占比98.1%。18.2万名非重度残疾人享受了个人缴费资助政策。52.7万人领取养老金。

全省完成托养3.8万余人，累计建成“残疾人之家”3017家，实现辅助性就业或就业3.2万人，在连云港、淮安两地开展居家托养试点，居家托养服务8700余人。

五、扶贫开发

扎实开展脱贫攻坚“三进三查”回头看工作，入户调查低收入和建档立卡残疾人32.5万人，排查整改220256条群众反映的问题，提高了脱贫攻坚质量，巩固了拓展脱贫成果，实现了全面小康残疾人一个都不能少的目标。

共有6876人次农村残疾人接受了实用技术培训，306名贫困残疾人获得康复扶贫贴息贷款扶持，146个残疾人扶贫基地安置2331名残疾人就业，辐射带动2356户残疾人家庭增收。

共完成692户农村贫困残疾人家庭危房改造，投入资金911.1万元，698名残疾人受益。

六、宣传文化

及时开设专题专栏“抗击疫情”“战‘疫’进行时”“残联改革进行时”宣传报道全省残联系统在抗击新冠疫情、残联改革方面所取得的成果。

截至2020年底，省地县三级公共图书馆共设立盲文及盲文有声读物阅览室80个，共开展残疾人文化周活动1053场次；省地两级残联共举办残疾人艺术类的比赛演出及展览53次。

七、体育

完成《群众性残疾人文化体育发展对策研究》课题，为群众性残疾人文化体育工作提供思路方向。指导各地利用“国际残疾人日”“全国助残日”等重要残疾人节日，开展基层文化体育服务活动，激励更多残疾人走出家门。

新增设立社区残疾人健身示范点84个，为834户重度残疾人提供康复体育进家庭服务，培养残疾人社会体育指导员156名。

八、维权

完成《江苏省残疾预防与残疾人康复实施办法》行政立法工作和《江苏省无障碍环境建设管理实施办法》立法调研工作。围绕脱贫攻坚开展残疾人家庭无障碍改造15000多户，配合民政开展老年重残家庭适老化改造7373户；联合省住建厅等部门组织开展无障碍环境市县村镇创建工作，12个地区通过省级验收，南京市江宁区等5个示范地区通过国家验收。

截至2020年底，全省成立残疾人法律救助工作协调机构110个，建立残疾人法律救助工作站110个。

县级以上人大开展《中华人民共和国残疾人保障法》执法检查和专题调研19次；政协开展视察和专题调研16次。开展省级普法宣传教育活动32次，2000多人参加。

残疾人参政议政工作稳步开展，各地残联协助人大代表、政协委员提出议案、建议、提案20件，办理议案、建议、提案91件。

九、组织建设

落实国务院办公厅关于加快推进政务服务“跨省通办”的指导意见，对标“38条重大改革举措”，以“强三性”“去四化”为主线统筹推动，选取8个县（市、区）开展基层残联组织专项改革试点，推动全省残联改革落实落地，实现十年换证工作的平稳过渡。

2020年，市县乡共有残联1389个，各地市已建残联13个，县（市、区）残联已建104个，乡镇（街道）残联已建1272个；社区（村）已建残协19557个。

省市县乡残联工作人员4652人，乡镇（街道）残联、村（社区）残协专职委员总计16260名。地市级配备了残疾人领导干部的残联9个，县级配备了残疾人干部的残联 48 个。

共建立各类残疾人专门协会 557 个，其中省级专门协会已建 5 个，市级专门协会已建 65 个，县级专门协会已建 487 个。助残社会组织 527 个。

十、服务设施

残疾人服务设施建设得到全面发展。

截至 2020 年底，已竣工的各级残疾人综合服务设施 79 个，总建设规模 47.5 万平方米，总投资 20.1 亿元；已竣工的各级残疾人康复设施 63 个，总建设规模 24.8 万平方米，总投资 10.0 亿元；已竣工的各级残疾人托养服务设施 113 个，总建设规模 33.5 万平方米，总投资 9.9 亿元。

十一、信息化建设

“智慧残联”信息化建设项目全面铺开，办公自动化系统上线运行，配合脱贫攻坚工作开发的“三进三查”系统被推荐参加 2020 年数字江苏建设优秀实践成果项目申报。

截至 2020 年底，13 个地级、57 个县级残联开通网站。

2020年浙江省残疾人事业发展统计公报

2020年，全省残疾人工作在省委省政府的坚强领导和中国残联的精心指导下，以习近平新时代中国特色社会主义思想为指导，深入贯彻习近平总书记考察浙江重要讲话精神，忠实践行“八八战略”，奋力打造“重要窗口”，统筹推进残联系统疫情防控和各项残疾人工作，圆满完成各项目标任务。

一、康复

2020年，全省64.1万名持证残疾人及残疾儿童得到基本康复服务，其中0—6岁残疾儿童0.8万人。得到康复服务的持证残疾人中，视力残疾人6.0万名、听力残疾人8.2万名、言语残疾人0.8万名、肢体残疾人19.0万名、智力残疾人10.9万名、精神残疾人14.6万名、多重残疾人4.4万名。全年共为7.0万名残疾人提供各类辅助器具适配服务。

截至2020年底，全省共有残疾人康复机构252个，其中，残联系统康复机构65个。康复机构在岗人员8822人，其中，管理人员1068人，业务人员6243人，其他人员1511人。

二、教育

2020年，全省各地完成残疾学生及残疾人家庭子女助学3.5万人，其中残疾儿童学前教育资助706人。

全省共有特殊教育普通高中（部、班）6个，在校生784人，其中聋生279人，盲生286人，其他219人。残疾人中等职业学校（班）16个，在校生1124人，毕业生249人，毕业生中82人获得职业资格证书。全省有436名残疾人被普通高等院校录取，475名残疾人进入浙江特殊教育职业学院学习。

2020年，有524名残疾青壮年文盲接受了扫盲教育。

三、就业

2020年，全省新增残疾人就业1.37万人，组织残疾人职业技能培训2.6万人次。截至2020年底，全省持证残疾人就业人数为30.7万人，其中按比例就业8.6万人，集中就业3.7万人，个体就业3.7万人，公益性岗位就业0.4万人，辅助性就业1.3万人，灵活就业（含社区、居家就业）8.3万人，从事农业种养殖4.7万人。

2020年，全省共培训盲人保健按摩人员563名、盲人医疗按摩人员327名。全省共有保健按摩机构1130个，医疗按摩机构89个。获得盲人医疗按摩初级专业技术职务任职资格33人、中级专业技术职务任职资格1人。

四、社会保障

截至2020年底，残疾居民参加城乡社会养老保险人数73.1万。60岁以下参保的重度残疾人中，13.6万人享受参保个人缴费资助政策，占比99.99%。21.3万名非重度残疾人享受个人缴费资助政策。36.8万人领取养老金。

全省共有残疾人托养服务机构1295个，其中寄宿制托养服务机构150个，日间照料机构1023个，综合性托养服务机构122个，为2万名残疾人提供托养服务。全年有3051名托养服务管理和服务人员接受各级各类专业培训。

五、扶贫

2020年，农村困难残疾人接受实用技术培训6004人次。388个残疾人扶贫基地安置1709名残疾人就业，辐射带动3665户残疾人家庭增收。

全省共完成3413户农村困难残疾人家庭危房改造，投入资金5301.9万元，3681名残疾人受益。

六、宣传文化

2020年，第三十个全国助残日期间，举办“云”相亲、“自强达人秀”微视频征集大赛和省第二届“最美残疾人”评选宣传等10项线上线下活动，共推出相关新闻报道1083篇。聚焦残疾人婚恋难题，开设《浙里同行》情感访谈类节目，举行首届残疾人集体婚礼，全省百对新人参加,相关话题进入新浪微博热搜榜前十，阅读量累计突破 500 万次。实施“五个一”文化助残服务和无障碍观影“百千万”行动。首届残疾人文化艺术季系列活动上下联动，书画摄影大赛网络展览馆阅读量破百万，44 名残疾人作家作品入刊《中国作家》。举行“新时代•共奋斗”特殊艺术线上演出，点击量超过 20 万次。在“中国残疾人事业好新闻奖”评选中我省一等奖数和获奖总数均居全国第一。截至 2020 年底，共有省级残疾人专题广播节目 1 个、电视手语栏目 4 个；市级残疾人专题广播节目 13 个、电视手语栏目 12 个。省市县三级公共图书馆共设立盲文及盲文有声读物阅览室 87 个，开展残疾人文化周活动 863 场次。省市两级残联有各类残疾人艺术团 35 个。

七、体育

备战北京冬残奥会、东京残奥会和全国十一残运会，组织 20 个项目 22 支项目队集训。承担国家备战东京残奥会游泳、射箭、盲人门球 3 个项目 4 支队伍的训练任务。开展健身周、特奥日、冰雪季活动。全省新增设立社区残疾人健身示范点 33 个，为 1.4 万户重度残疾人提供康复体育进家庭服务，培养残疾人社会体育指导员 258 名。

八、维权

2020 年，制定或修改保障残疾人权益的规范性文件市级 7 个、县级 19 个。全省已出台 69 个无障碍环境建设与管理法规、政府令和规范性文件。县级以上人大开展《中华人民共和国残疾人保障法》执法检查和专题调研 52 次，县级以上政协开展视察和专题调研 83 次。各地残联协助人大代表、政协委员提出议案、建议、提案 145 件，办理议案、建议、提案 173 件。

省级开展普法宣传教育活动 5 次，1100 人参加；省级举办法律培训班 2 个，760 人参加。截至 2020 年底，全省成立残疾人法律救助工作协调机构 102 个，建立残疾人法律救助工作站 102 个。

大力推进无障碍环境建设。省政协举办“推进无障碍环境建设”主题民生协商论坛，网上议政厅专题网页访问量达 16.43 万人次。成立省级无障碍环境促进会，全省开展无障碍环境建设检查 816 次，无障碍培训 8967 人次，实施困难残疾人家庭无障碍改造 1.1 万户，成功创建全国无障碍环境市县村镇 12 个、省级无障碍社区 118 个，发放残疾人机动轮椅车燃油补贴 1.3 万人次。

九、组织建设

2020 年，市县乡共有残联 1472 个，其中，设区市残联 11 个，县（市、区）残联 95 个，乡镇（街道）残联 1366 个。村（社区）已建残协 2.1 万个。

省市县乡残联实有工作人员 5068 人，乡镇（街道）、村（社区）选聘残疾人专职委员 2.0 万名。10 个设区市残联配备残疾人领导干部，65 个县级残联配备残疾人干部。

全省共建立各类残疾人专门协会 495 个，其中，省级 5 个、设区市 55 个、县级 435 个。全省共有助残社会组织 332 个。

十、服务设施

截至 2020 年底，全省已竣工的各级残疾人综合服务设施 89 个，总建设规模 64.2 万平方米，总投资 27.9 亿元；已竣工的各级残疾人康复设施 45 个，总建设规模 32.2 万平方米，总投资 13.0 亿元；已竣工的各级残疾人托养服务设施 51 个，总建设规模 35.6 万平方米，总投资 14.5 亿元。

十一、信息化建设

截至 2020 年底，全省入库持证残疾人 135.3 万人；10 个设区市、32 个县级残联开通网站。加强“数字残联”建设，持续完善与中国残联、省级相关厅局数据交换共享机制，实现中国残联残疾人证库、民政大救助平台低保低边库、民政殡仪火化库、卫健委医学死亡证明库、人社职工养老保险库、公安人口户籍库等数据库的联通和交换。推进助残服务体系数字化转型，完成省级 39 个助残服务事项梳理和残疾人证办理等 8 个事项的政务 2.0 提升工作。“浙里办”助残服务专区实现残疾人电子证照展示、助残服务事项申请、助残服务机构导航、辅助器具适配简介、心理咨询在线测评等五个特色服务板块上线运行，及时向社会公众发布助残服务政策法规、事项办理等相关信息。

2020年安徽省残疾人事业发展统计公报

2020年，安徽省残联系统以习近平新时代中国特色社会主义思想为指导，深入学习贯彻党的十九大和十九届二中、三中、四中、五中全会及习近平总书记考察安徽重要讲话指示精神，以党建为引领，以深入实施“六大行动”、倾情打造“五大残联”为抓手，围绕中心，服务大局，服务残疾人，聚焦残疾人脱贫攻坚和民生工程，多措并举，全力推动我省残疾人事业高质量发展。

一、康复

488078名持证残疾人及残疾儿童得到基本康复服务，其中0-6岁残疾儿童12742人。得到康复服务的持证残疾人中，有视力残疾人36846名、听力残疾人22505名、言语残疾人2222名、肢体残疾人185097名、智力残疾人33463名、精神残疾人170613名、多重残疾人30511名。全年共为93213名残疾人提供各类辅助器具。

截至2020年底，共有残疾人康复机构295个，其中残联系统康复机构63个。康复机构在岗人员达8570人，其中，管理人员765人，业务人员6945人，其他人员860人。

二、教育

实施残疾人事业专项彩票公益金助学项目，为920名家庭经济困难残疾儿童享受普惠性学前教育提供资助，带动各地对100残疾儿童给予学前教育资助。

2020年，共有特殊教育普通高中（部、班）1个，在校生40人，其中聋生9人，盲生1人，其他30人。残疾人中等职业学校（班）4个，在校生1240人，毕业生327人，毕业生中39人获得职业资格证书。有616名残疾人被普通高等院校录取。

1761名残疾青壮年文盲接受了扫盲教育。

三、就业

城乡持证残疾人就业人数为479729人，其中按比例就业10982人，集中就业6424人，个体就业40399人，公益性岗位就业3050人，辅助性就业9401人，灵活就业（含社区、居家就业）152582人，从事农业种养加256891人。

培训盲人保健按摩人员279名、盲人医疗按摩人员164名；现有保健按摩机构267个，医疗按摩机构4个。

四、社会保障

截至2020年底，残疾居民参加城乡社会养老保险人数1556743名，446637名60岁以下参保重度残疾人中，424499享受了参保个人缴费资助政策，占比95.0%。63680名非重度残疾人享受了个人缴费资助政策。605982人领取养老金。

残疾人托养服务机构410个，其中寄宿制托养服务机构192个，日间照料机构74个，综合性托养服务机构106个，为3501残疾人提供了托养服务。16333残疾人接受居家服务。417托养服务管理和服务人员接受了各级各类专业培训。

五、扶贫

共有18788人次农村残疾人接受了实用技术培训，15名贫困残疾人获得康复扶贫贴息贷款扶持，118个残疾人扶贫基地安置1316名残疾人就业，辐射带动1336户残疾人家庭增收。

共完成2554户农村贫困残疾人家庭危房改造，投入资金28948399.6元，3394名残疾人受益。

六、宣传文化

截至2020年底，全国共有省级残疾人专题广播节目1个、电视手语栏目1个；地级残疾人专题广播节目17个、电视手语栏目16个。

截至2020年底，省地县三级公共图书馆共设立盲文及盲文有声读物阅览室57个，共开展残疾人文化周活动328场次；省地两级残联艺术团8个。

七、体育

新增设立社区残疾人健身示范点16个，为593户重度残疾人提供康复体育进家庭服务，培养残疾人社会体育指导员280名。

八、维权

2020年，制定或修改保障残疾人权益的地级规范性文1个、县级4个。县级以上人大开展《中华人民共和国残疾人保障法》执法检查和专题调研14次；政协开展视察和专题调研7次。开展省级普法宣传教育活动1次，260人参加；举办省级法律培训班1个，60人参加。

截至2020年底，全省共建立残疾人法律救助协调机构97个，共建立残疾人法律救助工作站87个。

残疾人参政议政工作稳步开展，各地残联协助人大代表、政协委员提出议案、建议、提案17件，办理议案、建议、提案48件。

无障碍建设法规、标准进一步完善。共出台了8个省、地、县级无障碍环境建设与管理法规、政府令和规范性文件；82个地市、县系统开展无障碍环境建设；开展无障碍环境建设检查77次，无障碍培训571人次。

九、组织建设

2020年，市县乡共有残联1656个，各地市已建残联16个，县（市、区）残联已建117个，乡镇（街道）残联已建1523个；社区（村）已建残协15994个。

省市县乡残联工作人员3604人，乡镇（街道）残联、村（社区）残协专职委员总计16435名。地市级配备了残疾人领导干部的残联8个，县级配备了残疾人干部的残联49个。

共建立各类残疾人专门协会587个，其中省级专门协会已建5个，市级专门协会已建80个，县级专门协会已建502个。助残社会组织38个。

十、服务设施

截至2020年底，已竣工的各级残疾人综合服务设施89个，总建设规模250995.5平方米，总投资61912.8万元；已竣工的各级残疾人康复设施24个，总建设规模151344.3平方米，总投资52531.4万元；已竣工的各级残疾人托养服务设施16个，总建设规模49467.0平方米，总投资13415.0万元。

十一、信息化建设

截至2020年底，16个地市残联均已开通网站；省残联已建成省市残联视频会议系统。

2020年福建省残疾人事业发展统计公报

2020年，福建省残联坚持以习近平新时代中国特色社会主义思想为指导，深入学习贯彻习近平总书记关于残疾人事业的重要论述和指示批示精神，全面贯彻党的十九大和十九届二中、三中、四中、五中全会精神，贯彻落实党中央、国务院及省委、省政府的决策部署，残疾人脱贫攻坚、全面小康和疫情防控等重点工作成绩显著，残疾人工作更上新台阶。

一、康复

2020年，全省28.6万名持证残疾人及残疾儿童得到基本康复服务，其中，0-6岁残疾儿童1.4万人。得到康复服务的持证残疾人中，有视力残疾人1.5万名、听力残疾人2.9万名、言语残疾人404名、肢体残疾人12.1万名、智力残疾人3.3万名、精神残疾人6.3万名、多重残疾人1.5万名。全年共为5.7万名残疾人提供各类辅助器具。

截至2020年底，共有残疾人康复机构350个，其中，残联系统主管康复机构42个。康复机构从业人员达10123人，其中，管理人员1145人，业务人员7717人，其他人员1261人。

二、教育

实施残疾人事业专项彩票公益金助学项目，为517名家庭经济困难残疾儿童享受普惠性学前教育提供资助，带动各地对262名残疾儿童给予学前教育资助。

2020年，共有特殊教育普通高中（部、班）4个，在校生187人，其中：聋生76人，盲生34人，其他77人。残疾人中等职业学校（班）8个，在校生503人，毕业生109人。有212名残疾人被普通高等院校录取，2191名残疾青壮年文盲接受了扫盲教育。

三、就业

2020年，城乡持证残疾人就业人数为21.2万人，其中，按比例就业1.4万人，集中就业4445人，个体就业2.0万人，公益性岗位就业2401人，辅助性就业2405人，灵活就业（含社区、居家就业）6.9万人，从事农业种养加9.9万人。

培训盲人保健按摩人员250名、盲人医疗按摩人员135名；现有盲人保健按摩机构584个，盲人医疗按摩机构39个。

四、扶贫

圆满完成贫困残疾人脱贫攻坚任务。共有1.2万人次农村残疾人接受了实用技术培训，636名贫困残疾人获得康复扶贫贴息贷款扶持，56个残疾人扶贫基地安置599名残疾人就业，辐射带动1007户残疾人家庭增收。

共完成668户农村贫困残疾人家庭危房改造，投入资金1069.6万元。

五、社会保障

截至2020年底，残疾人居民参加城乡社会养老保险人数70.6万名，20.3万名60岁以下参保重度残疾人中，20.1万名享受了参保个人缴费资助政策，占比98.7%。14.5万名非重度残疾人享受了个人缴费资助政策。34.3万人领取养老金。

残疾人托养服务机构105个，其中：寄宿制托养服务机构46个，日间照料机构50个，综合性托养服务机构7个，为2024名残疾人提供了托养服务。1.6万残疾人接受居家服务。147名托养服务管理和服务人员接受了各级各类专业培训。

六、宣传体育

残疾人宣传文化工作持续推进。截至2020年底，全省共有省级残疾人电视手语栏目2个；地级残疾人专题广播节目3个、电视手语栏目8个。省地县三级公共图书馆共设立盲文及盲文有声读物阅览室46个，共开展残疾人文化周活动165场次。

残疾人群众体育活动日益活跃，残疾人竞技体育水平不断提高。新增设立社区残疾人健身示范点36个，为5575户重度残疾人提供康复体育进家庭服务，培养残疾人社会体育指导员280名。

七、维权

各级残联维权组织建设进一步加强，残疾人事业法律法规体系更加完善，无障碍环境建设取得新突破，残疾人维权工作全面开展。

2020年，制定或修改保障残疾人权益的省级规范性文件1个、县级8个。县级以上人大开展《中华人民共和国残疾人保障法》执法检查和专题调研1次；政协开展视察和专题调研6次。开展省级普法宣传教育活动7次，365人参加；举办省级法律培训班2个，100人参加。

残疾人参政议政工作稳步开展，各地残联协助人大代表、政协委员提出议案、建议、提案31件，办理议案、建议、提案58件。

无障碍建设法规、标准进一步完善。共出台了13个省、地、县级无障碍环境建设与管理法规、政府令和规范性文件；51个地市、县系统开展无障碍环境建设工作；开展无障碍环境建设检查69次，无障碍培训1751人次。

八、组织建设

2020年，市县乡共有残联1211个，其中：各地市已建残联9个，县（市、区）残联已建91个，乡镇（街道）残联已建1111个；社区（村）已建残协1.6万个。

省市县乡残联工作人员2744人，乡镇（街道）残联、村（社区）残协专职委员总计1.6万名。地市级配备了残疾人领导干部的残联8个，县级配备了残疾人干部的残联28个。

共建立各类残疾人专门协会454个，其中：省级专门协会已建5个，市级专门协会已建45个，县级专门协会已建404个。助残社会组织80个。

九、服务设施

截至2020年底，已竣工的各级残疾人综合服务设施84个，总建设规模27.3万平方米；已竣工的各级残疾人康复设施217个，总建设规模7.5万平方米；已竣工的各级残疾人托养服务设施47个，总建设规模7.5万平方米。

十、信息化建设

2020年，省残联门户网站共发稿2543篇，网站页面年浏览量40.3万人次，在残疾人事业新闻宣传、政务公开、信息服务等方面发挥了重要作用。与省人力资源和社会保障厅、省民政厅、省教育厅等厅局建立数据共享机制，提高部门协作水平。

2020年江西省残疾人事业发展统计公报

2020年，在省委省政府的坚强领导下和中国残联的悉心指导下，江西省残联围绕“全面建成小康社会，残疾人一个也不能少”的目标，坚决打赢脱贫攻坚战和新冠肺炎疫情防控阻击战，高质量推进残疾人事业发展。

一、康复

20万名持证残疾人及残疾儿童得到基本康复服务，其中0-6岁残疾儿童0.7万人。得到康复服务的持证残疾人中，有视力残疾人1.8万名、听力残疾人1.1万名、言语残疾人170名、肢体残疾人9万名、智力残疾人1.4万名、精神残疾人5.3万名、多重残疾人1.1万名。全年共为6.8万残疾人提供各类辅助器具。

截至2020年底，共有残疾人康复机构293个，其中残联系统康复机构43个。康复机构在岗人员达7905人，其中，管理人员1014人，业务人员5199人，其他人员1692人。

二、教育

实施残疾人事业专项彩票公益金助学项目，为1279名家庭经济困难残疾儿童提供学前教育资助，带动各地对715名残疾儿童给予学前教育资助。

2020年，共有特殊教育普通高中（部、班）1个，在校生30人，其中聋生24人，盲生6人。残疾人中等职业学校（班）7个，在校生1299人，毕业生247人，毕业生中93人获得职业资格证书。有536名残疾人被普通高等院校录取。513名残疾青壮年文盲接受了扫盲教育。

三、就业

城乡持证残疾人就业人数为37.1万人，其中按比例就业1.3万人，集中就业1.9万人，个体就业4.3万人，公益性岗位就业1万人，辅助性就业0.8万人，灵活就业（含社区、居家就业）16万人，从事农业种养加11.8万人。

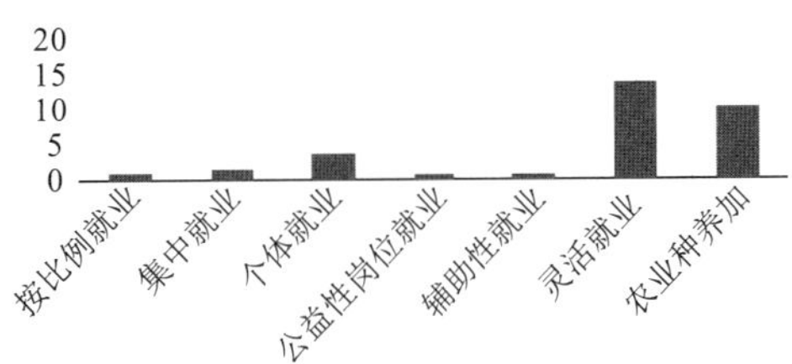

图1　城乡持证残疾人就业情况（单位：万人）

培训盲人保健按摩人员118名、盲人医疗按摩人员300名；现有保健按摩机构1000个，医疗按摩机构10个；8人获得盲人医疗按摩人员初级职务任职资格。

四、社会保障

截至2020年底，残疾居民参加城乡社会养老保险人数90.6万名，24.2万名60岁以下参保重度残疾人中，24万享受了参保个人缴费资助政策，占比99%。16.2万名非重度残疾人享受了个人缴费资助政策。30.9万人领取养老金。

残疾人托养服务机构172个，其中寄宿制托养服务机构30个，日间照料机构24个，综合性托养服务机构66个，为2418残疾人提供了托养服务。1.2万残疾人接受居家服务。382名托养服务管理和服务人员接受了各级各类专业培训。

五、扶贫

共有7948人次农村残疾人接受了实用技术培训，454个残疾人扶贫基地安置2419名残疾人就业，辐射带动2514户残疾人家庭增收。共完成1447户农村贫困残疾人家庭危房改造，投入资金2585.7万元，1716名残疾人受益。

六、宣传文化

截至2020年底，全省共有省级残疾人专题广播节目2个；地级残疾人专题广播节目6个、电视手语栏目8个。省地县三级公共图书馆共设立盲文及盲文有声读物阅览室30个，共开展残疾人文化周活动170场次；省地两级残联艺术团4个。

七、体育

新增设立社区残疾人健身示范点35个，为1117户重度残疾人提供康复体育进家庭服务，培养残疾人社会体育指导员382名。

八、维权

2020年，制定或修改保障残疾人权益的地级1个、县级13个。县级以上人大开展《中华人民共和国残疾人保障法》执法检查和专题调研12次；政协开展视察和专题调研20次。开展省级普法宣传教育活动9次，1321人参加；举办省级法律培训班3个，625人参加。

残疾人参政议政工作稳步开展，各地残联协助人大代表、政协委员提出议案、建议、提案43件，办理议案、建议、提案31件。

无障碍建设法规、标准进一步完善。共出台了16个包括省、市、县级无障碍环境建设与管理法规、政府令和规范性文件；127个市、县两级系统开展无障碍环境建设；开展无障碍环境建设检查60次，无障碍培训839人次。

九、组织建设

2020年，市县乡共有残联1776个，各地市已建残联11个，县（市、区）残联已建111个，乡镇（街道）残联已建1654个；社区（村）已建残协17795个。

省市县乡残联工作人员4008人，乡镇（街道）残联、村（社区）残协专职委员总计15028名。地市级配备了残疾人领导干部的残联10个，县级配备了残疾人干部的残联60个。

共建立各类残疾人专门协会482个，其中省级专门协会已建5个，市级专门协会已建55个，县级专门协会已建422个。助残社会组织29个。

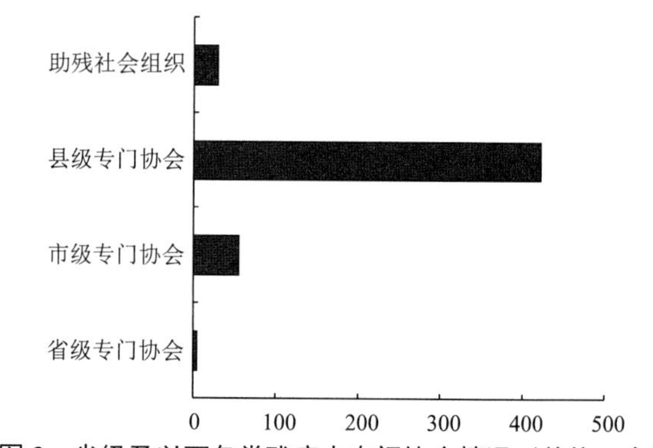

图2　省级及以下各类残疾人专门协会情况（单位：个）

十、服务设施

截至2020年底，已竣工的各级残疾人综合服务设施76个，总建设规模9.8万平方米，总投资22314.5万元；已竣工的各级残疾人康复设施30个，总建设规模21万平方米，总投资41248.4万元；已竣工的各级残疾人托养服务设施35个，总建设规模9.3万平方米，总投资20430.7万元。

十一、信息化

截至2020年底，6个地级、27个县级残联开通网站。全省残疾人6项办证事项接入“赣服通”“政务服务网”，初步实现“残疾人办证少跑路，数据多跑腿”的目标。建立了业务部门的数据共享机制，及时监测残疾人基础数据和政策服务数据，迈出了数据共享共用的第一步。

十二、民生工程

江西省残疾人民生工程项目稳步推进。全省已完成城乡残疾人职业培训0.3万个，为残疾人购买公益性岗位0.35万个，为残疾人购买农家书屋管理员岗位1.2万个，残疾人就业进一步得到保障。

2020年山东省残疾人事业统计公报

2020年，全省残联始终坚持围绕中心、服务大局，认真学习领会习近平新时代中国特色社会主义思想，全面贯彻落实省委省政府重大决策部署，牢牢把握工作重点，狠抓任务落实，推动各项工作取得了新成效。

一、康复

2020年，1219592名持证残疾人及残疾儿童得到基本康复服务，其中0-6岁残疾儿童19002人。得到康复服务的持证残疾人中，有视力残疾人89599名、听力残疾人76124名、言语残疾人9965名、肢体残疾人729604名、智力残疾人114185名、精神残疾人140397名、多重残疾人54486名。全年共为252214名残疾人提供各类辅助器具。

截至2020年底，共有残疾人康复机构870个，其中残联系统康复机构91个。康复机构在岗人员达31264人，其中，管理人员2651人，业务人员24158人，其他人员4455人。

二、教育

实施残疾人事业专项彩票公益金助学项目，为226名家庭经济困难残疾儿童享受普惠性学前教育提供资助，带动各地对117名残疾儿童给予学前教育资助。

2020年，共有特殊教育普通高中（部、班）7个，在校生889人，其中聋生382人，盲生263人，其他244人。残疾人中等职业学校（班）10个，在校生859人，毕业生228人，毕业生中49人获得职业资格证书。有1105名残疾人被普通高等院校录取，386名残疾人进入高等特殊教育学院学习。486名残疾青壮年文盲接受了扫盲教育。

三、就业

城乡持证残疾人就业人数为504746人，其中按比例就业68014人，集中就业16329人，个体就业29867人，公益性岗位就业4588人，辅助性就业2687人，灵活就业（含社区、居家就业）119018人，从事农业种养加264243人。

培训盲人保健按摩人员870名、盲人医疗按摩人员724名；现有保健按摩机构1770个，医疗按摩机构103个；62人获得盲人医疗按摩人员初级职务任职资格，6人获得中级职务任职资格。

四、社会保障

截至2020年底，残疾居民参加城乡社会养老保险人数1787349名，468722名60岁以下参保重度残疾人中，457796名享受了参保个人缴费资助政策，占比97.7%。88629名非重度残疾人享受了个人缴费资助政策。826754人领取养老金。

残疾人托养服务机构353个，其中寄宿制托养服务机构113个，日间照料机构89个，综合性托养服务机构61个，为4681名残疾人提供了托养服务。10524名残疾人接受居家服务。2164名托养服务管理和服务人员接受了各级各类专业培训。

五、扶贫

2020年共有15116人次农村残疾人接受了实用技术培训，184个残疾人扶贫基地安置3174名残疾人就业，辐射带动1842户残疾人家庭增收。

共完成5734户农村贫困残疾人家庭危房改造，投入资金55581668.49元，7945名残疾人受益。

六、文化体育

截至2020年底，全省共有省级残疾人专题广播节目1个、电视手语栏目1个；地级残疾人专题广播节目13个、电视手语栏目8个。

截至2020年底，省地县三级公共图书馆共设立盲文及盲文有声读物阅览室73个，共开展残疾人文化周活动308场次；省地两级残联艺术团18个。

新增设立社区残疾人健身示范点150个，为11162户重度残疾人提供康复体育进家庭服务，培养残疾人社会体育指导员1470名。

七、政策法规与维权

2020年，制定或修改保障残疾人权益的省级规范性文件4个、地级10个、县级9个。县级以上人大开展《中华人民共和国残疾人保障法》执法检查和专题调研15次；政协开展视察和专题调研9次。开展省级普法宣传教育活动5次，6000人参加；举办省级法律培训班2个，150人参加。

残疾人参政议政工作稳步开展，各地残联协助人大代表、政协委员提出议案、建议、提案47件，办理议案、建议、提案43件。

无障碍建设法规、标准进一步完善。共出台了49个省、地、县级无障碍环境建设与管理法规、政府令和规范性文件；94个地市、县系统开展无障碍环境建设；开展无障碍环境建设检查249次，无障碍培训2494人次。

八、组织建设

2020年，市县乡共有残联1908个，各地市已建残联16个，县（市、区）残联已建159个，乡镇（街道）残联已建1733个；社区（村）已建残协49624个。

省市县乡残联工作人员5958人，乡镇（街道）残联、村（社区）残协专职委员总计76141名。地市级配备了残疾人领导干部的残联11个，县级配备了残疾人干部的残联80个。

共建立各类残疾人专门协会719个，其中省级专门协会已建5个，市级专门协会已建80个，县级专门协会已建634个。助残社会组织87个。

九、服务设施

截至2020年底，已竣工的各级残疾人综合服务设施115个，总建设规模336368.5平方米，总投资89344.2万元；已竣工的各级残疾人康复设施110个，总建设规模701702.8平方米，总投资202975.5万元；已竣工的各级残疾人托养服务设施36个，总建设规模112655.9平方米，总投资29338.9万元。

十、信息化

截至2020年底，16个地级、45个县级残联开通网站。

2020 年河南省残疾人事业统计公报

2020 年，在省委省政府坚强领导和中国残联精心指导下，省残联坚持以习近平新时代中国特色社会主义思想为指导，统筹推进疫情防控和残疾人事业各项工作，全面完成了各项工作年度任务。现根据 2020 年度残疾人事业统计数据和实际情况，公报如下：

一、康复

2020 年，继续实施残疾人精准康复行动。全省 40.5 万名持证残疾人及残疾儿童得到基本康复服务，比上年下降 15.6%；其中 2.5 万 0-6 岁残疾儿童得到基本康复服务，比上年增长 31.6%。持证残疾人基本康复服务率达 94%，比上年提升 1.4 个百分点。在得到康复服务的持证残疾人中，有视力残疾人 3.3 万名、听力残疾人 2.9 万名、言语残疾人 1306 名、肢体残疾人 23.8 万名、智力残疾人 2.9 万名、精神残疾人 4.1 万名、多重残疾人 1.7 万名，得到康复服务的未持证残疾儿童 1.7 万名。全年共为 14.9 万残疾人提供各类辅助器具，比上年下降 18.1%，辅具适配服务率达 95%，比上年下降 0.2 个百分点。

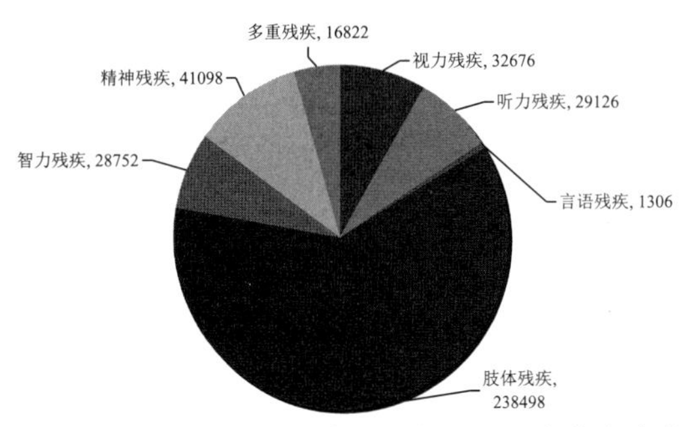

图 1　2020 年得到基本康复服务的持证残疾人分类（单位：人）

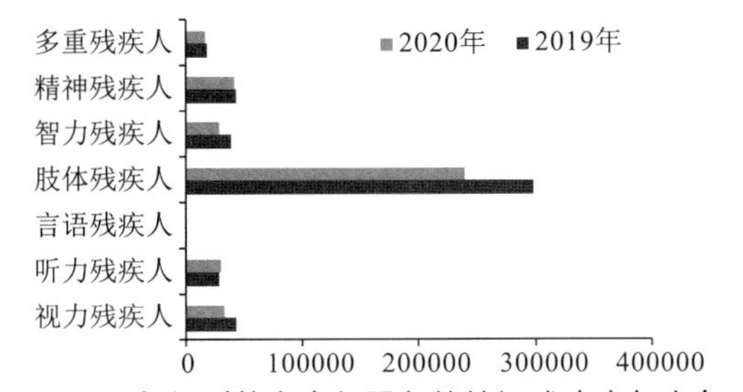

图 2　2020 年得到基本康复服务的持证残疾人与上年对比（单位：人）

截至 2020 年底，全省已建残疾人康复机构 498 个，比上年增加 35 个。其中残联系统已建康复机构 124 个，比上年增加 7 个。全省康复机构在岗人员达 1.8 万人，比上年增加 2150 人。在岗人员中有管理人员 1695 人，业务人员 1.4 万人，其他人员 1965 人。

二、教育

2020 年，我省继续实施残疾人事业专项彩票公益金助学项目，1325 名贫困家庭残疾儿童享受到普惠性学前教育资助，比上年增加 97 人。有 972 名残疾人被普通高等院校录取，比上年增加 44 人。有 340 名残疾人进入我省 3 所高等特殊教育学院学习。1312 名残疾青壮年文盲接受了扫盲教育。

三、就业

积极做好“稳就业、保就业”工作。2020 年，全省培训残疾人近 4 万人，帮扶就业 3.3 万人，分别完成年度任务的 133.27%和 181.54%。截至 2020 年底，全省已有 51.3 万城乡持证残疾人就业，比上年增长 18.8%。持证残疾人中，按比例就业 2.3 万人，比上年减少 0.2 万人；集中就业 1.2 万人、个体就业 8.7 万人，与上年持平；公益性岗位就业 4051 人，比上年增加 267 人；辅助性就业 1.7 万人，比上年增加 0.1 万人；灵活就业（含社区、居家就业）10.8 万人，比上年增加 4.7 万人，从事农业种养加 26.2 万人，比上年增加 3.6 万人。

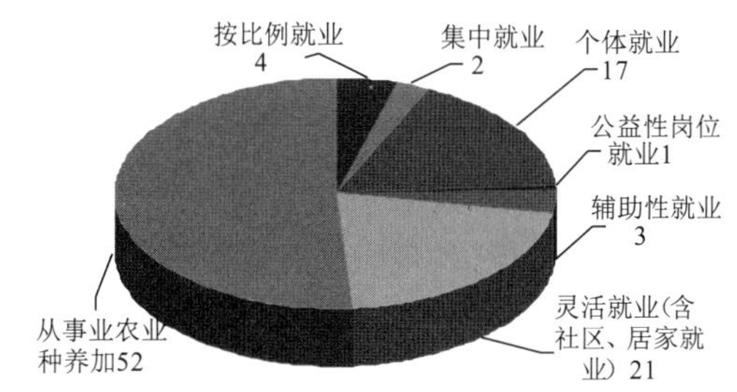

图 3　2020 年城乡持证残疾人就业状况（单位：%）

2020 年，全省培训盲人保健按摩人员 1340 名、盲人医疗按摩人员 1129 名，分别比上年增加 140 名和 379 名。获得盲人医疗按摩人员初级职务任职资格的 16 人，获得中级职务任职资格的 13 人。全省现有保健按摩机构 1200 个，医疗按摩机构 40 个。

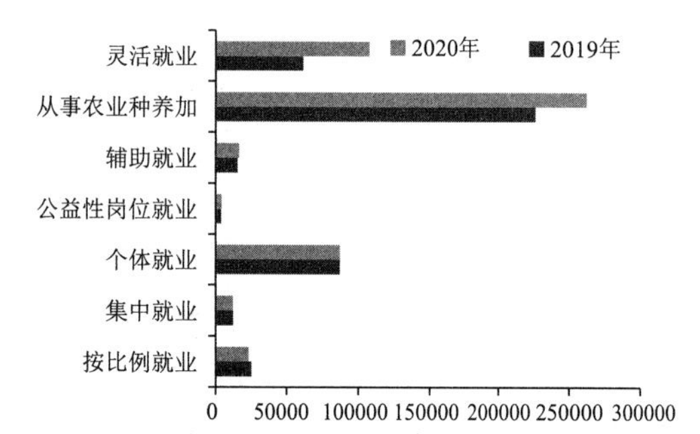

图 4　2020 年持证残疾人就业与上年对比（单位：人）

四、社会保障

持续加强残疾人社会保障。2020 年，全省 97.5 万人享受困难残疾人生活补贴，119 万人享受重度残疾人护理补贴，9.5 万残疾人纳入特困人员救助供养，分别是上年享受补助救助人数的 112.2%、103.6%和 206.5%。

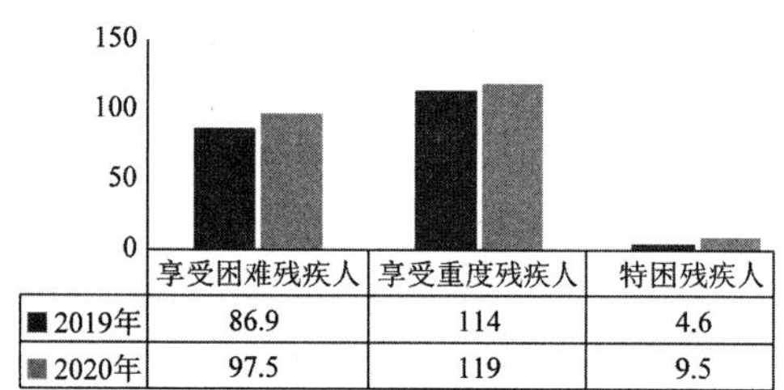

图 5　残疾人“两项补贴”同上年对比（单位：万人）

残疾人照护服务工作稳步推进。全省 17 个省辖市和济源示范区全部开展了残疾人照护服务工作，服务机构达到 1028 个。2020 年，继续实施“阳光家园计划”项目，对 461 个残疾人照护服务机构给予补贴，其中寄宿制照护服务机构 267 个，日间照料机构 22 个，综合性照护服务机构 117 个。共为 2 万名残疾人提供了照护服务，比上年增长 17.6%。2020 年全省专业培训各级各类照护服务管理和服务人员 869 名，比上年增长 75.6%。

五、扶贫

2020 年，全省农村贫困残疾人接受实用技术培训 3.3 万人次，比上年下降 19.5%；全省有残疾人扶贫基地 68 个，安置 4708 名残疾人就业，辐射带动 4464 户贫困残疾人家庭增收，分别比上年增加 123 名和 187 户。

六、宣传文化

协调省内主要媒体广泛宣传残疾人事业。2020 年，在和省广播电视台联办电视栏目《豫爱同行》中增设《残疾人无障碍改造》版块；对广播电台节目《残疾人之窗》进行全方位改版升级并更名为《共享阳光》，每期节目还以图文视频形式通过大象新闻客户端向社会推送，积极倡导全社会共同关爱残疾人。截至 2020 年底，全省共有省级残疾人专题广播节目 1 个、电视手语栏目 1 个；地级残疾人专题广播节目 11 个、电视手语栏目 6 个。全省各级组织新闻发布会 4 次。

不断丰富残疾人精神文化生活，广泛开展“残疾人文化周”、文化进家庭“五个一”等活动。2020 年，全省各级残联共开展残疾人文化周活动 231 场次，比上年增加 40 场次；残疾人参加活动 1.4 万人次；举办残疾人艺术类的比赛演出及展览 14 次；全省已有市级残疾人艺术团 6 个。截至 2020 年底，省地县三级公共图书馆已设立盲文及盲文有声读物阅览室 75 个。

七、体育

大力推进我省残疾人群众体育快速发展。2020 年，全省新增设立社区残疾人健身示范点 209 个；各级组织残疾人体育健身活动 139 次，残疾人参加活动 6746 人次；全省培养残疾人社会体育指导员 1355 名。

八、维权

2020 年，全省制定或修改关于残疾人的专门法规、规章 1 个；制定或修改保障残疾人权益的规范性文件 6 个。县级以上人大开展《中华人民共和国残疾人保障法》执法检查和专题调研 6 次；政协开展视察和专题调研 3 次。开展省级普法宣传教育活动 2 次，共 160 人参加。各地残联协助人大代表、政协委员提出议案、建议、提案 18 件，办理议案、建议、提案 29 件，分别比上年增加 10 件和 14 件。

无障碍建设法规、标准逐步完善。全省各级已出台无障碍环境建设与管理法规、政府令和规范性文件 98 个，比上年增加 6 个；62 个地市、县系统开展无障碍环境建设；全年各级残联开展无障碍环境建设检查 59 次；无障碍培训 575 人次。永城市等 5 个县市被命名全国无障碍环境示范市县；永城市演集镇等 5 个村镇被命名全国无障碍环境达标市县村镇。全年完成建档立卡重度残疾人家庭无障碍改造 6.7 万户，完成率达 416%。

燃油补贴工作有序开展，全年共为 1.9 万名符合条件的残疾人发放机动轮椅车燃油补贴。

九、组织建设

2020 年，全省围绕“强三性、去四化”，残联改革迈出新步伐，稳妥有序推进村（社区）残协建设。全省市县乡共有残联 2598 个，已建省辖市（含济源示范区）残联 18 个，县、市、区（含各类开发区等）残联已建 173 个，乡镇（街道）残联已建 2407 个；社区（村）已建残协 4.6 万个。

2020 年，全省残联系统工作人员 8030 人，乡镇（街道）残联、村（社区）残协专职委员 4.8 万人。6 个地市级残联配备残疾人领导干部，92 个县级残联配备了残疾人干部。

截至 2020 年底，全省已建立各类残疾人专门协会 886 个，其中省级专门协会已建 5 个，市级专门协会已建 90 个，县级专门协会已建 791 个。全省有助残社会组织 42 个。

十、服务设施

继续加强残疾人服务设施建设。2020 年，争取中央预算内投资项目 12 个，总投资 24999 万元，总建筑面积 8.1 万平方米，基层服务能力进一步提升。

截至 2020 年底，全省已竣工的各级残疾人综合服务设施 106 个，总建设规模 26.9 万平方米，比上年增加 2.5 万平方米；总投资 67776.2 万元，比上年增加 28354.4 万元。已竣工的各级残疾人康复设施 29 个，总建设规模 19.8 万平方米，比上年减少 0.1 万平方米；总投资 44499.5 万元，比上年增加了 86 万元。已竣工的各级残疾人托养服务设施 37 个，总建设规模 12 万平方米，比上年增加 1.6 万平方米；总投资 22602 万元，比上年增加了 1872 万元。

十一、信息化

信息化工作进一步拓展。2020 年，完善与中国残联数据共享交换机制，实现全国统建系统业务数据每日同步更新交换；开展与相关厅局数据共享交换比对工作，将业务数据纳入到全省残疾人大数据智慧平台中；“豫事办”河南省助残服务上线，在全国范围率先实现残疾人服务掌上办理。

门户网站建设进一步加强。2020 年，省残联网站信息无障碍访问工具全面升级，对网站业务版块内容进行补充及完善，在全国残联系统省级网站测评中排名第七。截至 2020 年底，全省残联已开通地市级网站 18 个、县级网站 38 个。

河南残疾人微信公众号影响力逐步提升。全年发布文章 788 篇，分享转发 14363 次，文章点赞量 17882 次，分别比上年增长 3.9%、43.5%和 112.6%。

2020 年湖北省残疾人事业发展统计公报

2020 年，在省委、省政府坚强领导和中国残联正确指导下，全省残联系统深入学习贯彻习近平新时代中国特色社会主义思想，砥砺奋进、勇于担当，以对残疾人群众和残疾人事业高度负责的精神，讲政治顾大局，扎实做好“六稳”工作，全面落实“六保”任务，在残疾人疫情防控、疫后重振、民生服务中淬炼初心、锤炼作风，残疾人事业各项工作取得了优异成绩。

一、康复

持续组织实施湖北省残疾儿童康复救助制度，指导全省残疾儿童康复救助定点机构开展形式多样的线上线下康复服务，44.9 万名持证残疾人及残疾儿童得到基本康复服务，其中 0-6 岁残疾儿童 1.2 万人。得到康复服务的持证残疾人中，有视力残疾人 5 万、听力残疾人 3 万、言语残疾人 0.3 万、肢体残疾人 19.9 万、智力残疾人 3.6 万、精神残疾人 10.1 万、多重残疾人 2.2 万。全年共为 9.9 万残疾人提供各类辅助器具，总体完成国家辅助器具华中区域中心和省残联康复医院建设任务，实现合作签约。国家残疾预防试点工作圆满成功。

截至 2020 年底，全省共有各类残疾人康复机构 254 个，其中残联系统康复机构 69 个。康复机构在岗人员达 8403 人，其中，管理人员有 1155 人，业务人员有 5820 人，其他人员 1428 人。

二、教育

联合省教育厅、团省委开展残疾大学生辅助器具适配助学行动。实施中央专项彩票公益金助学项目和交通银行助学项目。充分发挥高校教育资源优势，推动与华中师范大学融合教育战略合作。落实《湖北省第二期特殊教育提升计划（2018-2020）》，进一步提高适龄残疾儿童义务教育普及水平。实施残疾人事业专项彩票公益金助学项目，为 759 名家庭经济困难残疾儿童享受普惠性学前教育提供资助，带动各地对 29 名残疾儿童给予学前教育资助。2020 年，全省共有特殊教育普通高中（部、班）6 个，在校生 692 人，其中聋生 483 人，盲生 84 人，其他 125 人。残疾人中等职业学校（班）4 个，在校生 602 人，毕业生 193 人，毕业生中 117 人获得职业资格证书。有 469 名残疾人被普通高等院校录取。为 1745 名残疾青壮年文盲提供了扫盲教育。

三、就业

对受疫情灾情影响的盲人按摩机构、残疾儿童康复机构、残疾人托养机构和灵活就业残疾人、农村种养殖残疾人基地给予扶持。持续实施“十百千万”残疾人创业就业扶持计划，扶持 32 家品牌基地和就业创业基地、850 名农家小店主和集镇小老板、自主就业创业个人，培育 1000 名残疾人技术能手。

2020 年，全省城乡持证残疾人就业人数为 40.9 万人，其中按比例就业 3.2 万人，集中就业 1.9 万人，个体就业 2.4 万人，公益性岗位就业 0.4 万人，辅助性就业 0.6 万人，灵活就业（含社区、居家就业）13 万人，从事农业种养加 19.4 万人。全年共培训盲人保健按摩人员 388 人、盲人医疗按摩人员 274 人；各地共有保健按摩机构 1213 个，医疗按摩机构 45 个；42 人获得盲人医疗按摩人员初级职务任职资格，10 人获得中级职务任职资格。

四、社会保障

截至 2020 年底，全省有 124.4 万残疾居民参加城乡社会养老保险。60 岁以下有 36.9 万重度残疾人参保，其中 35.6 万人享受了参保个人缴费资助政策，占比 96.4%；8.1 万名非重度残疾人享受了个人缴费资助政策。49.7 万残疾人领取养老金。

全省残疾人托养服务机构达到 218 个，其中寄宿制托养服务机构 40 个，日间照料机构 56 个，综合性托养服务机构 42 个，为 3549 名残疾人提供了托养服务，为 6791 名残疾人提供居家服务。对 1363 名托养服务管理和服务人员进行了各级各类专业培训。

五、扶贫

圆满完成贫困残疾人脱贫攻坚任务。协调省扶贫办出台《关于深入推进残疾人脱贫攻坚的意见》，整合多方资源推动解决残疾人深度贫困难题。协调推进恩施州东西部残疾人扶贫协作。全省共有 2.3 万人次农村残疾人接受了实用技术培训，464 名贫困残疾人获得康复扶贫贴息贷款扶持，91 个残疾人扶贫基地安置 1437 名残疾人就业，辐射带动 2556 户残疾人家庭增收。共完成 1449 户农村贫困残疾人家庭危房改造，投入资金 1192.2 万元，1637 名残疾人受益。

六、宣传文化

以脱贫攻坚和疫情防控典型宣传为主线，精心组织"决胜全面小康、决战脱贫攻坚"重大主题宣传和"防控疫情湖北省残联系统在行动"专题综述。持续开展残疾人文化周、残疾人读书活动。组织实施"全国特奥日""残疾人健身周"等残疾人群众体育活动。

截至 2020 年底，全省目前现有省级残疾人专题广播节目 1 个，地市级残疾人专题广播节目 9 个、电视手语栏目 10 个。省、市、县三级公共图书馆共设立盲文及盲文有声读物阅览室 34 个，开展残疾人文化周活动 200 场次。省、市两级共有残疾人艺术团 4 个。

七、维权

2020 年，制定或修改保障残疾人权益的地市级规范性文件 2 个、县级 3 个。县级以上人大开展《中华人民共和国残疾人保障法》执法检查和专题调研 7 次；政协开展视察和专题调研 8 次。开展省级普法宣传教育活动 13 次，共有 2 万人参加；举办省级法律培训班 1 个，120 人参加。

残疾人参政议政工作稳步开展，各地残联协助人大代表、政协委员提出议案、建议、提案 39 件，办理议案、建议、提案 49 件。

无障碍建设法规、标准进一步完善，共出台了 13 个省、地、县级无障碍环境建设与管理法规、政府令和规范性文件；84 个地市、县系统开展无障碍环境建设；开展无障碍环境建设检查 61 次，无障碍培训 294 人次。

八、组织建设

2020 年，全省共有市、县、乡残联 1298 个，各地市已建残联 13 个，县（市、区）残联已建 108 个，乡镇（街道）残联已建 1177 个；社区（村）已建残协 2.2 万个。省市县乡残联共有工作人员 3299 人，乡镇（街道）残联、村（社区）残协专职委员总计 12422 名。地市级配备了残疾人领导干部的残联 5 个，县级配备了残疾人干部的残联 31 个。

共建立各类残疾人专门协会 519 个，其中省级专门协会已建 5 个，市级专门协会已建 65 个，县级专门协会已建 449 个。助残社会组织 655 个。

九、服务设施

截至 2020 年底，全省已竣工的各级残疾人综合服务设施有 89 个，总建设规模 203214.3 平方米，总投资 49747.4 万元；已竣工的各级残疾人康复设施有 21 个，总建设规模 109780.8 平方米，总投资 32992.0 万元；已竣工的各级残疾人托养服务设施有 30 个，总建设规模 67953.6 平方米，总投资 13014.2 万元。

十、信息化

加强与省政务服务平台、"一网通办""鄂汇办"等平台的对接，上线了省、市、县、乡、村 5 级 24 项公共服务事项，便民服务目录 5 项。联合省民政厅、省卫健委、省公安厅落实常态化疫情防控下的残疾人证核发管理和信息比对工作。

截至 2020 年底，全省 12 个地市级、30 个县级残联开通网站。

2020 年湖南省残疾人事业发展统计公报

2020 年，湖南省残联坚持以习近平新时代中国特色社会主义思想为指导，全面贯彻党的十九大和十九届二中、三中、四中、五中全会精神，落实中国残联和省残联七代会部署，不忘初心，牢记使命，全力决胜残疾人全面小康，决战残疾人脱贫攻坚，残疾人权益保障制度不断健全，残疾人基本公共服务体系进一步完善，全省残疾人事业在高质量发展的道路上迈出坚实步伐。

一、康复

坚持需求导向，提升康复服务能力。2020 年，省重点民生实事“10000 名残疾儿童康复救助”项目超额完成，通过省重点民生实事项目推动全省残疾儿童康复救助制度进一步建立实施，全省 90%的县市区出台残疾儿童救助制度。扎实推进残疾人精准康复服务行动，实施“启聪扶贫”“成人助听器”“低视力服务”“肢体残疾人矫治”等一批重点康复项目。2020 年，全省共有 350110 名持证残疾人及残疾儿童得到基本康复服务，其中 0-6 岁残疾儿童 13888 人。得到康复服务的持证残疾人中，有视力残疾人 42184 名、听力残疾人 20650 名、言语残疾人 940 名、肢体残疾人 168388 名、智力残疾人 19234 名、精神残疾人 72821 名、多重残疾人 16429 名。得到康复服务的 0-17 岁未持证残疾儿童 9464 名。全年共为 168174 残疾人提供各类辅助器具。

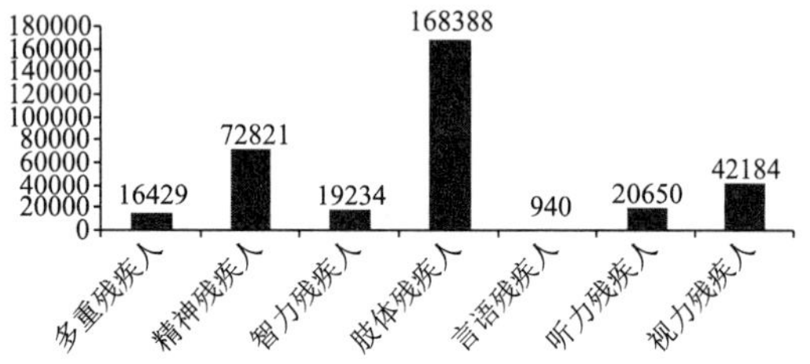

图 1　得到康复服务的持证残疾人（数量：人）

加强残疾人康复机构规范化建设，持续深化社区康复工作。制定《湖南省残疾儿童康复机构星级评定办法》，开展星级评定工作。为 118 个康复机构购买责任险、10513 名 0-14 岁残疾儿童购买意外伤害险，有效地降低残疾儿童康复机构运营风险，维护残疾儿童的康复权益。新建 50 个多功能残疾人社区康复综合服务站，配发康复器材和辅助器具。加强康复与辅具高技能人才队伍建设。康复技师辅具咨询师和残疾人健康照护师纳入全省新职业技能工种。举办全省残疾人康复与辅助器具服务技能大赛、第二届长沙康复辅助器具暨康养产业博览会。截至 2020 年底，全省共有残疾人康复机构 444 个，其中残联系统康复机构 109 个。康复机构在岗人员达 14109 人，其中，管理人员 1563 人，业务人员 10019 人，其他人员 2527 人。

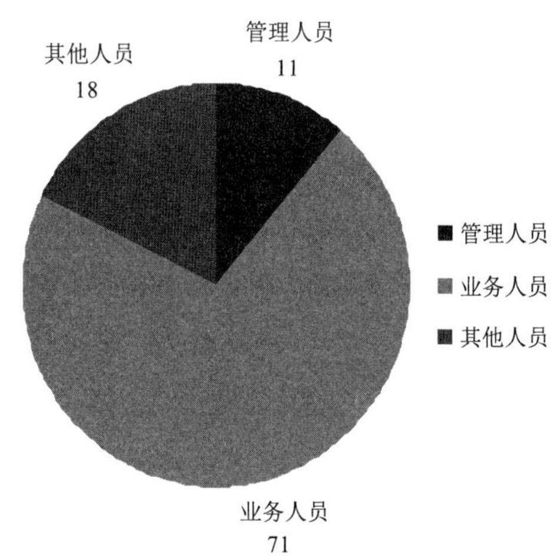

图 2　残疾人康复机构在岗人员情况（单位：%）

二、教育

2020 年，残疾人受教育权利进一步得到保障。将适龄残疾儿童少年接受义务教育情况纳入全省残疾人基础数据共享交换平台，协同教育部门共同稳定解决适龄残疾儿童少年接受义务教育问题，全省残疾儿童少年入率学达到 95.79%。实施残疾人事业专项彩票公益金助学项目，为 1320 名家庭经济困难残疾儿童享受普惠性学前教育提供资助。进一步加大通用盲文与手语推广，举办湖南省特教教师国家通用盲文推广过关挑战赛。通过政府购买服务的方式，21 家政府机关、企业、公共场所安装了通用手语服务系统。

2020 年，共有特殊教育普通高中（部、班）5 个，在校生 801 人，其中聋生 332 人，盲生 0 人，其他 469 人。残疾人中等职业学校（班）1 个，在校生 442 人，毕业生 191 人。高等特殊教育机构 1 所，78 名残疾人进入高等特殊教育学院学习。有 671 名残疾人被普通高等院校录取。

组织开展残疾人扫盲教育，举办首期残疾青壮年扫盲教员培训班。编写出版《湖南省残疾青壮年扫盲教育》（湖南教育出版社）教材，开发扫盲教学视频 181 个，建立扫盲教学网站。2020 年，全省 3161 名残疾青壮年文盲接受了扫盲教育。

三、就业

多措并举促进残疾人稳岗就业。印发实施《“点亮万家灯火”托底帮扶残疾人就业行动实施方案》，用三年时间，兜底帮扶全省劳动年龄段有就业意愿的残疾人就业。5000 余名残疾人已通过专项行动实现公益性岗位就业。开展残疾人就业援助活动，走访摸底 2459 户残疾人家庭的就业需求，举办 42 场残疾人专场招聘会，扶持 67 家盲人按摩机构。省残疾人创业孵化基地为 14 家残疾人企业提供创业孵化服务。成功举办第三届全省残疾人岗位能手职业技能竞赛。

2020 年，全省城乡持证残疾人就业人数为 404639 人，其中按比例就业 23836 人，集中就业 13176 人，个体就业 30800 人，公益性岗位就业 2385 人，辅助性就业 5898 人，灵活就业（含社区、居家就业 130395 人，从事农业种养加 198149 人。

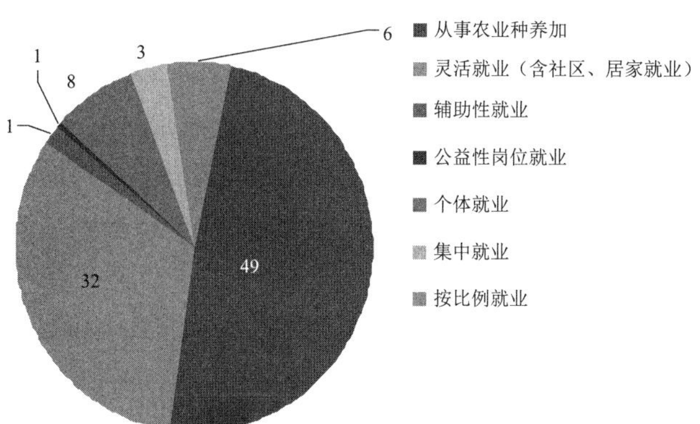

图 3　城乡持证残疾人就业情况（单位：%）

培训盲人保健按摩人员 568 名、盲人医疗按摩人员 338 名；现有保健按摩机构 732 个，医疗按摩机构 20 个；4 人获得中级职务任职资格。

四、社会保障

截至 2020 年底，全省残疾居民参加城乡社会养老保险人数 1570000 名。60 岁以下参保残疾居民有 914784 名，其中重度残疾人 474812 名，有 472047 名重度残疾人享受了参保个人缴费资助政策，占比 99.4%；非重度残疾人 439972 名，有 250298 名非重度残疾人享受了参保个人缴费资助政策，占比 56.9%。655216 人领取养老金。

残疾人托养服务工作稳步推进，残疾人托养服务机构达到 258 个，其中寄宿制托养服务机构 39 个，日间照料机构 68 个，综合性托养服务机构 57 个，为 23072 名残疾人提供了托养服务，其中 6193 名残疾人享受集中托养，16879 名残疾人接受居家托养服务。1006 名托养服务管理和服务人员接受了各级各类专业培训。

五、扶贫开发

我省圆满完成贫困残疾人脱贫攻坚任务。全省 56.2 万建档立卡残疾人全部脱贫，每名残疾人在解决“两不愁三保障”基础上，区分不同情况，额外享受一项以上的残疾人特惠政策。

2020 年，全省共有 19421 人次农村残疾人接受了实用技术培训，1410 名贫困残疾人获得康复扶贫贴息贷款扶持，429 个残疾人扶贫基地安置 6537 名残疾人就业，辐射带动 8623 户残疾人家庭增收。全省共完成 5992 户农村贫困残疾人家庭危房改造，投入资金 9235.1 万元，6478 名残疾人受益。

六、宣传文化

强化政治责任，围绕残疾人脱贫攻坚、第三十次全国助残日等重点工作、重要节点进行宣传报道，新湖南残联频道累计报道达到 1200 件次，湖南卫视、湖南日报、红网及地方各类媒体累计报道超过 500 件次。

开展为残疾人提供基本、均等公共文化服务工作，截至 2020 年底，全省共有地市级残疾人专题广播节目 7 个、电视手语栏目 3 个。扶持市县级公共图书馆盲人阅览室建设，实施文化进家庭“五个一”项目，截至 2020 年底，省地县三级公共图书馆共设立盲文及盲文有声读物阅览室 26 个，共开展残疾人文化周活动161场次;地市级残联艺术团28个。2020年，文化进家庭“五个一”项目惠及1560户农村残疾人家庭。

七、体育

积极配合中国残联，挑选、推荐10名优秀运动员入选国家队，备战北京冬残奥会、东京残奥会；选拔、培养100余名优秀运动员进入省队，以疫情“零报告”“零感染”的防控实效，备战第十一届全国残运会。不断推进残疾人群众体育，新增设立社区残疾人体育健身示范点66个，举办残疾人一级社会体育指导员培训班，培养残疾人体育社会指导员267名，新增设立1个省级残疾人体育训练基地。实施康复体育关爱家庭计划，为2498户重度残疾人提供康复体育进家庭服务。

八、维权

2020年，制定或修改保障残疾人权益的省级规范性文件1个、地级1个、县级5个。县级以上人大开展《中华人民共和国残疾人保障法》执法检查和专题调研28次；政协开展视察和专题调研20次。开展省级普法宣传教育活动1次，60人参加。

积极为残疾人提供法律援助。截至2020年底，建立省市县三级残疾人法律救助工作站共130个。残疾人参政议政工作稳步开展，各地残联协助人大代表、政协委员提出议案、建议、提案38件，办理议案、建议、提案28件。

大力推进无障碍环境建设。认真落实习近平总书记关于无障碍环境建设的重要指示，牵头开展全省无障碍环境建设工作调研，出台调研报告。起草全省无障碍环境建设五年行动计划，出台《湖南省无障碍环境建设管理办法》。2020年，我省共出台了19个省、地市、县级无障碍环境建设与管理法规、政府令和规范性文件；13个地市、县系统开展无障碍环境建设；开展无障碍环境建设检查79次，无障碍培训733人次；加大残疾人家庭无障碍改造力度，为16302户残疾人家庭实施了无障碍改造；为48376名残疾人发放了残疾人机动轮椅车燃油补贴。

九、组织建设

2020年，市县乡共有残联2054个，各地市、县（市、区）全部建立残联，97.9%的乡镇（街道）已建立残联，共1913个；97.7%的社区（村）已建立残协，共26947个。

省市县乡残联工作人员4814人，乡镇（街道）残联、村（社区）残协专职委员总计23952名。地市级配备了残疾人领导干部的残联6个，县级配备了残疾人干部的残联63个。2020年统计台账显示全省各级残联配备残疾人干部数共计138人。

共建立各类残疾人专门协会680个，其中省级专门协会已建5个，市级专门协会已建70个，县级专门协会已建605个。全省助残社会组织70个。

十、服务设施

残疾人服务设施建设得到全面发展。截至2020年底，已竣工的各级残疾人综合服务设施94个，总建设规模120556.4平方米，总投资23676.2万元；已竣工的各级残疾人康复设施47个，总建设规模185287.0平方米，总投资43943.5万元；已竣工的各级残疾人托养服务设施51个，总建设规模104122.2平方米，总投资22254.5万元。

十一、信息化建设

截至2020年底，14个地级、13个县级残联开通网站。全省残疾人基础数据共享交换平台运行良好，在助力残疾人脱贫攻坚中作用凸显。改造优化省残联门户网站，新版网站突出服务功能，以用户角色为主导，达到实用目的，增设网站无障碍浏览工具条实现语音播报、大字号阅览等功能。

2020年广东省残疾人事业发展统计公报

2020年，全省各级残联坚持以习近平新时代中国特色社会主义思想为指导，深入学习贯彻习近平总书记关于残疾人事业的重要论述和指示批示精神，认真落实国务院、中国残联、省委、省政府对残疾人事业的决策部署，残疾人脱贫攻坚、全面小康和疫情防控等重点工作成绩显著，残疾人工作再上一个新台阶。

一、残疾人康复

2020年，全省得到基本康复服务的儿童及持证残疾人共343930人。其中：0-6岁残疾儿童16830人；7-17岁残疾儿童20706人；18-59岁残疾人203092人；60岁以上残疾人103302人。从服务的残疾类型来看，服务视力残疾16129人，听力残疾19405人，言语残疾3116人，肢体残疾101573人，智力残疾28247人，精神残疾146788人，多重残疾21363人，0-17岁未持证残疾儿童7309人。从接受康复服务的内容来看，提供康复医疗服务142555人，提供功能训练服务26144人，提供辅助器具适配服务57054人，提供支持性服务130814人。为5704名视力残疾人配备助视器及盲杖，为10731名听力残疾人人配备助听器或人工耳蜗，为40153名肢体残疾人配备假肢、矫形器、轮椅等辅助器具。

截至2020年底，我省各级共有残疾人康复机构859个，其中158个机构提供视力残疾康复服务、158个机构提供听力言语残疾康复服务、382个机构提供肢体残疾康复服务、377个机构提供智力残疾康复服务、252个机构提供精神残疾康复服务、310个机构提供孤独症儿童康复服务、127个机构提供辅助器具服务。康复机构在岗人员30771人，其中管理人员2568人，专业技术人员21247人，其他人员6956人。

二、残疾人教育

普及适龄残疾儿童少年义务教育、推广国家通用手语和国家通用盲文，进一步改善残疾人教育支持保障条件。2020年底适龄残疾儿童少年义务教育入学率达到98.66%。残疾人事业专项彩票公益金助学项目的实施，为895名家庭经济困难的残疾儿童享受普惠性学前教育提供资助。各地也多渠道争取资金支持，对634名残疾儿童给予学前教育资助。

截至2020年底，共有特殊教育普通高中（部、班）7个，在校生390人。残疾人中等职业学校（班）9个，在校生1633人、毕业生394人、毕业生中24人获得职业资格证书。有687名残疾人被普通高等院校录取，122名残疾人进入高等特殊教育学院学习。2056名残疾青壮年文盲接受了扫盲教育。

三、残疾人就业

截至2020年底，我省城乡持证残疾人就业年龄段就业人数为302334人，其中按比例就业64699人、集中就业6351人、个体就业12421人、公益性岗位就业5368人、辅助性就业7825人、灵活就业（含社区、居家就业）72323人、从事农业种养加133347人。

四、残疾人社会保障

截至2020年底，城乡残疾居民参加社会养老保险人数达994756名；60岁以下参保重度残疾人448475名，其中得到政府参保扶助436893名，享受代缴比例达到97.4%；128436名非重度残疾人也享受了全额或部分代缴优惠缴费政策。领取养老金的残疾人达346631人。

残疾人托养服务工作稳步推进，残疾人托养服务机构达到1774个，其中寄宿制托养服务机构30个、日间照料机构1695个、综合性托养服务机构49个，为34974名残疾人提供了托养服务，1247名残疾人接受居家服务。全年共2564名托养管理和服务人员接受了各级各类专业培训。

五、残疾人扶贫

2020年度，农村实用技术培训残疾人11890人次；全省 55 个残疾人扶贫基地安置 1470 名残疾人就业，扶持带动 966 户残疾人家庭增收。2020 年度共完成 2087 户农村贫困残疾人危房改造，投入危房改造资金 1695 万元,2132 名残疾人受益。

六、残疾人宣传文化

截至 2020 年底，共有省级残疾人专题广播节目 1 个、电视手语栏目 1 个；地市级残疾人专题广播节目共 14 个、电视手语栏目 13 个。省地县三级公共图书馆共设立盲文及盲文有声读物阅览室 63 个。全年共开展残疾人文化周活动 684 场次，参加活动人数达 95531 人次；省地两级残联共有残疾人艺术团 13 个，举办残疾人文化艺术类的比赛及展览 55 次。

七、残疾人法制建设与维权

2020 年，制定或修改保障残疾人权益的地市级规范性文件 9 个、县级规范性文件 6 个；县级以上人大开展《中华人民共和国残疾人保障法》执法检查和专题调研 23 次；政协开展视察和专题调研 13 次;开展省级普法宣传教育活动 1 次，参加人数 9586 人；举办省级法律培训班 2 个，240 人参加。

残疾人参政议政工作稳步开展，各地残联协助人大代表、政协委员提出议案、建议、提案 46 件，办理议案、建议、提案 124 件。

无障碍建设法规、标准进一步完善。共出台了 34 个省、地市、县级无障碍环境建设与管理法规、政府令和规范性文件；145 个地市、县系统开展无障碍环境建设；开展无障碍环境建设检查 511 次，无障碍培训 862 人次。

八、残疾人组织建设

2020 年，地市县乡共成立残联 1798 个，其中各地市已建残联 21 个、县（市、区）残联已建 132 个、乡镇（街道）残联已建 1645 个；已建社区（村）残协 23272 个。

省市县乡残联工作人员共 7490 人，乡镇（街道）、村（社区）选聘残疾人专职委员总计 23507 名。16 个地市级残联配备了残疾人领导干部，38 个县级残联配备了残疾人干部。

全省共建立各类残疾人专门协会 695 个，其中省级专门协会已建 5 个、市级专门协会已建 105 个、县级专门协会已建 585 个。助残社会组织共有 133 个。

九、残疾人服务设施

截至 2020 年底，已竣工的各级残疾人综合服务设施 107 个，总建设规模 66.3 万平方米，总投资 22.9 亿元；已竣工的各级残疾人康复设施 53 个，总建设规模 22.8 万平方米，总投资 7.5 亿元；已竣工的各级残疾人托养服务设施 16 个，总建设规模 7.1 万平方米，总投资 1.5 亿元。

2020 年度广西壮族自治区残疾人事业统计公报

2020 年，在中国残联和自治区党委、政府的正确领导下，全区各级残联深入贯彻自治区党委、政府关于残疾人事业的新部署新要求，加快推进残疾人小康进程，积极推动落实“十三五”规划年度目标任务，残疾人事业发展取得良好的成效，广大残疾人得到更多福祉。现根据我区 2020 年度残疾人事业统计年报数据和实际情况进行分析，并公报如下：

一、康复

截至 2020 年底，全区共有残疾人康复机构 416 个，其中残联系统康复机构 83 个。全区康复机构在岗人员 10349 人，其中，管理人员 1083 人，专业技术人员 6815 人，其他人员 2451 人。

2020 年，209031 名残疾儿童及持证残疾人得到基本康复服务，其中包括 0-6 岁残疾儿童 9515 人。得到康复服务的持证残疾人中，有视力残疾人 18052 人、听力残疾人 12229 人、言语残疾人 303 人、肢体残疾人 102462 人、智力残疾人 17647 人、精神残疾人 39767 人、多重残疾人 12693 人、未持证残疾儿童 5878 人。全年共为 69996 名残疾人提供各类辅助器具适配服务。

二、教育

2020 年度实施残疾人事业专项彩票公益金助学项目，为 1104 名家庭经济困难的残疾儿童享受普惠性学前教育提供资助。各地也积极多渠道争取资金支持，对 8 名残疾儿童给予学前教育资助。

共有特殊教育普通高中学校（班）3 个，在校生 159 人，其中聋生 128 人，盲生 5 人，其他 26 人。残疾人中等职业学校（班）1 个，在校生 196 人，毕业生 55 人。有 358 名残疾人被普通高等院校录取。

314 名残疾青壮年文盲接受了扫盲教育。

三、就业

城乡持证残疾人就业人数为 321680 人，其中按比例就业 11373 人，集中就业 1632 人，个体就业 12535 人，公益性岗位就业 1622 人，辅助性就业 2009 人，灵活性就业（含社区、居家就业）66350 人，从事农业种养加 226159 人。

培训盲人保健按摩人员 1496 人、盲人医疗按摩人员 126 人；保健按摩机构 250 个，医疗按摩机构 4 个。

四、扶贫

2020 年，共有 12154 人次农村残疾人接受了实用技术培训，6 名贫困残疾人获得康复扶贫贴息贷款扶持。

残疾人扶贫基地 134 个，共安置 796 名残疾人就业，辐射带动 15459 户残疾人家庭。

共完成 1822 户农村贫困残疾人危房改造，各地投入危房资金 1422.5 万元，1979 名残疾人受益。

五、社会保障

截至 2020 年底，残疾居民参加城乡社会养老保险人数 986431 名，265600 名 60 岁以下参保重度残疾人中，255524 名残疾人享受了参保个人缴费资助政策，享受比例达到 96.2%；117688 名非重度残疾人享受了个人缴费资助政策；460380 人领取养老金。

残疾人托养服务机构 166 个，其中寄宿制托养服务机构 27 个，日间照料机构 12 个，综合性托养服务机构 21 个；为 4277 名残疾人提供了托养服务、27871 名残疾人接受居家服务。培训托养服务管理和服务人员 1304 人。

六、宣传文化

截至 2020 年底，共有省级残疾人专题广播节目 1 个、电视手语栏目 1 个；地市级残疾人专题广播节目 4 个、电视手语栏目 5 个。

省地县三级公共图书馆共设立盲文及盲文有声读物阅览室 29 个，共开展残疾人文化周活动 242 场次；省地两级残联共举办残疾人文化艺术类的比赛及展览 3 次，共有各类残疾人艺术团 5 个。

七、体育

各地深入开展残疾人体育工作，全区县级以上残联组织残疾人群众体育健身活动 92 次，5552 人次参加。

八、维权

2020 年，县级以上人大开展《中华人民共和国残疾人保障法》执法检查和专题调研 6 次；政协开展视察和专题调研 3 次；开展省级普法宣传教育活动 3 次，500 人参加；举办省级法律培训班 1 个，50 人参加。

残疾人参政议政工作稳步开展，各地残联协助人大代表、政协委员提出议案、建议、提案 14 件，办理议案、建议、提案 27 件。

125 个地市、县系统开展无障碍环境建设；开展无障碍环境建设检查 89 次，无障碍培训 981 人次。

各级残联共处理残疾人群众来信 214 件；接待残疾人群众来访 3097 人次，其中集体访 6 批次、38 人次；来电 382 通。

九、组织建设

2020 年，市县乡共成立残联 1376 个，其中地级市残联 15 个，县（市、区）残联 111 个，乡镇（街道）残联 1250 个；已建社区（村）残协 15705 个。省市县乡残联实有人员达 3370 人，乡镇（街道）、村（社区）选聘残疾人专职委员总计 16919 名。地市级配备了残疾人领导干部的残联 11 个，县级配备了残疾人干部的残联 39 个。

共建立省级及以下各类残疾人专门协会 628 个，其中省级专门协会 5 个，市级专门协会 70 个，县级专门协会 553 个。助残社会组织共有 13 个。

十、服务设施

残疾人服务设施建设得到全面发展。截至 2020 年底，已竣工的各级残疾人综合服务设施 98 个，总建设规模 148739.6 平方米，总投资 26718.2 万元；已竣工的各级残疾人康复设施 14 个，总建设规模 95362.8 平方米，总投资 22561.7 万元；已竣工的各级残疾人托养服务设施 25 个，总建设规模 61669.6 平方米，总投资 16098.1 万元。

十一、信息化

截至 2020 年底，11 个地级、45 个县级残联开通网站。

2020 年海南省残疾人事业发展统计公报

2020 年，在海南省委、省政府正确领导下，在中国残联有力指导下，全省残联系统坚决贯彻落实习近平总书记关于残疾人事业的重要论述和党中央、国务院关于残疾人事业的决策部署，围绕打赢贫困残疾人脱贫攻坚战、残联改革发展任务积极进取、主动担当、改革创新，推动残疾人事业和残联各项工作实现了新发展，为实现残疾人小康目标又向前推进了一步。

一、康复

2020 年，4 万名持证残疾人及残疾儿童得到基本康复服务，其中 0-6 岁残疾儿童 2127 人。得到康复服务的持证残疾人中，有视力残疾人 1983 名、听力残疾人 1649 名、言语残疾人 83 名、肢体残疾人 1.1 万名、智力残疾人 1965 名、精神残疾人 2 万名、多重残疾人 1623 名。全年共为 6826 名残疾人提供各类辅助器具。

截至 2020 年底，共有残疾人康复机构 42 个，其中残联系统康复机构 7 个。康复机构在岗人员达 1550 人，其中，管理人员 241 人，业务人员 925 人，其他人员 384 人。

二、教育

实施残疾人事业专项彩票公益金助学项目，为 347 名家庭经济困难残疾儿童享受普惠性学前教育提供资助，带动各地对 165 残疾儿童给予学前教育资助。

2020 年，残疾人中等职业学校（班）1 个，在校生 133 人，毕业生 36 人。有 66 名残疾人被普通高等院校录取。

904 名残疾青壮年文盲接受了扫盲教育。

三、就业

2020 年，城乡持证残疾人就业人数为 3.9 万人，其中按比例就业 4438 人，集中就业 435 人，个体就业 1058 人，公益性岗位就业 486 人，辅助性就业 156 人，灵活就业（含社区、居家就业）7747 人，从事农业种养加 2.4 万人。

培训盲人保健按摩人员 143 名、盲人医疗按摩人员 22 名；现有保健按摩机构 164 个，医疗按摩机构 1 个。

四、社会保障

截至 2020 年底，残疾居民参加城乡社会养老保险人数 16 万名，5.2 万名 60 岁以下参保重度残疾人中，5 万人享受了参保个人缴费资助政策，占比 97.7%。1.8 万名非重度残疾人享受了个人缴费资助政策。6.1 万人领取养老金。

残疾人托养服务机构 51 个，其中寄宿制托养服务机构 13 个，日间照料机构 2 个，综合性托养服务机构 1 个，为 733 残疾人提供了托养服务。3 万名残疾人接受居家服务。60 名托养服务管理和服务人员接受了各级各类专业培训。

五、扶贫

共有 5259 人次农村残疾人接受了实用技术培训，36 个残疾人扶贫基地安置 383 名残疾人就业，扶持带动 255 户残疾人家庭增收。

共完成 72 户农村贫困残疾人家庭危房改造，投入资金 22.6 万元，89 名残疾人受益。

六、宣传文化

截至 2020 年底，全国共有省级残疾人电视手语栏目 1 个；电视手语栏目 1 个。

截至 2020 年底，省地县三级公共图书馆共设立盲文及盲文有声读物阅览室 3 个，共开展残疾人文化周活动 12 场次；省地两级残联艺术团 3 个。

七、维权

2020 年，制定或修改省级关于残疾人的专门法规、规章 1 个；制定或修改保障残疾人权益的省级规范性文件 2 个。县级以上人大开展《中华人民共和国残疾人保障法》执法检查和专题调研 2 次；政协开展视察和专题调研 1 次。开展省级普法宣传教育活动 32 次，1.1 万人参加；举办省级法律培训班 1 个，102 人参加。

残疾人参政议政工作稳步开展，各地残联协助人大代表、政协委员提出议案、建议、提案 12 件，办理议案、建议、提案 15 件。

无障碍建设法规、标准进一步完善。共出台了 6 个省、地、县级无障碍环境建设与管理法规、政府令和规范性文件；6 个地市、县系统开展无障碍环境建设；开展无障碍环境建设检查 55 次，无障碍培训 1732 人次。

八、组织建设

2020 年，市县乡共有残联 248 个，各地市已建残联 3 个，县（市、区）残联已建 20 个，乡镇（街道）残联已建 225 个；社区（村）已建残协 2358 个。

省市县乡残联工作人员 742 人，乡镇（街道）残联、村（社区）残协专职委员总计 2906 名。地市级配备了残疾人领导干部的残联 2 个，县级配备了残疾人干部的残联 7 个。

共建立各类残疾人专门协会 114 个，其中省级专门协会已建 5 个，市级专门协会已建 15 个，县级专门协会已建 94 个。助残社会组织 3 个。

九、服务设施和信息化建设

截至 2020 年底，已竣工的各级残疾人综合服务设施 10 个，总建设规模 1.4 万平方米，总投资 4190 万元；已竣工的各级残疾人康复设施 3 个，总建设规模 1.3 万平方米，总投资 4590 万元；已竣工的各级残疾人托养服务设施 4 个，总建设规模 9885 平方米，总投资 3381.2 万元。

截至 2020 年底，1 个地级、4 个县级残联开通网站。

2020 年重庆市残疾人事业发展统计公报

2020 年，重庆市残疾人联合会坚持以习近平新时代中国特色社会主义思想为指导，认真贯彻落实党的十九大和十九届二中、三中、四中、五中全会精神，深入学习贯彻习近平总书记视察重庆重要讲话精神和关于残疾人事业的重要论述，抢抓成渝地区双城经济圈建设重大战略机遇，着力加强和改善残疾人民生，如期打赢残疾人脱贫攻坚战，全市残疾人事业发展迈上新台阶。

一、康复

扎实开展精准康复服务行动。2020 年，全市 283731 名持证残疾人及残疾儿童得到基本康复服务，其中 0-6 岁残疾儿童 4897 人。得到康复服务的持证残疾人中，有视力残疾人 37150 名、听力残疾人 16380 名、言语残疾人 1179 名、肢体残疾人 124074 名、智力残疾人 21847 名、精神残疾人 67408 名、多重残疾人 12713 名。全年共为 49090 残疾人提供各类辅助器具。参加 2020 年全国辅助器具技能竞赛，获一等奖 5 个、二等奖 5 个、三等奖 1 个。

截至 2020 年底，共有残疾人康复机构 305 个，其中残联系统康复机构 43 个。康复机构在岗人员达 9188 人，其中，管理人员 1026 人，业务人员 6435 人，其他人员 1727 人。

二、教育

切实保障残疾人受教育权利，全市适龄残疾儿童少年义务教育入学率为 97.5%。实施残疾人事业专项彩票公益金助学项目，为 301 名家庭经济困难残疾儿童享受普惠性学前教育提供资助，带动各区县对 89 名残疾儿童给予学前教育资助。

2020 年，全市共有特殊教育普通高中（部、班）2 个，在校生 196 人，其中聋生 94 人，盲生 102 人。残疾人中等职业学校（班）1 个，在校生 34 人。有 403 名残疾人被普通高等院校录取。

1730 名残疾青壮年文盲接受了扫盲教育。

三、就业

着力提升残疾人就业服务水平。开展就业援助月活动，举办专场招聘会 67 场（次）。2020 年，全市城乡持证残疾人就业人数为 240835 人，其中按比例就业 16412 人，集中就业 9497 人，个体就业 18403 人，公益性岗位就业 2414 人，辅助性就业 2597 人，灵活就业（含社区、居家就业）73156 人，从事农业种养加 118356 人。

四、社会保障

切实加大残疾人社会保障工作力度。截至 2020 年底，残疾居民参加城乡社会养老保险人数 566381 名，136002 名 60 岁以下参保重度残疾人中，129946 享受了参保个人缴费资助政策，占比 95.5%。67392 名非重度残疾人享受了个人缴费资助政策。244647 人领取养老金。

残疾人托养服务机构 147 个，其中寄宿制托养服务机构 37 个，日间照料机构 57 个，综合性托养服务机构 21 个，为 2241 残疾人提供了托养服务。21432 残疾人接受居家服务。1581 托养服务管理和服务人员接受了各级各类专业培训。

五、扶贫

坚决打赢打好残疾人脱贫攻坚战，持续推动残疾人“两不愁三保障”突出问题动态清零，全市 98750 名建档立卡贫困残疾人全部如期实现脱贫。2020 年，共有 10875 人次农村残疾人接受了实用技术培训，196 个残疾人扶贫基地安置 1434 名残疾人就业，辐射带动 1567 户残疾人家庭增收。

共完成 1525 户农村贫困残疾人家庭危房改造，投入资金 20429708 元，1615 名残疾人受益。

六、宣传文化

加大残疾人事业宣传力度，在中央、市级媒体刊发宣传报道 1095 条。截至 2020 年底，共有市级电视手语栏目 1 个；区级残疾人专题广播节目 10 个、电视手语栏目 27 个。

不断丰富残疾人精神文化生活。大力发展残疾人特殊艺术，开展“决胜小康 奋斗有我”2020 年重庆市特殊艺术巡演 60 场，成功举办第六届重庆市残疾人艺术汇演。积极培育残疾人文化产业，打造残疾人陶艺项目培育基地 10 个。组织残疾人优秀文创文旅产品参展 2020 年重庆国际文化旅游产业博览会。开展残疾人“梦想课堂”公益艺术培训课，让更多残疾儿童免费接受艺术教育。开展文化进家庭“五个一”活动，惠及 900 户重度贫困残疾人家庭。开展“书香有爱 阅读无碍”残健融合阅读活动，被市委宣传部评为全民阅读活动重点项目。

截至 2020 年底，市区县公共图书馆共设立盲文及盲文有声读物阅览室 41 个，共开展残疾人文化周活动 480 场次；市级残疾人艺术团 1 个。

七、体育

疫情期间，为了维护运动员的竞技状态，向各市级训练队提出改基地训练为居家训练，改集中训练为分散训练的策略，有效减轻了疫情对训练的影响。出台《重庆市残疾人群众体育和特奥运动项目训练基地建设管理（试行）办法》规范残疾人体育训练基地建设管理，建设残疾人群众体育和特奥运动项目训练基地 15 个。加强市级 200 个文体示范点监管指导，积极推进全国残疾人啦啦操运动发展模范市创建，做好重庆市第六届残疾人运动会筹备工作。

八、维权

加强残疾人法律服务网络体系建设，建立、完善残疾人法律援助工作站 42 个，实现残疾人法律救助工作站区县全覆盖。

2020 年，制定或修改保障残疾人权益的省级规范性文件 2 个、区县级 3 个。县级以上人大开展《中华人民共和国残疾人保障法》执法检查和专题调研 7 次；政协开展视察和专题调研 8 次。开展市级普法宣传教育活动 9 次，1397 人参加；举办市级法律培训班 4 个，833 人参加。

残疾人参政议政工作稳步开展，各地残联协助人大代表、政协委员提出议案、建议、提案 30 件，办理议案、建议、提案 39 件。

无障碍建设法规、标准进一步完善。全市共出台了 10 个市、区县级无障碍环境建设与管理法规、政府令和规范性文件；38 个区县系统开展无障碍环境建设；开展无障碍环境建设检查 58 次，无障碍培训 1746 人次。全市残联系统实施残疾人家庭无障碍改造 11228 户，其中建档立卡重度残疾人家庭 6212 户，实现建档立卡重度残疾人家庭无障碍改造全覆盖目标。

九、组织建设

强化残联系统组织建设。目前，全市共有各级残联 1072 个，其中区县残联 41 个，乡镇（街道）残联 1031 个；社区（村）已建残协 11052 个。

加强残联系统工作队伍建设。全市各级残联工作人员 1968 人，乡镇（街道）残联、村（社区）残协专职委员总计 11059 名。区县级配备了残疾人干部的残联 20 个。

加强专门协会管理，提高专门协会建设制度化、规范化水平。共建立各类残疾人专门协会 199 个，其中市级专门协会 5 个，区县级专门协会 194 个。全市助残社会组织 66 个。

十、服务设施

大力推进残疾人服务设施建设。推进市残疾人康复中心和黔江、沙坪坝等 8 个区县贫困失能残疾人区域性集中供养中心建设。万州区、石柱县等 8 个区县残疾人服务设施建设纳入社会服务兜底工程中央预算。

截至 2020 年底，已竣工的各级残疾人综合服务设施 28 个，总建设规模 88259.2 平方米，总投资 29163.1 万元；已竣工的各级残疾人康复设施 19 个，总建设规模 153650 平方米，总投资 55356.4 万元；已竣工的各级残疾人托养服务设施 12 个，总建设规模 52188.9 平方米，总投资 15168.3 万元。

十一、信息化建设

严格实施数据质量控制，如期完成 2020 年残疾人基本服务状况和需求信息数据动态更新工作。开展智能化残疾人证换发工作，目前全市已完成制卡量 60 余万张。完成重庆市残疾人综合信息系统的升级改造工作，搭建了全市残疾人信息数据资源仓库。推进残疾人数据上云，将残疾人数据纳入政府政务信息大数据资源，启动和完善残疾人工作数据资源池建设。通过市政府政务信息共享平台，加强了与政府涉残部门之间的数据共享交换机制建设，为残联与政府涉残部门之间整合政策资源、开展业务协同创造了条件。截至 2020 年底，全市有 10 个区县级残联开通网站。

2020年四川省残疾人事业发展统计公报

2020年，四川省各级残联深入贯彻习近平新时代中国特色社会主义思想和习近平总书记关于残疾人事业重要论述，准确把握新时代残疾人事业发展历史方位，聚焦主责主业，持续深化“量体裁衣”式残疾人服务，各项工作取得新进展，迈上新台阶，为广大残疾人带来更多福祉。现将我省2020年度残疾人事业统计数据公报如下：

一、康复

2020年，共为272万名残疾儿童及持证残疾人提供基本康复服务。其中0-6岁残疾儿童1.5万名，视力残疾人41.1万名，听力言语残疾人22.8万名，肢体残疾人152.2万名，智力残疾人19万名，精神残疾人25.6万名,多重残疾人10.8万名。

截至2020年底，全省共建有残疾人康复机构320个，其中残联系统管理的康复机构111个。康复机构在岗人员达1万人，其中管理人员1047人，业务人员6840人，其他人员2229人。

二、教育

2020年，通过实施残疾人事业专项彩票公益金助学项目，为107名家庭经济困难残疾儿童提供普惠性学前教育资助；通过多渠道争取资金支持，对446名残疾儿童给予学前教育资助。

截至2020年底，全省共有特殊教育普通高中班（部）4个，在校生331人；残疾人中等职业学校（班）2个，在校生250人；全年共有709名残疾考生被普通高等院校录取，65名残疾人进入特殊教育学院学习。

全年共对5069名残疾青壮年文盲开展扫盲教育。

三、就业

截至2020年底，城乡持证残疾人就业人数为80.5万人。其中按比例就业2.2万人，集中就业1.1万人，个体就业4.6万人，公益性岗位就业5909人，辅助性就业1.5万人，灵活就业37.4万人，从事农业种养加33.2万人。

2020年共培训盲人保健按摩人员650名、盲人医疗按摩人员21名。

四、扶贫

2020年，共为农村残疾人提供实用技术培训6.8万人次。

截至2020年底，全省残疾人扶贫基地达到240个，共安置4038名残疾人就业，辐射带动4424户残疾人家庭增收；

全年共完成5432户农村贫困残疾人家庭危房改造，使5587名残疾人受益。

五、社会保障

截至2020年底，城乡残疾居民参加城乡社会养老保险人数达到247.4万名；60岁以下的参保残疾人中有54.1万名重度残疾人，其中有52.2万名享受参保个人缴费资助政策，占比96.5%；有26.9万名非重度残疾人享受参保个人缴费资助政策；领取养老金的残疾人达到107.3万名。

全省残疾人托养服务机构达到206个，2020年共为4333名残疾人提供机构托养服务；有3.3万名残疾人接受居家托养服务。

六、宣传文化体育

截至2020年底，全省共有残疾人专题广播节目7个，电视手语新闻栏目9个；共设立盲文及盲文有声读物阅览室71个；共有各类残疾人艺术团16个。

2020年共开展残疾人文化周活动356场。

2020年共为5.7万户重度残疾人家庭提供康复体育进家庭服务。

七、维权

2020年，残疾人参政议政工作稳步开展，各级残联协助人大代表、政协委员提出议案、建议、提案36件，办理议案、建议、提案56件。

在无障碍建设领域，全省已有61个市、县、区系统开展无障碍建设；2020年共开展无障碍培训3419人次。

八、组织建设

截至2020年底，市县乡共有残联3065个，其中市级残联21个，县级残联188个，乡镇（街道）残联2856个；村（社区）残协已建3.4万个。

省、市、县、乡残联实有人员达到7815人，乡镇（街道）、村（社区）选聘残疾人专职委员共计4.2万人。

截至2020年底，共建立各类残疾人专门协会937个，其中省级专门协会5个，市级专门协会100个，县级专门协会832个；共建立助残社会组织169个。

九、服务设施

深入推进残疾人服务设施建设。截至2020年底，已竣工的各级残疾人综合服务设施达170个，总建设规模49.1万平方米；已竣工的各级残疾人康复设施达45个，总建设规模21.1万平方米；已竣工的各级残疾人托养服务设施达34个，总建设规模8.6万平方米。

十、个性化服务

持续深化优化“量体裁衣”式残疾人服务。根据四川省“量体裁衣”式残疾人服务平台统计结果，2020年，全省各级残联共为280.5万名残疾人提供657.2万项次的个性化服务，服务覆盖率达99.6%。

2020年贵州省残联人事业发展统计公报

2020年，贵州省各级残联坚持以习近平新时代中国特色社会主义思想为指导，深入学习贯彻习近平总书记关于残疾人事业的重要论述和指示批示精神，全面贯彻党的十九大和十九届二中、三中、四中、五中全会精神，按照党中央、国务院及贵州省委、省政府决策部署，积极开展残疾人脱贫攻坚、全面小康和疫情防控等重点工作，成绩显著，残疾人工作上了一个新台阶。

一、康复

25.2万名持证残疾人及残疾儿童得到基本康复服务，其中0-6岁残疾儿童5122人。得到康复服务的持证残疾人中，有视力残疾人2.9万名、听力残疾人1.5万名、言语残疾人3334名、肢体残疾人14.9万名、智力残疾人1.4万名、精神残疾人2.0万名、多重残疾人2.0万名。全年共为7.6万残疾人提供各类辅助器具。

截至2020年底，共有残疾人康复机构257个，其中残联系统康复机构51个。康复机构在岗人员达9958人，其中，管理人员1215人，业务人员6687人，其他人员2056人。

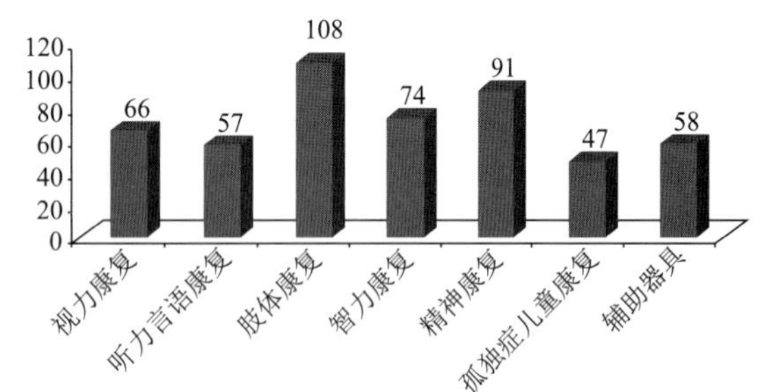

图1　2020年度开展康复业务的康复机构数（单位：个）

二、教育

实施残疾人事业专项彩票公益金助学项目，为960名家庭经济困难残疾儿童享受普惠性学前教育提供资助。

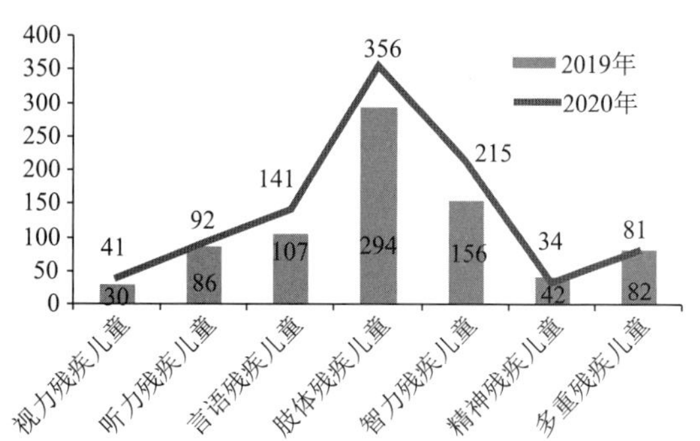

图2　2020年与2019年度接受残疾人事业专项彩票公益金助学项目资助人数对比（单位：人）

三、就业

城乡持证残疾人就业人数为33.8583万人。

四、扶贫

共有1.3万人次农村残疾人接受了实用技术培训。

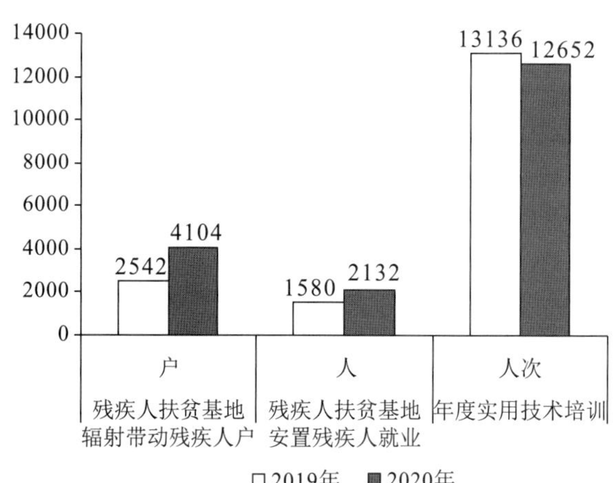

图3　2020年与2019年扶贫情况比较

五、社会保障

截至2020年底，残疾居民参加城乡社会养老保险人数89.4万名，21.1万名60岁以下参保重度残疾人中，20.4万人享受了参保个人缴费资助政策，占比96.3%。5.6万名非重度残疾人享受了个人缴费资助政策。40.3万人领取养老金。

残疾人托养服务机构122个，其中寄宿制托养服务机构16个，日间照料机构8个，综合性托养服务机构 53 个，为 1350 名残疾人提供了托养服务。6168 名残疾人接受居家服务。518 名托养服务管理和服务人员接受了各级各类专业培训。

六、宣传文化

截至 2020 年底，全省共有省级残疾人专题广播节目 1 个、电视手语栏目 1 个；地级残疾人专题广播节目 3 个、电视手语栏目 7 个。

截至 2020 年底，省地县三级公共图书馆共设立盲文及盲文有声读物阅览室 27 个，共开展残疾人文化周活动 192 场次；省地两级残联艺术团 2 个。

七、体育

新增设立社区残疾人健身示范点 9 个，为 833 户重度残疾人提供康复体育进家庭服务，培养残疾人社会体育指导员 55 名。

八、维权

2020 年，制定或修改保障残疾人权益的县级规范性文件 5 个。县级以上人大开展《中华人民共和国残疾人保障法》执法检查和专题调研 1 次；政协开展视察和专题调研 2 次。开展省级普法宣传教育活动 2 次，400 人参加。

残疾人参政议政工作稳步开展，各地残联协助人大代表、政协委员提出议案、建议、提案 11 件，办理议案、建议、提案 10 件。

无障碍建设法规、标准进一步完善。共出台了 2 个省、地、县级无障碍环境建设与管理法规、政府令和规范性文件；26 个地市、县系统开展无障碍环境建设；开展无障碍环境建设检查 9 次，无障碍培训 58 人次。

九、组织建设

2020 年，市县乡共有残联 1515 个，各地市已建残联 10 个，县（市、区）残联已建 91 个，乡镇（街道）残联已建 1414 个；社区（村）已建残协 1.5 万个。

省市县乡残联工作人员 3353 人，乡镇（街道）残联、村（社区）残协专职委员总计 1.5 万名。地市级配备了残疾人领导干部的残联 8 个，县级配备了残疾人干部的残联 62 个。

共建立各类残疾人专门协会 432 个，其中省级专门协会已建 5 个，市级专门协会已建 45 个，县级专门协会已建 382 个。助残社会组织 19 个。

十、服务设施

截至 2020 年底，已竣工的各级残疾人综合服务设施 56 个，总建设规模 6.5 万平方米，总投资 1.4 亿元；已竣工的各级残疾人康复设施 19 个，总建设规模 16.4 万平方米，总投资 4.3 亿元；已竣工的各级残疾人托养服务设施 61 个，总建设规模 22.0 万平方米，总投资 5.1 亿元。

十一、信息化

截至 2020 年底，4 个地级、9 个县级残联开通网站。

2020 年云南省残疾人事业发展统计公报

2020 年，全省各级残联始终坚持以习近平新时代中国特色社会主义思想为指导，深入学习贯彻习近平总书记关于残疾人事业的重要论述及考察云南重要讲话精神，全面贯彻党的十九大和十九届二中、三中、四中、五中全会精神和省委十届十次、十一次全会精神，按照省委、省政府决策部署，切实增强“四个意识”，坚定“四个自信”，做到“两个维护”，紧扣“全面建成小康社会，残疾人一个也不能少”目标，聚焦解决贫困残疾人“两不愁、三保障”突出问题，统筹做好疫情防控和残疾人“六稳”“六保”工作，圆满完成各项任务，团结带领全省残疾人攻坚克难，自立自强，开创了残疾人事业新局面。

一、康复

2020 年，省残联积极推进全省残疾人精准康复服务行动，全面贯彻落实残疾儿童康复救助制度，实施重点残疾人康复救助工程，加快实现残疾人“人人享有康复服务”的目标，残疾人康复水平不断提高。全省共有 25.4 万名残疾儿童和持证残疾人获得基本康复服务，其中，共为 5.3 万名残疾人提供各类辅助器具适配服务，共为 1.14 万名建档立卡贫困残疾人提供服务，服务因病致（返）贫残疾人 3,469 名。

按照年龄结构划分，2020 年全省共有 1.56 万名残疾儿童得到基本康复服务，其中包括 0-6 岁残疾儿童 4,086 名，7-17 岁残疾儿童 11,537 名；共有 23.85 万名成年残疾人得到康复服务，其中 18-59 岁残疾人 14.58 万名，60 岁以上残疾人 9.27 万名。

按照残疾类别划分，2020 年得到康复服务的持证残疾人中，视力残疾人占 10.1%，为 2.56 万名；听力残疾人占 7.9%，为 2 万名；言语残疾人占 0.7%，为 1,703 名；肢体残疾人占 45.1%，为 11.47 万名；智力残疾人占 6.1%，为 1.56 万名；精神残疾人占 23.3%，为 5.94 万名；多重残疾人占 6.2%，为 1.58 万名；非持证的残疾儿童占 0.6%，为 1,442 名。

按照服务内容划分（包括获得多项服务情况），2020 年获得康复医疗服务 4.1 万名，获得康复训练 1.3 万名，获得辅助器具服务 5.3 万名，获得支持性服务 15.7 万名。

截至 2020 年底，全省 104 个县（市、区）开展了社区康复服务，共建设康复服务设施 993 个，总共 13,990 个社区（村）中配备了 13,123 名社区康复协调员，康复协调员覆盖率 93.8%；其中 12,000 名社区协调员接受过系统培训，接受培训率 91.4%。

截至 2020 年底，全省共有残疾人康复机构 297 个，其中，59 个机构提供视力残疾康复服务，78 个机构提供听力语言残疾康复服务，119 个机构提供肢体残疾康复服务，107 个机构提供智力残疾康复服务，97 个机构提供精神残疾康复服务，116 个机构提供辅助器具适配服务。在这 297 个康复机构中，属于残联系统的有 105 个，属于卫生系统的有 98 个，属于民政系统的有 9 个，属于教育系统的有 24 个，属于民办机构的有 40 个，其他机构有 21 个。各类康复机构在岗服务人员达 10,235 名，其中，管理人员 976 名，业务人员 7,814 名，其他人员 1,445 名。各类机构服务人员中，有 1,283 名提供视力残疾康复服务，有 639 名提供听力语言残疾康复服务，有 2,615 名提供肢体残疾康复服务，有 2,086 名提供智力残疾康复服务，有 3,340 名提供精神残疾康复服务，有 272 名提供辅助器具适配服务。全年共培训康复管理人员 1,847 名，培训康复业务人员 7,805 名。

二、教育

2020 年全省共有 575 名学龄前残疾儿童接受中央残疾人事业专项彩票公益金项目资助,共有 231 名学龄前残疾儿童接受资助新入园。

截至 2020 年底，全省累计共有残疾人中等职业学校（班）5 个，均为教育部门办学，本年度招生 326 名，其中盲生 31 名，聋生 153 名，肢残生 83 名，其他 59 名；本年度总计在校生 1039 名，其中盲生 124 名，聋生 491 名，肢残生 250 名，其他 174 名；本年度毕业生 245 名，其中有盲生 35 名，聋生 130 名，肢残生 58 名，其他 22 名。

2020年，云南省共有高等特殊教育机构1所，办学层次为高职，录取残疾考生100名，其中盲生4名，聋生41名，其他55名。本年度全省共有1118名残疾人考生达到普通高等院校招生考试录取分数线，在被录取的1098名残疾考生中，本科生录取365名，其中，盲生45名，聋生28名，肢残生265名，其他27名；专科（高职）生733名，其中，盲生91名，聋生59名，肢残生475名，其他108名。

三、就业

2020年，各级残联严格落实党中央、国务院和省委、省政府以及中国残联关于新冠疫情防控工作的一系列重要指示精神和决策部署要求，配合做好残保金减半征收工作，出台疫情防控盲人按摩行业稳岗就业措施，发放稳岗补助121.4万元，会同省人社厅、省扶贫办、省总工会、省妇联在全省开展了“2020年春风行动暨就业援助月”活动，积极探索“互联网+职业培训”模式，开展“技能在线”网上培训，集中帮扶残疾人就业困难人员就业创业。

截至2020年底，全省城乡持证残疾人就业人数为42.24万名，按照就业形式划分，其中按比例就业1.62万名，集中就业6,913名，个体就业1.66万名，公益性岗位就业1,662名，辅助性就业4,120名，从事农业种养加27.49万名，灵活就业（包括社区就业、居家就业）10.2万名。

2020年，在全省736家规范化盲人按摩店开展爱国卫生“七个专项行动”，率先在全国出台疫情防控盲人按摩行业稳岗就业措施和盲人按摩机构复工复业疫情防控指南，发放稳岗补助121.4万元，稳住近万盲人群体就业。全年完成盲人保健按摩培训902人次，共培养269名盲人医疗按摩人员，共有20名盲人医疗按摩人员获得专业技术职务任职资格评审初级资格。全省保健按摩机构累计达948个，全省注册医疗按摩机构12个。

四、扶贫

2020年，各级残联主动作为，根据省委、省政府的决策部署，协调推进将残疾人脱贫攻坚纳入全省脱贫攻坚大局。2020年11月13日，云南省人民政府正式宣布，镇雄县、会泽县等9个贫困县（市）退出贫困县序列，全省纳入建档立卡的41万贫困残疾人与健全人一道实现全面脱贫。

2020年度共组织残疾人实用技术培训3.4万人次，其中扫盲教育4,693人次，实用技术培训投入经费1,985.4万元；全省投入扶贫资金666.9万元，其中省级财政投入629.4万元，社会募集资金37.5万元。

2020年全省累计建设残疾人扶贫基地386个，累计安置残疾人就业2,694名，扶持带动残疾人户1.49万户。

截至2020年底，全年完成危房改造925户，受益残疾人1,421名，总共投入资金1,394万元，其中省级投入资金1,325.8万元，各州（市）投入资金37.2万元，各县（市、区）投入资金31万元。

五、社会保障与托养

2020年省残联与省住建厅、省财政厅等部门联合下发《关于做好城乡残疾人基本住房保障工作的通知》，农村贫困残疾人家庭存量危房改造完成率达100%。

2020年，全省符合参加城乡社会养老保险条件的残疾居民为116.75万人，其中重度残疾人有43.72万名。本年度实际参保残疾居民107.53万名中，领取待遇的有41.02万名，领取待遇的残疾人中有重度残疾人15.85万名，60周岁以下还未领取待遇的残疾人有66.5万名，其中有重度残疾人24.73万名，非重度残疾人41.78万人。参保重度残疾人中有21.05万名获得全额代缴保险费用，1.86万名获得部分代缴保险费用，非重度参保残疾人中有10.31万人获得全额代缴保险费用，14.83万人获得部分代缴保险费用。

全省残疾人托养服务工作稳步推进，截至2020年底，全省共建设残疾人托养服务机构189个。其中寄宿制托养服务机构36个，托养残疾人1,681名；日间照料托养服务机构20个，托养残疾人135名；综合性托养服务机构33个，托养残疾人926名；各类托养机构中托养的残疾人中，托养智力残疾人472名，托养精神残疾人1858名，托养重度肢体残疾人361名。享受居家托养服务残疾人1.9万名。

全省共培训托养服务管理人员和服务人员1,519名，其中有259名托养机构的管理人员，有1,260名居家托养服务人员。接收培训的托养机构的管理人员中有4名接受了国家级培训，有255名接受了地市及区县级培训。

六、宣传文化体育

2020年，全省各级残联积极做好残疾人脱贫攻坚和疫情防控阻击战宣传。开设“防控新型冠状病毒肺炎基层在行动”和《众志成城齐心协力云南省残联抗击新冠肺炎疫情在行动》专栏，撰写和转发207条信息，通过工作群发布消息168条，向中残联报送消息19篇，中残联综合报道云南抗疫消息3篇。省残联与省委宣传部联发了《中共云南省委宣传部云南省残疾人联合会关于开展“决战脱贫攻坚决胜全面小康”秋冬季主题宣传活动的通知》，组织中央媒体和省级主流媒体深入基层宣传报道。人民日报、新华每日电讯、中央人民广播电视台、新华网、《三月风》《华夏时报》等媒体对我省残疾人脱贫攻坚工作进行了大力报道。省残联持续提升省残联官方网站、微信公众号质量和影响力，探索微博、抖音、快手等新媒体手段，以群众喜闻乐见的方式拓展宣传渠道，提升省残联宣传平台社会影响力，报道新闻近千条，其中35条被中国残联网站转载引用，400余条被各网站引用，浏览次数近300万次，微信公众号多次进入“十佳榜”，同时进一步推进提升云南广播电视台澜湄卫视《追梦》节目和手语新闻《我们同行》栏目的质量和影响力。持续推动州（市）级电视台开设手语栏目，在综合新闻类栏目加载同步文字，推进和鼓励公共服务机构、公共场所提供语音和文字提示、盲文等信息交流方式。

截至2020年底，省级共有残疾人专题电视手语栏目1个，广播电台残疾人专题节目1个，开通1个省级残疾人联合会官方微信；州（市）残联残疾人广播电台残疾人专题节目4个、电视手语栏目9个。

截至2020年底，全省各级公共图书馆共设立盲文及盲文有声读物图书室51个，其中省级1个，州市级15个，县区级35个。全年共开展残疾人文化周活动240场次，其中省残联举办1场次，参与390人次，州（市）残联举办25场次，参与人次4,753人次，县（市、区）残联举办214场次，参与1.47万人次。州（市）级残联共举办残疾人文化艺术类的比赛及展览5次。

2020年全省各级共组织残疾人群众进行体育健身活动396场次，参与残疾人2.36万人次。其中省级举办3场次，参与残疾人200人次；各州（市）举办81场次，参与残疾人3,769人次；县区级举办312场次，参与残疾人1.96万人次。

共有省级残疾人体育训练基地6个，聘任教练员20名。

七、维权与信访

2020年，省残联继续认真做好残疾人信访工作，采取法律顾问、律师坐班、领导包案制度，做到件件有答复、事事有着落，未发生群体性、政治性信访事件，把依法维护残疾人合法权益作为残联一项重要的政治任务常抓不懈，同时加强对残疾人的法制宣传教育，残疾人依法维权意识不断提高。

2020年全省各级残联累计接到来信1,730件，来电242通。来信来电中，残疾人涉法涉诉类17例，占比0.86%；医疗康复类559例，占比28.35%；教育类135例，占比6.85%；就业扶贫类330例，占比16.73%；社会保障类299例，占比15.16%；权益保障类239例，占比12.12%；意见建议类19例，占比0.96%；控告检举类10例，占比0.51%；非残及其他类364例，占比18.46%。

2020年全省各级残联累计接待残疾人个人来访7,189人次，没有残疾人集体来访。个人来访中涉法涉诉类65人次，占比0.9%；医疗康复类1,868人次，占比25.98%；教育类421人次，占比5.86%；就业扶贫类976人次，占比13.58%；社会保障类2,255人次，占比31.37%；权益保障类660人次，占比9.18%；意见建议类29人次，占比0.4%；控告检举类10人次，占比0.1%；非残及其他类905人次，占比12.59%。

2020全省累计共有2个州市和6个县区制定或修改了保障残疾人权益的规范性文件。县（市、区）以上人大开展执法检查或专题调研9次，政协开展视察或专题调研4次。组织普法宣传教育活动2次，参加人120人，组织法律培训班1场，参加人80人。

全省残疾人参政议政工作稳步开展，全省各级共有84名残疾人担任人大代表，其中省级1人，州（市）级10人，县级代表34人，乡镇（街道）代表39人；各级共有145名残疾人担任政协委员，其中州（市）级18人，县（市、区）级127人。各级残联协助人大代表提出议案、建议5件，协助政协委员提出议案、建议 18 件；各级残联办理人大建议 6 件，办理政协提案 11 件。

全省共有 4 个州市修改或发布了无障碍建设与管理法规、政府令，15 个县区发布了县级无障碍环境建设与管理规范性文件。本年度累计建设有无障碍领导协调组织 64 个，其中州市级 18 个，县区级 46 个。全省各级共有 4 个州市和 41 个县区系统开展无障碍环境建设。全省各级共进行无障碍环境建设检查 61 次，进行无障碍建设培训 780 人次。

八、组织建设

2020 年，各级残联扎实推进残联系统改革，按照《中国残联关于扎实做好地方残联改革工作的通知》要求，云南 16 个州（市）、129 个县（市、区）残联改革方案全部出台，率先在全国完成中国残联部署的改革工作任务，推动五个省级专门协会成立功能型党支部，全面提升专门协会党建工作水平，并着力解决专门协会和助残社会组织办公场所困难的问题，加快培育和发展助残社会组织，深入推进志愿助残服务，积极支持省残疾人福利基金会、中国狮子联会云南代表处等更好为残疾人服务，加强残协专职委员和各级专门协会负责人线上、线下培训，提升能力素质和工作水平。

云南省残联机关有编制 62 个，实有人员 65 名，其中残疾人干部有 7 名。省残联直属 7 个事业单位，共有编制 206 个，实有人员 159 名。省级共举办 2 期综合培训班，参加 180 人次。

16 个州（市）残联中的 13 个配备了残疾人领导干部，共有编制 212 个，实有工作人员 224 名，其中残疾人领导干部 13 名，一般残疾人干部 27 名。州（市）残联共有直属事业单位共 27 个，共有编制 159 个，实有人员 130 名，其中残疾人工作者 13 名；各州（市）2020 年共举办综合培训班 16 期，参加培训人次达 798 人次；共举办残疾人干部培训班 5 期，参加培训人次 339 人次；共有 99 名助残志愿者为 4,465 名残疾人提供了志愿助残服务。

全省共有 129 个县（市、区）和 3 个开发区建立了残联，其中 101 个残联机关配备了残疾人领导干部，县（市、区）残联机关共有编制 1,057 个，实有人员 1,298 名，其中残疾人干部 181 名；县（市、区）残联共有直属事业单位 112 个，共有编制 357 个，实有人员 403 名。各县（市、区）共举办 176 期干部培训班，参加培训人次 6,491 人次；共有 2,945 名助残志愿者为 7.56 万名残疾人提供了志愿助残服务。

全省共有 1,409 个乡镇（街道）建立了残联，共有编制 1,414 个，实有人员 1,527 名，其中专职残联理事长有 426 名，兼职残联理事长有 444 名，乡镇级残疾人专职委员 2,756 名。乡镇（街道）残联共举办培训班 912 期，参加培训人次 1.73 万人次；共有 5,080 名助残志愿者为 8.01 万名残疾人提供了志愿助残服务。

全省已建村（农村社区）残协 12,574 个，已建城市社区残协 1,640 个；全省共建设残疾人活动室 4,389 个，其中村（农村社区）建立 3,748 个，城市社区建立 641 个；全省各村、社区共配备残疾人专职委员 24,987 名，其中农村（农村社区）配备 22,257 名,城市社区配备 2,730 名。共有 3,271 名助残志愿者为 9.01 万名残疾人提供了志愿助残服务。

截至 2020 年底，全省共建立省级及以下各类残疾人专门协会 681 个，其中盲人协会省级 1 个、州（市）级 16 个、县（市、区）级 125 个；聋人协会省级 1 个、州（市）级 15 个、县（市、区）级 125 个；肢残人协会省级 1 个、州（市）级 16 个、县（市、区）级 127 个；智力残疾人及亲友协会省级 1 个、州（市）级 15 个、县（市、区）级 111 个；精神残疾人及亲友协会省级 1 个、州（市）级 15 个、县（市、区）级 111 个。

截至 2020 年，全省各级共有助残社会组织为 21 个，其中，社会团体 8 个，基金会 1 个，社会服务机构 9 个。

九、服务设施

截至 2020 年底，全省累计已竣工的各级残疾人综合服务设施 125 个，总建设规模 16.41 万平方米，总投资 3.19 亿元。2020 年在建项目 3 个，总建设规模 2.13 万平方米，总投资 5,813 万元。

截至 2020 年底，全省已竣工的各级残疾人托养服务设施 39 个，总建设规模 10.13 万平方米，总投资 2.77 亿元。其中本年度新竣工项目 10 个，总建设规模 2.87 万平方米，总投资 7,009 万元。2020 年筹建中的项目 2 个，总建设规模 3,948 平方米，总投资 1,429 万元，在建项目 18 个，总建设规模 5.32 万平方米，总投资 1.64 亿元。

截至2020年底，全省已竣工的各级残疾人康复服务设施12个，总建设规模7.64万平方米，总投资2.2亿元。其中本年度新竣工项目3个，总建设规模2.03万平方米，总投资5,528万元。2020年在建项目14个，总建设规模12.42万平方米，总投资3.63亿元。

十、信息化建设

截至2020年底，全省6个地州、8个县区独立建立网站，2个地州和4个县区搭载同级政府部门网站。省残联依托“智慧残联”平台建设，基于残疾人人口基础数据库和“云南省按比例安排残疾人就业年审”数据，与民政、扶贫、税务等部门建立了数据共享机制，落实残联重点业务应用建设，推动“一网通办”。

全省残疾人事业统计部分数据连续5年纳入省统计局编撰的云南省统计年鉴面向社会公开发布。

2020年西藏自治区残疾人事业发展统计公报

2020年，在西藏自治区党委、政府的坚强领导和中国残联的有力指导下，全区各级残联始终坚持以习近平新时代中国特色社会主义思想为指导，全面贯彻落实党的十九大和十九届二中、三中、四中、五中全会精神、中央第七次西藏工作座谈会精神以及习近平总书记关于残疾人事业的重要论述和指示精神，切实将党中央、国务院和自治区党委、政府关于残疾人事业的决策部署贯彻落实到实际工作中，围绕决战决胜脱贫攻坚、全面建成小康社会的工作目标，切实履行“代表、服务、管理”的职能，不断开拓进取，全区残疾人事业及各项工作取得长足发展。现将我区残疾人事业情况公报如下：

一、康复

2020年，全区共有12890名持证残疾人及残疾儿童得到基本康复服务，其中0-6岁残疾儿童324人。得到康复服务的持证残疾人中，有视力残疾人1635名、听力残疾人1778名、言语残疾人330名、肢体残疾人7279名、智力残疾人116名、精神残疾人287名、多重残疾人1460名。全年共为10741名残疾人提供各类辅助器具。

截至2020年底，全区已投入使用的残疾人康复机构共有11个。全区各级残疾人康复机构在岗人员达共75人，其中，管理人员20人，业务人员47人，其他人员8人。

二、教育、就业

2020年，全区共有37名残疾学生达到了录取分数线并被普通高等院校录取，其中本科7人，专科30人。全区122名残疾青壮年文盲接受了扫盲教育。

2020年，城乡持证残疾人就业人数为16589人，其中按比例就业573人，集中就业373人，个体就业645人，公益性岗位就业165人，辅助性就业57人，灵活就业（含社区、居家就业）8809人，从事农业种养加596人。

全年培训了盲人保健按摩人员2名、盲人医疗按摩人员6名；全区现有保健按摩机构67个。

三、扶贫、社会保障

2020年，围绕“决战决胜脱贫攻坚，全面建成小康社会，残疾人一个也不能少的目标。”为全区1194人次农村残疾人提供了实用技术培训。为改善贫困残疾人的居住条件，共计投入119880元为贫困残疾人家庭进行危房改造。

努力健全覆盖惠及全体残疾人的社会保障系统。截至2020年底，残疾居民参加城乡社会养老保险人数101691名，22774名60岁以下参保重度残疾人中，22774名享受了参保个人缴费资助政策，实现全覆盖。共计12184名非重度残疾人享受了个人缴费资助政策，有32561人领取养老金。

截至2020年底，全区共有残疾人托养服务机构2个，其中寄宿制托养服务机构1个，为11名残疾人提供了托养服务，23名残疾人接受居家服务。不断增强广大残疾群众的获得感、幸福感安全感，切实实现全面建成小康社会残疾人一个也不能少的目标。

四、宣传文化、维权

不断提升公共文化服务水平。为广大残疾人开展群众性文化活动提供活动场所，截至2020年底，省地县三级公共图书馆共设立盲文及盲文有声读物阅览室4个，共计开展残疾人文化周活动5场次；

为切实增强残疾人知法懂法意识。2020年，开展省级普法宣传教育活动7次，共计475人参加；举办省级法律培训班2个，共有120人参加。

残疾人参政议政工作稳步开展，各地残联协助人大代表、政协委员提出议案、建议、提案1件，办理议案、建议、提案2件。

五、组织建设

积极健全残联系统，配备工作人员，为打通服务残疾人最后一公里，切实为残疾人提供更好的服务。2020 年，市县乡共有残联 81 个，各地市已建残联 7 个，县（市、区）残联已建 74 个，社区（村）已建残协 1060 个。

省市县乡残联工作人员 336 人，乡镇（街道）残联、村（社区）残协专职委员总计 33 名。地市级配备了残疾人领导干部的残联 2 个，县级配备了残疾人干部的残联 8 个。

截至 2020 年底，共建立各类残疾人专门协会 8 个，其中省级专门协会已建 3 个，市级专门协会已建 5 个，

六、服务设施

截至 2020 年底，已竣工的各级残疾人综合服务设施 48 个，总建设规模 60899.9 平方米，总投资 19875 万元；已竣工的各级残疾人康复设施 14 个，总建设规模 31850.1 平方米，总投资 11721 万元；已竣工的各级残疾人托养服务设施 4 个，总建设规模 15294.1 平方米，总投资 4865.8 万元。

2020 年陕西省残疾人事业统计公报

2020 年，全省残联系统深入学习贯彻习近平新时代中国特色社会主义思想，坚决贯彻落实习近平总书记关于残疾人事业的重要论述和党中央、国务院关于残疾人事业的决策部署，紧扣推进“五个聚力”工作思路和建设“三个残联”目标，不断开拓进取、真抓实干，为实现残疾人对美好生活的向往作出了新的贡献。

一、康复

2020 年，全面落实《国务院关于建立残疾儿童康复救助制度的意见》，全省普遍建立残疾儿童康复救助工作体系和服务网络。以贫困残疾人为重点，持续组织实施残疾人精准康复服务行动，534398 名持证残疾人及残疾儿童得到基本康复服务，其中 0-6 岁残疾儿童 6747 人。得到康复服务的持证残疾人中，有视力残疾人 58902 名、听力残疾人 49042 名、言语残疾人 7107 名、肢体残疾人 275153 名、智力残疾人 34128 名、精神残疾人 71497 名、多重残疾人 32803 名。全年共为 182595 名残疾人提供各类辅助器具。

截至 2020 年底，全省共有残疾人康复机构 342 个，其中残联系统康复机构 78 个。康复机构在岗人员达 8948 人，其中，管理人员 1041 人，业务人员 6840 人，其他人员 1067 人。

二、教育

通过实施残疾人事业专项彩票公益金助学项目，为 10 名家庭经济困难残疾儿童享受普惠性学前教育提供资助，带动各地对 53 名残疾儿童给予学前教育资助。

2020 年，残疾人中等职业学校（班）5 个，在校生 1143 人，毕业生 525 人，毕业生中 469 人获得职业资格证书。有 194 名残疾人被普通高等院校录取。829 名残疾青壮年文盲接受了扫盲教育。

三、就业

截至 2020 年底，全省城乡持证残疾人就业人数 236524 人，其中按比例就业 10460 人，集中就业 4098 人，个体就业 14957 人，公益性岗位就业 4243 人，辅助性就业 4445 人，灵活就业（含社区、居家就业）67916 人，从事农业种养加 130405 人。培训盲人保健按摩人员 455 名、盲人医疗按摩人员 211 名；现有保健按摩机构 454 个，医疗按摩机构 36 个；39 人获得盲人医疗按摩人员初级职务任职资格。

四、社会保障

截至 2020 年底，全省残疾居民参加城乡社会养老保险人数 969795 名，181355 名 60 岁以下参保重度残疾人，174525 名享受了参保个人缴费资助政策，占比 96.2%。201747 名非重度残疾人享受了个人缴费资助政策。424564 人领取养老金。残疾人托养服务机构 180 个，其中寄宿制托养服务机构 61 个，日间照料机构 22 个，综合性托养服务机构 33 个，为 2722 名残疾人提供了托养服务。7749 名残疾人接受居家服务。914 名托养服务管理和服务人员接受了各级各类专业培训。

五、扶贫

2020 年，共有 20603 人次农村残疾人接受了实用技术培训，126 个残疾人扶贫基地安置 2201 名残疾人就业，辐射带动 3449 户残疾人家庭增收。共完成 165 户农村贫困残疾人家庭危房改造，投入资金 1516200 元，167 名残疾人受益。

六、宣传文化

截至 2020 年底，全省共有省级残疾人专题广播节目 1 个、电视手语栏目 1 个；地级残疾人专题广播节目 1 个、电视手语栏目 2 个。省市县三级公共图书馆共设立盲文及盲文有声读物阅览室 54 个，共开展残疾人文化周活动 124 场次；省市两级残联艺术团 6 个。

七、体育

新增设立社区残疾人健身示范点 1 个，新增竞技体育项目 13 个，大众体育 3 个。

八、维权

2020 年，制定或修改保障残疾人权益的规范性文件 6 个。县级以上人大开展《中华人民共和国残疾人保障法》执法检查和专题调研 1 次；政协开展视察和专题调研 1 次。开展省级普法宣传教育活动 3 次，2000 人参加；举办省级法律培训班 1 个，70 人参加。

残疾人参政议政工作稳步开展，各地残联协助人大代表、政协委员提出议案、建议、提案 7 件，办理议案、建议、提案 13 件。

无障碍建设法规、标准进一步完善。共出台了 28 个省、市、县级无障碍环境建设与管理法规、政府令和规范性文件；55 个地市、县系统开展无障碍环境建设；开展无障碍环境建设检查 56 次，无障碍培训 870 人次。

九、组织建设

2020 年，市县乡共有残联 1398 个，各地市已建残联 11 个，县（市、区）残联已建 117 个，乡镇（街道）残联已建 1270 个；社区（村）已建残协 20411 个。

省市县乡残联工作人员 4747 人，乡镇（街道）残联、村（社区）残协专职委员总计 22347 名。地市级配备了残疾人领导干部的残联 9 个，县级配备了残疾人干部的残联 72 个。

共建立各类残疾人专门协会 578 个，其中省级专门协会已建 5 个，市级专门协会已建 51 个，县级专门协会已建 522 个。助残社会组织 7 个。

十、服务设施

截至 2020 年底，已竣工的各级残疾人综合服务设施 80 个，总建设规模 176587.8 平方米，总投资 46966.0 万元；已竣工的各级残疾人康复设施 41 个，总建设规模 115317 平方米，总投资 30257.2 万元；已竣工的各级残疾人托养服务设施 56 个，总建设规模 141367.7 平方米，总投资 27441 万元。

十一、信息化

截至 2020 年底，9 个市级、25 个县级残联开通网站。与扶贫办、民政厅、审计厅、教育厅、医保局等部门进行数据交换，并向西安市残联提供残疾人数据接口和每日推送服务。

2020年甘肃省残疾人事业发展统计公报

2020年，全省残疾人工作以习近平新时代中国特色社会主义思想为指导，全面贯彻党的十九大和十九届二中、三中、四中、五中全会精神，认真落实习近平总书记关于残疾人事业的重要论述、习近平总书记对甘肃重要讲话和指示精神，按照中国残联和省委省政府的决策部署，紧扣“全面建成小康社会，残疾人一个也不能少”的目标，全面推进残联改革发展，着力完善残联工作机制，助力打赢贫困残疾人脱贫攻坚战，持续提升残疾人社会保障和公共服务水平，“十三五”残疾人事业发展规划圆满收官，广大残疾人的获得感、幸福感、安全感进一步提高，为决胜全面建成小康社会和加快建设幸福美好新甘肃、不断开创富民兴陇新局面作出积极贡献。

一、康复

2020年，各市（州）继续推进残疾儿童康复救助制度建设工作，进一步健全政策措施，市（州）、县（市、区）全部出台残疾儿童救助制度或实施细则，积极协调财政部门将残疾儿童康复救助制度经费纳入本级财政预算，保障残疾儿童康复救助制度安全、高效运行。各级残联普遍确定残疾儿童定点康复机构，建立残疾儿童康复救助经办队伍，提高经办队伍服务能力，确保残疾儿童应救尽救。12.8万持证残疾人及残疾儿童得到基本康复服务，其中0-6岁残疾儿童0.4万人。得到康复服务的人中有视力残疾人1.3万、听力残疾人1.3万、言语残疾人0.03万、肢体残疾人6.4万、智力残疾人0.9万、精神残疾人1.4万、多重残疾人1.1万。全年共为4.8万残疾人提供各类辅助器具适配服务。（见图1）

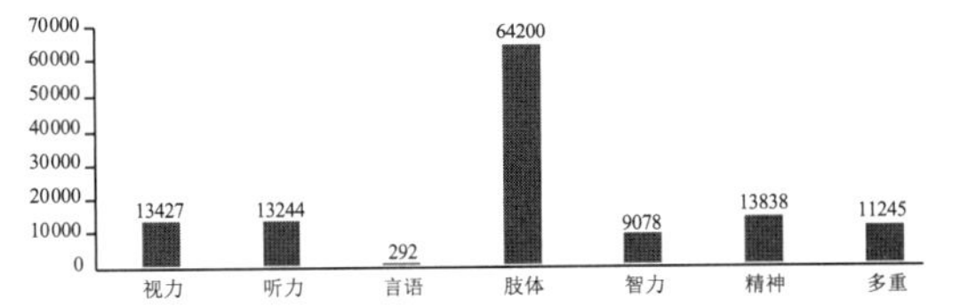

图1　全省各类别残疾人得到基本康复服务情况（单位：人）

截至2020年底，全省共有残疾人康复机构208个，其中残联办70个、卫生办76个、民政办6个、教育办6个、民办45个、其他5个。全省康复机构在岗人员4695人，其中，管理人员539人、业务人员3561人、其他人员595人。

二、教育

以普及适龄残疾儿童义务教育、推广国家通用手语和国家通用盲文为重点，进一步改善残疾人教育支持保障条件。进一步完善残疾人综合救助体系和“一人一案”助学措施，切实解决城乡贫困残疾人家庭的实际困难，鼓励残疾儿童少年和大中专学生发奋自强，平等接受各类教育。

实施残疾人事业专项彩票公益金助学项目，为283名家庭经济困难的残疾儿童享受普惠性学前教育提供资助。多渠道争取资金支持，对27名残疾儿童给予学前教育资助。

全省共有特殊教育普通高中班（部）1个。在校生195人，毕业生20人。残疾人中等职业学校（班）2个，在校生325人，毕业生82人，有560名被普通高等院校录取。2518名残疾青壮年文盲接受了扫盲教育。

三、就业

全省城乡持证残疾人新增就业6513人，其中，城镇新增就业1513人，农村新增就业5000人，城乡新增残疾人培训7982人。

截至2020年底，全省城乡持证残疾人就业人数为24.4万人，其中按比例就业0.6万人，集中就业0.2万人，个体就业1.5万人，公益性岗位就业0.3万人，辅助性就业0.3万人，灵活就业（含社区、居家就业）6.4万人，从事农业种养加15万人（见图2）

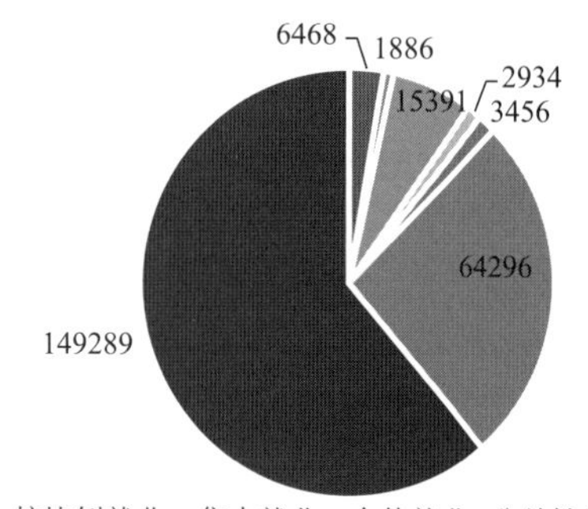

图 2 全省城乡持证残疾人就业情况（单位：人）

盲人按摩事业稳步发展，全年培训盲人保健按摩 749 名，盲人医疗按摩 266 名；保健按摩机构达 394 个，医疗按摩机构达 32 个。

四、社会保险

截至 2020 年底，全省残疾居民参加城乡社会养老保险人数 97 万；21.9 万 60 岁以下参保重度残疾人中，21 万享受参保个人缴费资助政策，占比 95.9%。8.6 万非重度残疾人享受个人缴费资助政策。36.7 万残疾人领取养老金。

残疾人托养服务工作稳步推进，残疾人托养服务机构 104 个，为 135 名残疾人提供托养服务。2.6 万残疾人接受居家服务。354 名托养服务管理人员接受各级各类专业培训。

五、扶贫

圆满完成贫困残疾人脱贫攻坚任务。残疾人接受实用技术培训 1.7 万人次。212 个残疾人扶贫基地安置 3398 名残疾人就业，扶持带动 5489 户残疾人家庭增产增收。

六、宣传文化

深入推进文化进家庭、进社区等项目，实施残疾人文化进家庭“五个一”项目 5000 户，推动各地将残疾人文化工作纳入基层文化服务体系，大力扶持特殊艺术人才培养和残疾人文创产业发展，打造残疾人文化服务、文化产业品牌。向中国残联推荐并成功申报 5 个文化创意示范基地。参加“决战脱贫 同奔小康”微电影微视频征集活动，其中《轮椅上的站姿》被中国残联评为优秀奖；参加省委宣传部组织的甘肃省第四届“践行社会主义核心价值观 脱贫攻坚奔小康”主题微电影微视频活动，其中《笑对人生》被省委宣传部评为二等奖。开展第八届全省残疾人艺术汇演，持续推进“数字阅读工程”，丰富基层残疾人文化生活。以“助残脱贫 决胜小康”为主题，组织第三十次全国助残日活动。

开展新冠疫情防控宣传工作，微信公众号连续刊登“抗击疫情残联在行动”系列报道；配合各类媒体刊登有关疫情防控、残疾人复工复产信息 21 条。各类媒体全方位宣传残疾人脱贫攻坚和全面小康现状稿件 270 余篇。开展“决战脱贫攻坚，决胜全面小康”秋冬季主题宣传活动。配合中国残联艺术团赴通渭开展 2 场公益演出。中央媒体刊登稿件 50 余篇，省级媒体 80 余条。每日甘肃网微信公众号、省残联网站开设主题活动专栏发布稿件 100 余条。联合省电视台制作《决战脱贫同奔小康》主题节目 20 期。组织全省新闻发布会 1 次，省、市（州）残疾人专题广播节目 28 个、电视手语栏目 13 个，省、市（州）、县（市、区）三级公共图书馆共设立盲文及盲文有声读物阅览室 56 个，全省共开展残疾人文化周活动 246 场次，省市残联共举办残疾人文化艺术类的比赛及展览 19 次。

七、体育

做好 2021 年全国第十一届残运会暨第八届特奥会的备战工作。全省组织开展残疾人群体活动 274 次，参加人数 22149 人，全省新建残疾人体育健身示范点 31 个，其中省级命名资助 20 个。向中国残联推荐培养残疾人社会体育指导员 7 名。

八、维权

全省县级以上人大常委会开展《中华人民共和国残疾人保障法》执法检查和专题调研 15 次；政协开展视察和专题调研 12 次。开展普法宣传教育活动 8 次，1200 人参加。

残疾人参政议政工作得到加强。全省残联协助人大代表、政协委员提出议案、建议、提案 27 件，办理议案、建议、提案 19 件。

无障碍建设法规、标准进一步完善。省市县三级无障碍环境建设与管理法规、政府令和规范性文件共出台 46 个；101 个市（州）、县（市、区）开展无障碍环境建设；开展无障碍环境建设检查 56 次，组织无障碍环境建设工作培训 704 人次。

九、组织建设

2020 年，全省市（州）、县（市、区）全部建立残联。乡镇（街道）已建立残联 1365 个，已建立社区（村）残协 17051 个。省市县乡残联工作人员达 4253 人，乡镇（街道）、村（社区）选聘残疾人专职委员 1.6 万。各市州残联配备残疾人领导干部 11 人，县级残联配备残疾人领导干部 78 人。

全省共建立各类残疾人专门协会 510 个，其中省级专门协会 5 个，市级专门协会 75 个，县级专门协会 430 个。助残社会组织 49 个。

十、服务设施

2020 年底，已竣工的综合服务设施（含办公楼）93 个，总建筑面积 978 万平方米，总投资 3 亿元；2020 年中央预算内投资项目 8 个，其中，康复设施 4 个，托养设施 4 个。总投资 5379 万元。

十一、信息化

截至 2020 年底，10 个市（州）、22 个县（市、区）残联开通网站。落实省政府关于“放管服”改革要求，为更多的残疾人在网上办理残疾人证，实现了一网通办，让“数据多跑腿，残疾人少跑路”。甘肃省政务服务网网上办理残疾人证累计受理 89 万次。全年在甘肃省残联门户网站各类栏目刊发信息 2838 条。

2020年青海省残疾人事业发展统计公报

2020年，青海省残联坚持以习近平新时代中国特色社会主义思想为指引，认真落实习近平总书记关于残疾人事业的重要论述，深入贯彻党的十九大和十九届二中三中四中全会精神和省委十三届四次五次六次七次全会精神，全面落实党中央、国务院和省委省政府关于残疾人事业决策部署，深入实施"五四战略"，奋力推进"一优两高"，主动融入群团协同化发展，着力推进残联改革，圆满完成"十三五"小康规划各项任务，团结带领广大残疾人讲政治、勇担当、善作为，全省残疾人工作取得新的进步。

一、康复

5.8万持证残疾人及残疾儿童得到基本康复服务，其中0-6岁残疾儿童1355名。得到康复服务的持证残疾人中，有视力残疾人7298名、听力残疾人7760名、言语残疾人791名、肢体残疾人3.3万名、智力残疾人4036名、精神残疾人2117名、多重残疾人3316名。全年共为2.8残疾人提供各类辅助器具。

截至2020年底，共有残疾人康复机构59个，其中残联系统康复机构12个。康复机构在岗人员达2161人，其中，管理人员292人，业务人员1552人，其他人员317人。

二、教育

实施残疾人事业专项彩票公益金助学项目，为168名家庭经济困难残疾儿童享受普惠性学前教育提供资助，带动各地对12残疾儿童给予学前教育资助。

2020年，共有特殊教育普通高中1个，在校生151人，其中聋生151人。残疾人中等职业学校1个，在校生333人，毕业生50人。有178名残疾人被普通高等院校录取。

566名残疾青壮年文盲接受了扫盲教育。

三、就业

城乡持证残疾人就业人数为4.4万人，其中按比例就业1952人，集中就业1662人，个体就业2707人，公益性岗位就业1173人，辅助性就业556人，灵活就业（含社区、居家就业）1.6万人，从事农业种养加2.0万人。

培训盲人保健按摩人员70名、盲人医疗按摩人员120名；现有保健按摩机构77个，医疗按摩机构8个；7人获得盲人医疗按摩人员初级职务任职资格。

四、社会保障

截至2020年底，残疾居民参加城乡社会养老保险人数12.0万名，3.4万名60岁以下参保重度残疾人中，3.2万名享受了参保个人缴费资助政策，占比93.4%。26740名非重度残疾人享受了个人缴费资助政策。5.3万人领取养老金。

残疾人托养服务机构74个，其中寄宿制托养服务机构35个，日间照料机构43个，综合性托养服务机构20个，为2924残疾人提供了托养服务。1337残疾人接受居家服务。131名托养服务管理和服务人员接受了各级各类专业培训。

五、扶贫

共有3656人次农村残疾人接受了实用技术培训，53个残疾人扶贫基地安置807名残疾人就业，辐射带动517户残疾人家庭增收。

共完成18户农村贫困残疾人家庭危房改造，投入资金8万元，18名残疾人受益。

六、宣传文化

截至2020年底，全国共有省级残疾人专题广播节目1个、电视手语栏目1个；地市级残疾人电视手语栏目5个。

截至2020年底，省地县三级公共图书馆共设立盲文及盲文有声读物阅览室16个，共开展残疾人文化周活动84场次；省地两级残联艺术团2个。

七、体育

新增设立社区残疾人健身示范点8个,为27户重度残疾人提供康复体育进家庭服务，培养残疾人社会体育指导员85名。

八、维权

2020年，制定或修改省级关于残疾人的专门法规、规章1个；制定或修改保障残疾人权益的省级规范性文件1个、地级1个、县级6个。县级以上人大开展《中华人民共和国残疾人保障法》执法检查和专题调研1次；政协开展视察和专题调研3次。开展省级普法宣传教育活动1次，10.6万人参加；举办省级法律培训班1个，80人参加。

残疾人参政议政工作稳步开展，各地残联协助人大代表、政协委员提出议案、建议、提案20件，办理议案、建议、提案7件。

无障碍建设法规、标准进一步完善。共出台了5个省、地市、县级无障碍环境建设与管理法规、政府令和规范性文件；14个地市、县系统开展无障碍环境建设；开展无障碍环境建设检查34次，无障碍培训10人次。

九、组织建设

2020年，市县乡共有残联433个，各地市已建残联8个，县（市、区）残联已建45个，乡镇（街道）残联已建380个；社区（村）已建残协4408个。

省市县乡残联工作人员1201人，乡镇（街道）残联、村（社区）残协专职委员总计2253名。地市级配备了残疾人领导干部的残联5个，县级配备了残疾人干部的残联14个。

共建立各类残疾人专门协会266个，其中省级专门协会已建5个，市级专门协会已建40个，县级专门协会已建221个。助残社会组织11个。

十、服务设施

截至2020年底，已竣工的各级残疾人综合服务设施23个，总建设规模94204.2平方米，总投资30033.3万元；已竣工的各级残疾人康复设施7个，总建设规模37858.4平方米，总投资14810.0万元；已竣工的各级残疾人托养服务设施32个，总建设规模61667.0平方米，总投资18364.2万元。

十一、信息化

截至2020年底，4个地级、8个县级残联开通网站。

2020年宁夏回族自治区残疾人事业发展统计公报

2020年，在自治区党委、政府的正确领导下，在中国残联的大力指导和支持下，在社会各界的热心帮助下，全区残疾人事业持续发展，在残疾人康复、教育、就业、扶贫、社会保障、组织建设、维权、宣传文化、体育、服务设施建设等业务领域取得了突出的进步和工作成效，为广大残疾人带来了更多福祉，现将2020年全区残疾人事业统计数据公报如下：

一、康复

2020年，全面落实残疾儿童康复救助制度，会同教育、民政、财政等8部门联合建立“545”制度体系，实现残疾儿童应救尽救。以贫困残疾人为重点，持续组织实施残疾人精准康复服务行动，61144名持证残疾人及残疾儿童得到基本康复服务，其中0-6岁残疾儿童1677人。得到康复服务的持证残疾人中，有视力残疾人7416名、听力残疾人6007名、言语残疾人223名、肢体残疾人30121名、智力残疾人3905名、精神残疾人8866名、多重残疾人3746名，0-17岁未持证残疾儿童860名。推行辅助器具补贴办法，实施“爱心接力、循环使用”辅助器具免费借用公益项目，全年共为21518名残疾人提供各类辅助器具。积极维护残疾人健康，保障贫困残疾人基本医疗，推进贫困残疾人家庭医生签约服务。

加强残疾人康复机构规范化建设，持续深化社区康复工作。承担中国残联、国家民政部、卫生健康委联合开展的全国残疾儿童康复救助定点服务机构管理试点工作。联合自治区民政厅、卫生健康委印发《关于进一步加强残疾人社区康复工作实施方案》。印发《2020年全区“十百千”康复人才实名制培养实施方案》。截至2020年底，全区共有残疾人康复机构42个，其中残联系统康复机构20个。康复机构在岗人员达986人，其中，管理人员106人，业务人员722人，其他人员158人。贯彻落实《宁夏回族自治区残疾预防行动计划（2016—2020年）》，组织开展第四次全国残疾预防日宣传活动。

二、教育

2020年底，全区义务教育阶段适龄残疾儿童共有7133人，入学6961人，入学率达到96%以上，圆满实现“十三五”任务目标。特殊教育学校发展到15所，在校学生2143人，实现30万人以上人口县（市、区）特殊教育学校全覆盖，其中特殊教育普通高中1个，在校生66人；特殊教育中等职业学校（部）2个。招收5人以上的普通学校116个，其中资源教室211个。有1028名残疾青壮年接受扫盲培训。实施扶残助学项目，有266名经济困难残疾儿童和156名残疾大中专学生享受资助。

三、就业

全区城乡持证残疾人就业人数为56944人，其中按比例就业5159人，集中就业1386人，个体就业4767人，公益性岗位就业1034人，辅助性就业1097人，灵活就业（含社区、居家就业）19397人，从事农业种养加24104人。

2020年，城乡持证残疾人新增就业2195人，其中，城镇新增就业792人，农村新增就业1403人；城乡新增残疾人实名培训3005人。

全区共培训盲人保健按摩人员97名、盲人医疗按摩人员228名；现有保健按摩机构207个，医疗按摩机构10个。13人获得盲人医疗按摩人员初级职务任职资格。

四、社会保障

截至2020年底，全区参加城乡居民养老保险残疾人153221名。已领取养老保险金61363名。60岁以下参保残疾人91858名,享受参保个人缴费资助65166名，其中：重度残疾人46381名，轻度残疾人18785名。享受贫困残疾人生活补贴105075人次，享受重度残疾人护理补贴100363人次。支持建成残疾人托养服务机构66个，其中：寄宿制托养服务机构 17 个，日间照料机构 19 个，居家托养机构 26 个，综合性托养服务机构 4 个。为 5956 名有需求的残疾人提供托养服务，其中：寄宿制托养服务 526 名，日间照料托养服务 331 名，居家托养服务 5095 名。培训托养服务管理和服务人员 109 名，其中：培训托养机构服务和管理人员 31 名，培训居家服务人员 78 名。

五、扶贫

圆满完成贫困残疾人脱贫攻坚任务，截至 2020 年底，55495 名建档立卡贫困残疾人全部脱贫。

2020 年，全区共有 5538 人次农村残疾人接受了实用技术培训，1290 名贫困残疾人获得康复扶贫贴息贷款扶持，39 个残疾人扶贫基地安置 516 名残疾人就业，辐射带动 1607 户残疾人家庭增收。全区共完成 578 户农村贫困残疾人家庭危房改造，投入资金 1710.5 万元，596 名残疾人受益。

六、宣传文化

开展第三十次全国助残日系列活动和“决胜全面小康、决战脱贫攻坚”主题宣传季活动，组织全区自强与助残典型宣传暨巡回宣讲活动，我区残疾人脱贫代表辛宝同参加中国残联与国务院新闻办举办的残疾人脱贫攻坚基层代表中外记者见面会。各大媒体累计刊发残疾人事业宣传报道共计 520 多篇（次）。

组织全区残联开展残疾人文化周系列活动 104 场次，实施文化残疾人进家庭“五个一”项目 500 人（次）。全区 3 个残疾人文创基地被命名为全国第二批文化创意产业基地。积极争取中国残疾人艺术团来宁赴基层脱贫攻坚一线慰问演出 3 场。截至 2020 年底，全区共有自治区级残疾人专题广播节目 1 个、电视手语栏目 1 个；地级残疾人专题广播节目 1 个、电视手语栏目 5 个。自治区、市、县三级公共图书馆共设立盲文及盲文有声读物阅览室 29 个，现有残疾人艺术团 3 个。

七、体育

开展冰雪运动季、残疾人健身周、全国特奥日等群众性体育活动。做好第十一届全国残疾人运动会暨第八届特殊奥林匹克运动会备战工作，组织开展运动员选拔和分级测试。参加第三届全国基层残疾人机构旱地冰壶比赛总决赛，取得了 1 金 1 银的优异成绩。全区新增设立社区残疾人健身示范点 3 个，为 412 户重度残疾人提供康复体育进家庭服务，培养残疾人社会体育指导员 90 名。

八、维权

2020 年，自治区制定或修改关于残疾人的专门法规、规章 1 个；地级市制定或修改保障残疾人权益的规范性文件 3 个。县级以上人大开展《中华人民共和国残疾人保障法》执法检查和专题调研 1 次；政协开展视察和专题调研 3 次。自治区开展普法宣传教育活动 4 次，240 人参加；残疾人参政议政工作稳步开展，各地残联协助人大代表、政协委员提出议案、建议、提案 6 件，办理议案、建议、提案 12 件；为残疾人提供法律援助案件 149 件。

无障碍建设法规、标准进一步完善。全区共出台了 5 个区、市、县级无障碍环境建设与管理法规、政府令和规范性文件；25 个地市、县系统开展无障碍环境建设；开展无障碍环境建设检查 36 次，无障碍培训 156 人次。

2020 年度，为 3265 名残疾人家庭实施了无障碍改造，为 4287 名残疾人发放了残疾人机动轮椅车燃油补贴。

九、组织建设

2020 年，市县乡共有残联 261 个，5 个地市残联已全部成立，22 个县（市、区）已建残联 21 个，235 个乡镇（街道）已全部建立残联；95.8%的村（社区）已建残协，共 1989 个。

各级残联工作人员 629 人，乡镇（街道）残联、村（社区）残协专职委员总计 818 名。有 3 个地市级残联配备了残疾人领导干部，有 14 个县级残联配备了残疾人干部。

全区共建立各类残疾人专门协会 133 个，其中自治区级专门协会已建 5 个，市级专门协会已建 25 个，县级专门协会已建 103 个。助残社会组织 38 个。

十、服务设施

截至 2020 年底，已竣工的各级残疾人综合服务设施 15 个，总建设规模 30450.3 平方米，总投资

7685.2 万元；已竣工的各级残疾人康复设施 21 个，总建设规模 139044.3 平方米，总投资 48432.7 万元；已竣工的各级残疾人托养服务设施 13 个，总建设规模 31990.0 平方米，总投资 10242.0 万元。

十一、信息化

截至 2020 年底，自治区、3 个地市级、2 个县级残联开通网站；开通并运行宁夏残联微信公众号；建成 OA 办公系统，纵向打通各级残联系统，横向打通各部门文件传输；在宁夏政务服务网建成 10 个助残服务事项线上申请办理，其中，4 项实现表单式办理，2 项实现业务系统办理。全区共有持证残疾人 216537 人。

2020 年新疆维吾尔自治区残疾人事业发展统计公报

2020 年，在自治区党委、人民政府的正确领导和中国残联的指导下，新疆残联紧紧围绕党中央、国务院关于残疾人事业的决策部署和习近平总书记关于残疾人事业的重要论述，在全区各族人民众志成城共同抗击“疫情”的情况下，自治区残联统筹推进疫情防控和残疾人事业各项工作，努力降低疫情带来的影响，确保完成全年目标任务。

一、康复

2020 年，自治区康复服务水平不断提升，康复服务覆盖率大幅提高，10.4 万名持证残疾人及残疾儿童得到基本康复服务，其中 0-6 岁残疾儿童 0.36 万人。得到康复服务的持证残疾人中，有视力残疾人 1.2 万名、听力残疾人 0.88 万名、言语残疾人 183 名、肢体残疾人 5.3 万名、智力残疾人 0.6 万名、精神残疾人 1.4 万名、多重残疾人 1.0 万名（图 1）。全年共为 3.8 万残疾人提供各类辅助器具。

截至 2020 年底，全区共有残疾人康复机构 176 个，其中残联系统康复机构 46 个。康复机构在岗人员达 2564 人，其中，管理人员 300 人，业务人员 1971 人，其他人员 293 人。为加快推进全国残疾预防综合试验区创建工作，喀什市、昌吉市全国残疾预防综合试验区创建工作受到国家通报表扬。

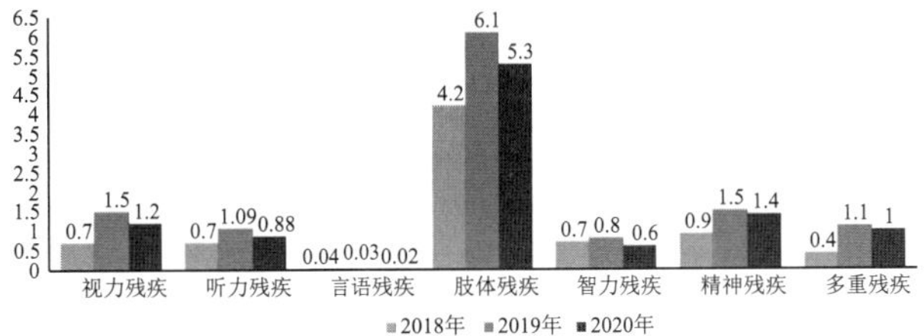

图 1　2018–2020 年新疆残疾人康复服务对照表
（单位：万人）

二、教育

2020 年，自治区实施“爱心天使”助学项目，对 250 名考入普通高等院校本、专科和家庭生活困难的残疾学生给予资助；继续实施残疾人远程开放教育项目，2020 年共招收学生 261 人；全区有 398 名残疾人被普通高等院校录取；全年共 1157 名残疾青壮年文盲接受了扫盲教育。

截至 2020 年底，全区共有特殊教育普通高中部 1 个，在校生 209 人，其中聋生 209 人。残疾人中等职业学校 2 个，其中毕业生 140 人，毕业生中 35 人获得职业资格证书。

三、就业

2020 年城乡持证残疾人就业人数为 17.3 万人，其中按比例就业 2 万人，集中就业 0.4 万人，个体就业 1.6 万人，公益性岗位就业 0.5 万人，辅助性就业 0.18 万人，灵活就业（含社区、居家就业）4.4 万人，从事农业种养加 8.2 万人。

全年共培训盲人保健按摩人员 79 名、盲人医疗按摩人员 51 名；全疆现有保健按摩机构 117 个，医疗按摩机构 13 个。

自治区残联不断探索残疾人就业创业新模式、新途径，建立新疆残疾人文化创意产业基地和就业创业孵化基地（简称“双创基地”），受到中国残联高度肯定。目前已入驻 20 余家残疾人文创工作室和就业创业孵化项目。

四、社会保障

截至 2020 年底，全区残疾居民参加城乡社会养老保险人数 37.5 万名，10.1 万名 60 岁以下参保重度残疾人中，9.5 万人享受了参保个人缴费资助政策，占比 94.6%。9.7 万名非重度残疾人享受了个人缴费资助政策。10.9 万人领取养老金。

2020 年，全区共有残疾人托养服务机构 152 个，其中寄宿制托养服务机构 79 个，日间照料机构 37 个，综合性托养服务机构 31 个，为 1020 名残疾人提供了托养服务。98 名残疾人接受居家服务，202 名托养服务管理和服务人员接受了各级各类专业培训。

2020 年疫情发生以来，自治区残联高度重视疫情期间的残疾人民生保障工作，在全国率先出台残疾人民生保障措施，制定了《疫情防控期间做好全区残疾人帮扶解困工作的意见》，印发了《新冠肺炎疫情期间对就业创业残疾人发放生活困难补贴的通知》。全区累计发放残疾人就业创业生活困难补贴资金 3225.3 万元，惠及残疾人 1 万余人。疫情期间，全区残联系统开通热线电话 1066 部，受理解决残疾人诉求 1.1 万余件次，临时救助残疾人 6.4 万余人次，累计减免房屋租金达 40 余万元；累计向 5.3 万名残疾人发放慰问金和各类生活用品折合 1323 万元；2126 名残疾儿童参加线上康复教学，累计达到 3.5 万余人次。

五、扶贫

截至 2020 年底，全区共有 8121 人次农村残疾人接受了实用技术培训，136 个残疾人扶贫基地安置 801 名残疾人就业，辐射带动 1085 户残疾人家庭增收。

积极开展消费扶贫，购买帮扶村农副产品 49 万余元。“访惠聚”驻村、支教及第一书记工作成效显著，全年累计实施扶贫项目 62 个，6 个村全部实现整村脱贫退出。

实施阳光助残扶贫、电商助残扶贫、产业助残扶贫、残疾妇女手工编制、助盲就业脱贫等扶贫助残活动，帮助贫困残疾人实现就业，全区实现就业残疾人 16 万余人。投入 287.7 万元开展残疾人技能培训，通过开展种植养殖、家用电器维修、美容美发、电子商务等方式培训残疾人 8202 人。22705 名建档立卡贫困残疾人通过扶贫车间、安置公益性岗位、自主就业等方式实现就业。全区 12 万建档立卡贫困残疾人实现全部脱贫。

六、宣传文化

截至 2020 年底，自治区设立电视手语栏目 1 个；地级残疾人专题广播节目 1 个、电视手语栏目 3 个；全疆各级公共图书馆共设立盲文及盲文有声读物阅览室 12 个，共开展残疾人文化周活动 66 场次。

2020 年，自治区残疾人文化体育活动有序开展。组织开展以“助残脱贫决胜小康”为主题第三十次全国助残日活动，采取线上方式推动各类残疾人宣传文化工作顺利开展。

七、维权

2020 年，自治区无障碍建设法规、标准进一步完善，自治区残联会同住建厅、卫健委、民政厅、工信厅等部门联合印发了《关于加强无障碍环境市（县）创建工作的通知》，开展无障碍环境市县、村镇创建工作，加强无障碍环境建设督导，全疆各级共出台了 3 个无障碍环境建设与管理法规、政府令和规范性文件；开展无障碍环境建设检查 33 次，无障碍培训 131 人次。

2020 年，全区共制定或修改保障残疾人权益的地级规范性文 3 个、县级 2 个。县级以上人大开展《中华人民共和国残疾人保障法》执法检查和专题调研 2 次；政协开展视察和专题调研 1 次。残疾人参政议政工作稳步开展，各地残联协助人大代表、政协委员提出议案、建议、提案 5 件，办理议案、建议、提案 10 件。认真开展残疾人矛盾纠纷排查化解工作。通过 12385 残疾人服务热线等方式，处理来信来访及网上咨询服务共 1652 件次。

八、组织建设

2020 年，全区已建各地（州、市）级残联 14 个，县（市、区）级残联 97 个，市、县（乡）级残联共有 974 个，乡镇（街道）级残联 863 个；社区（村）已建残协 5506 个。

自治区地、县、乡残联工作人员 2349 人，乡、镇（街道）残联、村（社区）残协专职委员总计 2379 名。地市级配备了残疾人领导干部的残联 11 个，县级配备了残疾人干部的残联 47 个。共建立各类残疾人专门协会 497 个，其中自治区级专门协会已建 5 个，地级专门协会已建 68 个，县级专门协会已建 424 个。助残社会组织 13 个。

自治区残联为加快推进地（州、市）残联改革工作，地（州、市）、县（市、区）残联改革方案已全部出台实施。

九、服务设施

截至 2020 年底，已竣工的各级残疾人综合服务设施 83 个，总建设规模 25.5 万平方米，总投资 6.3 亿元；已竣工的各级残疾人康复设施 39 个，总建设规模 16.4 万平方米，总投资 34150.7 万元；已竣工的各级残疾人托养服务设施 60 个，总建设规模 10.8 万平方米，总投资 1.9 亿元。

十、信息化

2020 年自治区残联继续运用大数据平台提升残疾人服务能力建设，加快推进“智慧残联”建设，加快推进残疾人第三代残疾人证（智能化）项目的实施，在克拉玛依市、乌鲁木齐市、哈密市、博州、伊犁州直、塔城、阿勒泰地区、吐鲁番市、巴州、阿克苏地区、昌吉州推进智能化残疾人证的换发。

残疾人大数据平台服务能力不断增强。建立与扶贫、民政等相关部门残疾人信息数据实时对接，助力残疾人脱贫攻坚。加强精准数据比对促脱贫。认真做好与扶贫、民政等相关部门数据比对，确保各项惠残政策有效落实，不漏一人。做好对易致贫返贫贫困残疾人的预警监测和帮扶工作，7690 名残疾人边缘户和 6503 名残疾人脱贫监测户纳入低保。

2020 年新疆生产建设兵团残疾人事业发展统计公报

2020 年，在中国残联的关心指导和兵团党委的正确领导下，兵团残联系统以习近平新时代中国特色社会主义思想为指导，认真学习宣传贯彻党的十九大和十九届二中、三中、四中、五中全会精神，深入贯彻以习近平同志为核心的党中央治疆方略和对兵团的定位要求，贯彻落实党中央、国务院关于新时代中国特色残疾人事业新部署新要求，按照第三十四次全国残联工作会议、兵团残联第二十八次工作会议确定的目标任务，扎实做好残疾人基本民生保障，千方百计促进残疾人及其家庭就业增收，着力提升残疾人基本公共服务水平，不断健全残疾人权益保障，残疾人生活质量进一步提升，平等参与共享的社会环境更加优化。现根据 2020 年度残疾人事业统计数据公报如下：

一、康复

2020 年，10169 名持证残疾人及残疾儿童得到基本康复服务，其中 0-6 岁残疾儿童 106 人。得到康复服务的持证残疾人中，有视力残疾人 651 名、听力残疾人 617 名、言语残疾人 5 名、肢体残疾人 3395 名、智力残疾人 599 名、精神残疾人 4342 名、多重残疾人 541 名。全年共为 3169 名残疾人提供各类辅助器具。

截至 2020 年底，共有残疾人康复机构 34 个，其中残联系统康复机构 6 个。康复机构在岗人员达 910 人，其中，管理人员 63 人，业务人员 543 人，其他人员 304 人。

二、教育

2020 年，共有 35 名残疾人被普通高等院校录取，471 名残疾青壮年文盲接受了扫盲教育。

三、就业

2020 年，城乡持证残疾人就业人数为 21143 人，其中按比例就业 8558 人，集中就业 832 人，个体就业 2413 人，公益性岗位就业 451 人，辅助性就业 202 人，灵活就业（含社区、居家就业）5648 人，从事农业种养加 3039 人。

培训盲人保健按摩人员 22 名、盲人医疗按摩人员 8 名；现有保健按摩机构 18 个，医疗按摩机构 1 个。

四、社会保障

截至 2020 年底，残疾居民参加城乡社会养老保险人数 21932 名，8557 名 60 岁以下参保重度残疾人中，8238 名享受了参保个人缴费资助政策，占比 96.3%。4689 名非重度残疾人享受了个人缴费资助政策。3829 人领取养老金。

残疾人托养服务机构 63 个，其中寄宿制托养服务机构 33 个，日间照料机构 5 个，综合性托养服务机构 25 个，为 492 名残疾人提供了托养服务。495 名残疾人接受居家服务。15 名托养服务管理和服务人员接受了各级各类专业培训。

五、扶贫开发

2020 年，共有 4175 人次农村残疾人接受了实用技术培训，0 名贫困残疾人获得康复扶贫贴息贷款扶持，37 个残疾人扶贫基地安置 353 名残疾人就业，辐射带动 773 户残疾人家庭增收。

共完成 34 户农村贫困残疾人家庭危房改造，投入资金 850000 元，38 名残疾人受益。

六、宣传文化

截至 2020 年底，共有地级残疾人专题广播节目 1 个、电视手语栏目 1 个。

截至 2020 年底，省地县三级公共图书馆共设立盲文及盲文有声读物阅览室 2 个，共开展残疾人文化周活动 190 场次；省地两级残联艺术团 1 个。

七、体育

2020 年，为 204 户重度残疾人提供康复体育进家庭服务，培养残疾人社会体育指导员 43 名。

八、维权

2020年，残疾人参政议政工作稳步开展，各地残联协助人大代表、政协委员办理议案、建议、提案2件。

无障碍建设法规、标准进一步完善。共出台了1个地市、县系统开展无障碍环境建设；开展无障碍环境建设检查1次，无障碍培训32人次。

九、组织建设

2020年，市县乡共有残联14个，县（市、区）残联已建14个；社区（村）已建残协1个。

省市县乡残联工作人员77人，乡镇（街道）残联、村（社区）残协专职委员总计151名。县级配备了残疾人干部的残联2个。

共建立各类残疾人专门协会39个，其中省级专门协会已建5个，市级专门协会已建9个，县级专门协会已建25个。助残社会组织1个。

十、服务设施

截至2020年底，已竣工的各级残疾人综合服务设施9个，总建设规模10384.0平方米，总投资2315.0万元；已竣工的各级残疾人康复设施13个，总建设规模78136.2平方米，总投资29254.8万元；已竣工的各级残疾人托养服务设施54个，总建设规模93523.3平方米，总投资20058.5万元。

十一、信息化建设

截至2020年底，1个县级残联开通网站。

6

附录

Appendix

关于使用2010年末全国残疾人总数及各类、不同残疾等级人数的通知

残联〔2012〕25号

各省、自治区、直辖市及计划单列市残联，新疆生产建设兵团残联，黑龙江农垦总局残联：

根据第六次全国人口普查我国总人口数，及第二次全国残疾人抽样调查我国残疾人占全国总人口的比例和各类残疾人占残疾人总人数的比例，推算了2010年末我国残疾人总人数及各类、不同等级的残疾人数，现通知如下：

全国残疾人总数为8502万人。

各类残疾人的人数分别为：视力残疾1263万人；听力残疾2054万人；言语残疾130万人；肢体残疾2472万人；智力残疾568万人；精神残疾629万人；多重残疾1386万人。

各残疾等级人数分别为：重度残疾2518万人；中度和轻度残疾人5984万人。

以上数据可在工作中使用并对外公开。

中国残疾人联合会

二〇一二年三月五日

中国残联统计调查项目目录

审批项目一览表

统计调查项目名称	批准文号	有效期截止时间
中国残疾人事业统计调查制度	国统制[2021]102 号	2024 年 9 月
全国残疾人基本服务状况和需求信息数据动态更新	国统制[2021]70 号	2024 年 6 月
全国残疾人家庭收入状况调查制度	国统制[2018] 60 号	2021 年 5 月

中国残疾人联合会文件

残联发[2006]1 号

关于印发《全国残联系统统计工作管理办法》的通知

各省、自治区、直辖市及计划单列市残联，新疆生产建设兵团残联、黑龙江农垦总局残联：

为了加强统计工作的管理，规范统计调查行为，提高统计调查的整体效益，充分发挥统计工作的服务和监督作用，中国残联依据《中华人民共和国统计法》《中华人民共和国统计法实施细则》《部门统计调查管理暂行办法》，结合工作实际，对原有的《中国残联系统统计工作暂行规定》《中国残联系统专项业务统计调查项目管理暂行办法》《中国残联机关统计资料管理暂行办法》等进行了修订和整合，制定了《全国残联系统统计工作管理办法》，现予以印发，请遵照执行。

中国残疾人联合会

二〇〇六年一月三日

全国残联系统统计工作管理办法

一、总　则

第一条　为了科学、有效地组织全国残联系统统计工作，规范统计调查行为，提高统计调查的整体效益，充分发挥统计工作的服务和监督作用，依据《中华人民共和国统计法》(以下简称《统计法》)、《中华人民共和国统计法实施细则》(以下简称《实施细则》)、《部门统计调查管理暂行办法》，结合工作实际，制定本办法。

第二条　全国残联系统统计工作的基本任务是：对全国残疾人事业的发展状况和残联系统的业务工作进行统计调查、统计分析、统计预测和统计监督，为国家和各级人民政府制定与残疾人事业相关的政策、法规提供依据，为领导运筹决策和残联系统工作的发展提供有效的服务。

第三条　全国残联系统统计工作由：中国残疾人事业统计年报制度、中国残疾人事业统计快报制度、中国残疾人事业基础统计台账制度、专项业务统计调查工作组成。

第四条　各级残联应加强统计现代化建设，积极利用信息技术手段，使残疾人事业统计数据更加科学、准确、及时，逐步实现残疾人事业统计数据的电子化和统计数据的社会共享与服务。

二、统计机构、职责和统计人员

第五条　全国残联系统统计工作实行统一领导、分级负责。中国残联负责全国残疾人事业统计工作的组织、协调与管理，并对地方残联统计工作进行指导，具体由中国残联设置的统计机构负责组织实施。地方各级残联的统计工作由地方各级残联设置的统计机构或统计主管部门负责管理和组织实施，并接受上级残联统计机构和同级人民政府统计部门的指导、监督与管理。

第六条　中国残联的统计机构设在中国残联信息中心，负责组织、协调和管理全国残联系统的统计工作。其主要职责是：制定残疾人事业统计调查计划和项目，制定统计标准；组织协调各级残联搜集、整理、提供统计资料，管理统计资料的发布，开展统计分析、统计预测和统计监督工作；指导、检查全国残联系统统计工作，组织统计业务经验交流，开展全国残联系统统计科学研究；做好统计人员培训工作；制订全国残联系统统计工作现代化规划。

各省级残联应设置统计机构或明确统计主管部门并设专职统计人员，负责指导本行政区域内各级残联统计工作，组织管理本级残联的统计工作。其主要职责是：在完成好中国残联和上级残联下达的各项统计调查工作的同时，为本级残疾人事业提供各项统计数据，并开展统计调查活动。

各地级市残联应明确统计主管部门并设专(兼)职统计人员，其主要职责是：在完成好中国残联和上级残联下达的各项统计调查工作的同时，为本级残疾人事业提供各项统计数据，并开展统计调查活动。

各县级残联应明确统计工作主管部门或主管负责人，确定兼职统计人员。其主要职责是：做好基础数据工作，建立统计台账，完成好中国残联和上级残联下达的统计调查任务，为本级残疾人事业提供各项统计数据，并开展统计调查活动。

第七条　各级残联统计人员应保持相对稳定。统计人员的调动，应当征得本级统计主管部门或统计工作负责人的同意；省级专职统计人员的调动，应当征得中国残联统计机构的同意。统计人员调动工作或离职，应当由经过统计业务培训、能够胜任统计业务工作的人员接替，并办理交接手续。各级残联的统计人员应取得同级人民政府统计机构颁发的统计上岗证，具有残联系统业务知识和计算机操作能力。

三、统计报表制度的编制、修改与审批

第八条　中国残疾人事业统计年报、快报制度和统计台账制度中的指标、指标涵义、调查范围、

分类目录、计算方法和统计报表表式、统计编码以及报送时间，由中国残联统一规定，按照国家统计局的要求报送国家统计局进行审批备案。按规定程序经国家统计局批准或备案的统计报表，在报表的右上角标明制表机关名称、表号、批准或备案机关名称及其批准文号。被调查的部门、人员应当准确、及时地按报表规定填报。

不符合前款规定的统计报表（包括以搜集数字为主的调查提纲）是非法报表，被调查的部门可以拒绝填报。

第九条 中国残疾人事业统计年报、快报和统计台账应根据中国残疾人事业发展的需要及时进行调整和补充。中国残联各业务部门因工作需要，调整和补充有关指标时，应进行充分论证并与中国残联统计管理部门联系与协商，经中国残联理事会批准后，报国家统计局批准或备案。

四、统计台账管理

第十条 为了规范中国残联系统统计工作，做到依法统计，发挥统计服务和监督作用，根据《中华人民共和国统计法》和国家相关统计工作的规定，中国残联将制定中国残疾人事业统计台账制度，加强统计台账的管理与数据的报送。

第十一条 中国残疾人事业统计台账（卡）充分利用电子网络化的方式、将科学合理、准确实用的动态管理，与中国残疾人事业统计报表制度相衔接。台账填写内容要符合法律法规政策的要求，填写对象真实、准确；先填卡，后建账，做到由台账中提取统计数字。

第十二条 各级残联必须依据中国残疾人事业统计台账（卡）中的数据，报送中国残疾人事业统计快报、年报和各项专项业务统计调查的统计报表，做到填报统计报表的数据全面、准确、及时、数出一门。

第十三条 中国残疾人事业统计台账在统一格式、统一软件下实施，由各级地方残联统计人员协调业务部门和人员用计算机或纸质台账、台卡方式进行专门管理。统计人员发生变动时，要严格履行交接手续。

第十四条 省级、地（市）级残联都应建立电子化台账。有条件的县级残联也要实行电子化台账，各级残联应积极推动电子化台账建设，加强统计台账的管理工作。在没有实行全面电子化台账之前，将实行电子化台账和纸质台账、台卡的同时保存。

第十五条 中国残疾人事业统计台账、台卡按中国残疾人事业统计报表逐级汇总上报。

五、专项业务统计调查管理

第十六条 中国残联和地方各级残联开展的专项业务统计调查，以及残联各业务部门与其他部门或单位联合组织实施的统计调查，其调查的统计指标与中国残联年报、快报指标交叉重复或需要对外公布统计数据的统计调查，均属于专项业务统计调查管理范畴。

第十七条 中国残联系统各级统计机构统一管理和协调本级业务部门专项业务统计调查。

第十八条 专项业务统计调查项目必须符合国家统计局《部门统计调查项目管理暂行办法》的基本原则与要求。专项业务统计调查项目的立项必须有充分的理由。调查要有明确的目的和资料使用范围。调查项目应当与中国残联职能范围和各项业务工作相对应。

第十九条 中国残联系统各级统计机构通过建立审批备案制度、调查项目公布制度、跟踪检查制度、举报制度，对会内专项业务统计调查进行管理。

第二十条 专项业务统计调查项目中的统计标准和分类必须与政府综合统计机构规定使用的标准和分类相一致。涉及政府综合统计机构规定以外的专业标准和分类，要与国家有关标准或行业标准相一致。尚无国家标准和行业标准的，必须严格按照标准化及分类科学的原则进行归纳和设计，并在使用前征求政府综合统计机构的意见。

第二十一条 中国残联新增设的统计调查项目在制定好统计调查方案后，须提交中国残联统计机构审核，报国家统计局批准后统一组织实施。

地方残联新增设的统计调查项目，由本级残联统计机构统一管理，报上级残联统计机构和同级人民政府统计局批准后组织实施。地方残联制发的统计调查表内容、指标涵义、计算方法、完成期限等，均不得与中国残联制发的有关统计调查表相抵触。

六、统计资料的管理与发布

第二十二条 残联系统统计资料实行归口管理。全国性残联系统 统计资料，由中国残联统计机构统一管理；地方性残联系统统计资料，由地方残联统计机构或统计人员统一管理。统计机构和统计人员必须建立统计工作责任制和统计资料整理、审查、管理制度，不断提高工作质量和工作效率，保证残联系统统计资料的准确、及时。

各级残联的文件、报告、简报、情况反映、信息等引用综合性的统计数字，必须经本级统计机构或统计人员复核。对外提供和公布的统计资料，必须经本级统计机构或统计人员统一复核和办理并由主管理事长批准。任何部门和个人不得擅自公开和使用未经正式公布的残联系统统计资料。

第二十三条 各级残联统计机构、统计人员必须建立健全统计资料档案，对原始记录、统计台账和综合分析等统计资料，按有关规定保管，不得损坏。对于属于国家秘密的残联系统统计资料，要按照《中华人民共和国保守国家秘密法》、国家统计局《统计资料保密管理办法》等有关规定，妥善保管。

七、奖励和惩罚

第二十四条 各级残联对有下列表现之一的残联统计机构或者人员，给予表扬或奖励：

一、在改革和完善残联系统统计制度、统计方法等方面，有重要贡献的；

二、在完成规定的残联系统统计调查任务，保障残联系统统计资料的准确性、及时性方面，做出显著成绩的；

三、在进行残联系统统计分析、统计预测和统计监督方面取得重要成绩的；

四、在运用和推广现代化信息技术方面，有显著效果的；

五、在残联系统统计科学研究方面有所创新的；

六、坚持实事求是，依法办事，同违反统计法规和本办法的行为作斗争，表现突出的。

第二十五条 各级残联对有下列行为之一的机构或者人员，给予批评或处分：

一、虚报、瞒报、拒报残联系统统计资料的；

二、伪造、篡改残联系统统计资料的；

三、无故迟报残联系统统计资料的；

四、侵犯统计机构、统计人员行使统计法规及本办法所规定的职权或打击报复统计人员的；

五、违反统计法规及本办法，未经批准，自行编制发布残联系统统计报表的；

六、违反统计法规及本办法，未经核定批准，擅自对外提供或公布残联系统统计资料的。

八、附 则

第二十六条 本办法由中国残联负责解释。

第二十七条 本办法自发布之日起试行。

中华人民共和国统计法

（1983 年 12 月 8 日第六届全国人民代表大会常务委员会第三次会议通过。根据 1996 年 5 月 15 日第八届全国人民代表大会常务委员会第十九次会议《关于修改〈中华人民共和国统计法〉的决定》修正。2009 年 6 月 27 日第十一届全国人民代表大会常务委员会第九次会议修订。）

第一章　总　则

第一条　为了科学、有效地组织统计工作，保障统计资料的真实性、准确性、完整性和及时性，发挥统计在了解国情国力、服务经济社会发展中的重要作用，促进社会主义现代化建设事业发展，制定本法。

第二条　本法适用于各级人民政府、县级以上人民政府统计机构和有关部门组织实施的统计活动。

统计的基本任务是对经济社会发展情况进行统计调查、统计分析，提供统计资料和统计咨询意见，实行统计监督。

第三条　国家建立集中统一的统计系统，实行统一领导、分级负责的统计管理体制。

第四条　国务院和地方各级人民政府、各有关部门应当加强对统计工作的组织领导，为统计工作提供必要的保障。

第五条　国家加强统计科学研究，健全科学的统计指标体系，不断改进统计调查方法，提高统计的科学性。

国家有计划地加强统计信息化建设，推进统计信息搜集、处理、传输、共享、存储技术和统计数据库体系的现代化。

第六条　统计机构和统计人员依照本法规定独立行使统计调查、统计报告、统计监督的职权，不受侵犯。

地方各级人民政府、政府统计机构和有关部门以及各单位的负责人，不得自行修改统计机构和统计人员依法搜集、整理的统计资料，不得以任何方式要求统计机构、统计人员及其他机构、人员伪造、篡改统计资料，不得对依法履行职责或者拒绝、抵制统计违法行为的统计人员打击报复。

第七条　国家机关、企业事业单位和其他组织以及个体工商户和个人等统计调查对象，必须依照本法和国家有关规定，真实、准确、完整、及时地提供统计调查所需的资料，不得提供不真实或者不完整的统计资料，不得迟报、拒报统计资料。

第八条　统计工作应当接受社会公众的监督。任何单位和个人有权检举统计中弄虚作假等违法行为。对检举有功的单位和个人应当给予表彰和奖励。

第九条　统计机构和统计人员对在统计工作中知悉的国家秘密、商业秘密和个人信息，应当予以保密。

第十条　任何单位和个人不得利用虚假统计资料骗取荣誉称号、物质利益或者职务晋升。

第二章　统计调查管理

第十一条　统计调查项目包括国家统计调查项目、部门统计调查项目和地方统计调查项目。

国家统计调查项目是指全国性基本情况的统计调查项目。部门统计调查项目是指国务院有关部门的专业性统计调查项目。地方统计调查项目是指县级以上地方人民政府及其部门的地方性统计调查项目。

国家统计调查项目、部门统计调查项目、地方统计调查项目应当明确分工，互相衔接，不得重复。

第十二条　国家统计调查项目由国家统计局制定，或者由国家统计局和国务院有关部门共同制定，报国务院备案；重大的国家统计调查项目报国务院审批。

部门统计调查项目由国务院有关部门制定。统计调查对象属于本部门管辖系统的，报国家统计局备案；统计调查对象超出本部门管辖系统的，报国家统计局审批。

地方统计调查项目由县级以上地方人民政府统计机构和有关部门分别制定或者共同制定。其中，由省级人民政府统计机构单独制定或者和有关部门共同制定的，报国家统计局审批；由省级以下人民政府统计机构单独制定或者和有关部门共同制定的，报省级人民政府统计机构审批；由县级以上地方人民政府有关部门制定的，报本级人民政府统计机构审批。

第十三条 统计调查项目的审批机关应当对调查项目的必要性、可行性、科学性进行审查，对符合法定条件的，作出予以批准的书面决定，并公布；对不符合法定条件的，作出不予批准的书面决定，并说明理由。

第十四条 制定统计调查项目，应当同时制定该项目的统计调查制度，并依照本法第十二条的规定一并报经审批或者备案。

统计调查制度应当对调查目的、调查内容、调查方法、调查对象、调查组织方式、调查表式、统计资料的报送和公布等作出规定。

统计调查应当按照统计调查制度组织实施。变更统计调查制度的内容，应当报经原审批机关批准或者原备案机关备案。

第十五条 统计调查表应当标明表号、制定机关、批准或者备案文号、有效期限等标志。

对未标明前款规定的标志或者超过有效期限的统计调查表，统计调查对象有权拒绝填报；县级以上人民政府统计机构应当依法责令停止有关统计调查活动。

第十六条 搜集、整理统计资料，应当以周期性普查为基础，以经常性抽样调查为主体，综合运用全面调查、重点调查等方法，并充分利用行政记录等资料。

重大国情国力普查由国务院统一领导，国务院和地方人民政府组织统计机构和有关部门共同实施。

第十七条 国家制定统一的统计标准，保障统计调查采用的指标涵义、计算方法、分类目录、调查表式和统计编码等的标准化。

国家统计标准由国家统计局制定，或者由国家统计局和国务院标准化主管部门共同制定。

国务院有关部门可以制定补充性的部门统计标准，报国家统计局审批。部门统计标准不得与国家统计标准相抵触。

第十八条 县级以上人民政府统计机构根据统计任务的需要，可以在统计调查对象中推广使用计算机网络报送统计资料。

第十九条 县级以上人民政府应当将统计工作所需经费列入财政预算。

重大国情国力普查所需经费，由国务院和地方人民政府共同负担，列入相应年度的财政预算，按时拨付，确保到位。

第三章 统计资料的管理和公布

第二十条 县级以上人民政府统计机构和有关部门以及乡、镇人民政府，应当按照国家有关规定建立统计资料的保存、管理制度，建立健全统计信息共享机制。

第二十一条 国家机关、企业事业单位和其他组织等统计调查对象，应当按照国家有关规定设置原始记录、统计台账，建立健全统计资料的审核、签署、交接、归档等管理制度。

统计资料的审核、签署人员应当对其审核、签署的统计资料的真实性、准确性和完整性负责。

第二十二条 县级以上人民政府有关部门应当及时向本级人民政府统计机构提供统计所需的行政记录资料和国民经济核算所需的财务资料、财政资料及其他资料，并按照统计调查制度的规定及时向本级人民政府统计机构报送其组织实施统计调查取得的有关资料。

县级以上人民政府统计机构应当及时向本级人民政府有关部门提供有关统计资料。

第二十三条 县级以上人民政府统计机构按照国家有关规定，定期公布统计资料。

国家统计数据以国家统计局公布的数据为准。

第二十四条 县级以上人民政府有关部门统计调查取得的统计资料，由本部门按照国家有关规定公布。

第二十五条 统计调查中获得的能够识别或者推断单个统计调查对象身份的资料，任何单位和个人不得对外提供、泄露，不得用于统计以外的目的。

第二十六条 县级以上人民政府统计机构和有关部门统计调查取得的统计资料，除依法应当保密的外，应当及时公开，供社会公众查询。

第四章　统计机构和统计人员

第二十七条　国务院设立国家统计局，依法组织领导和协调全国的统计工作。

国家统计局根据工作需要设立的派出调查机构，承担国家统计局布置的统计调查等任务。

县级以上地方人民政府设立独立的统计机构，乡、镇人民政府设置统计工作岗位，配备专职或者兼职统计人员，依法管理、开展统计工作，实施统计调查。

第二十八条　县级以上人民政府有关部门根据统计任务的需要设立统计机构，或者在有关机构中设置统计人员，并指定统计负责人，依法组织、管理本部门职责范围内的统计工作，实施统计调查，在统计业务上受本级人民政府统计机构的指导。

第二十九条　统计机构、统计人员应当依法履行职责，如实搜集、报送统计资料，不得伪造、篡改统计资料，不得以任何方式要求任何单位和个人提供不真实的统计资料，不得有其他违反本法规定的行为。

统计人员应当坚持实事求是，恪守职业道德，对其负责搜集、审核、录入的统计资料与统计调查对象报送的统计资料的一致性负责。

第三十条　统计人员进行统计调查时，有权就与统计有关的问题询问有关人员，要求其如实提供有关情况、资料并改正不真实、不准确的资料。

统计人员进行统计调查时，应当出示县级以上人民政府统计机构或者有关部门颁发的工作证件；未出示的，统计调查对象有权拒绝调查。

第三十一条　国家实行统计专业技术职务资格考试、评聘制度，提高统计人员的专业素质，保障统计队伍的稳定性。

统计人员应当具备与其从事的统计工作相适应的专业知识和业务能力。

县级以上人民政府统计机构和有关部门应当加强对统计人员的专业培训和职业道德教育。

第五章　监督检查

第三十二条　县级以上人民政府及其监察机关对下级人民政府、本级人民政府统计机构和有关部门执行本法的情况，实施监督。

第三十三条　国家统计局组织管理全国统计工作的监督检查，查处重大统计违法行为。

县级以上地方人民政府统计机构依法查处本行政区域内发生的统计违法行为。但是，国家统计局派出的调查机构组织实施的统计调查活动中发生的统计违法行为，由组织实施该项统计调查的调查机构负责查处。

法律、行政法规对有关部门查处统计违法行为另有规定的，从其规定。

第三十四条　县级以上人民政府有关部门应当积极协助本级人民政府统计机构查处统计违法行为，及时向本级人民政府统计机构移送有关统计违法案件材料。

第三十五条　县级以上人民政府统计机构在调查统计违法行为或者核查统计数据时，有权采取下列措施：

（一）发出统计检查查询书，向检查对象查询有关事项；

（二）要求检查对象提供有关原始记录和凭证、统计台账、统计调查表、会计资料及其他相关证明和资料；

（三）就与检查有关的事项询问有关人员；

（四）进入检查对象的业务场所和统计数据处理信息系统进行检查、核对；

（五）经本机构负责人批准，登记保存检查对象的有关原始记录和凭证、统计台账、统计调查表、会计资料及其他相关证明和资料；

（六）对与检查事项有关的情况和资料进行记录、录音、录像、照相和复制。

县级以上人民政府统计机构进行监督检查时，监督检查人员不得少于二人，并应当出示执法证件；未出示的，有关单位和个人有权拒绝检查。

第三十六条　县级以上人民政府统计机构履行监督检查职责时，有关单位和个人应当如实反映情况，提供相关证明和资料，不得拒绝、阻碍检查，不得转移、隐匿、篡改、毁弃原始记录和凭证、统计台账、统计调查表、会计资料及其他相关证明和资料。

第六章　法律责任

第三十七条　地方人民政府、政府统计机构或者有关部门、单位的负责人有下列行为之一的，由任免机关或者监察机关依法给予处分，并由县级以上人民政府统计机构予以通报：

（一）自行修改统计资料、编造虚假统计数据的；

（二）要求统计机构、统计人员或者其他机构、人员伪造、篡改统计资料的；

（三）对依法履行职责或者拒绝、抵制统计违法行为的统计人员打击报复的；

（四）对本地方、本部门、本单位发生的严重统计违法行为失察的。

第三十八条 县级以上人民政府统计机构或者有关部门在组织实施统计调查活动中有下列行为之一的，由本级人民政府、上级人民政府统计机构或者本级人民政府统计机构责令改正，予以通报；对直接负责的主管人员和其他直接责任人员，由任免机关或者监察机关依法给予处分：

（一）未经批准擅自组织实施统计调查的；

（二）未经批准擅自变更统计调查制度的内容的；

（三）伪造、篡改统计资料的；

（四）要求统计调查对象或者其他机构、人员提供不真实的统计资料的；

（五）未按照统计调查制度的规定报送有关资料的。

统计人员有前款第三项至第五项所列行为之一的，责令改正，依法给予处分。

第三十九条 县级以上人民政府统计机构或者有关部门有下列行为之一的，对直接负责的主管人员和其他直接责任人员由任免机关或者监察机关依法给予处分：

（一）违法公布统计资料的；

（二）泄露统计调查对象的商业秘密、个人信息或者提供、泄露在统计调查中获得的能够识别或者推断单个统计调查对象身份的资料的；

（三）违反国家有关规定，造成统计资料毁损、灭失的。

统计人员有前款所列行为之一的，依法给予处分。

第四十条 统计机构、统计人员泄露国家秘密的，依法追究法律责任。

第四十一条 作为统计调查对象的国家机关、企业事业单位或者其他组织有下列行为之一的，由县级以上人民政府统计机构责令改正，给予警告，可以予以通报；其直接负责的主管人员和其他直接责任人员属于国家工作人员的，由任免机关或者监察机关依法给予处分：

（一）拒绝提供统计资料或者经催报后仍未按时提供统计资料的；

（二）提供不真实或者不完整的统计资料的；

（三）拒绝答复或者不如实答复统计检查查询书的；

（四）拒绝、阻碍统计调查、统计检查的；

（五）转移、隐匿、篡改、毁弃或者拒绝提供原始记录和凭证、统计台账、统计调查表及其他相关证明和资料的。

企业事业单位或者其他组织有前款所列行为之一的，可以并处五万元以下的罚款；情节严重的，并处五万元以上二十万元以下的罚款。

个体工商户有本条第一款所列行为之一的，由县级以上人民政府统计机构责令改正，给予警告，可以并处一万元以下的罚款。

第四十二条 作为统计调查对象的国家机关、企业事业单位或者其他组织迟报统计资料，或者未按照国家有关规定设置原始记录、统计台账的，由县级以上人民政府统计机构责令改正，给予警告。

企业事业单位或者其他组织有前款所列行为之一的，可以并处一万元以下的罚款。

个体工商户迟报统计资料的，由县级以上人民政府统计机构责令改正，给予警告，可以并处一千元以下的罚款。

第四十三条 县级以上人民政府统计机构查处统计违法行为时，认为对有关国家工作人员依法应当给予处分的，应当提出给予处分的建议；该国家工作人员的任免机关或者监察机关应当依法及时作出决定，并将结果书面通知县级以上人民政府统计机构。

第四十四条 作为统计调查对象的个人在重大国情国力普查活动中拒绝、阻碍统计调查，或者提供不真实或者不完整的普查资料的，由县级以上人民政府统计机构责令改正，予以批评教育。

第四十五条 违反本法规定，利用虚假统计资料骗取荣誉称号、物质利益或者职务晋升的，除对其编造虚假统计资料或者要求他人编造虚假统计资料的行为依法追究法律责任外，由作出有关决定的单位或者其上级单位、监察机关取消其荣誉称号，追缴获得的物质利益，撤销晋升的职务。

第四十六条 当事人对县级以上人民政府统计机构作出的行政处罚决定不服的，可以依法申请行政复议或者提起行政诉讼。其中，对国家统计局在省、自治区、直辖市派出的调查机构作出的行政处罚决定不服的，向国家统计局申请行政复议；对国家统计局派出的其他调查机构作出的行政处罚决定不服的，向国家统计局在该派出机构所在的省、自治区、直辖市派出的调查机构申请行政复议。

第四十七条 违反本法规定，构成犯罪的，依法追究刑事责任。

第七章 附 则

第四十八条 本法所称县级以上人民政府统计机构，是指国家统计局及其派出的调查机构、县级以上地方人民政府统计机构。

第四十九条 民间统计调查活动的管理办法，由国务院制定。

中华人民共和国境外的组织、个人需要在中华人民共和国境内进行统计调查活动的，应当按照国务院的规定报请审批。

利用统计调查危害国家安全、损害社会公共利益或者进行欺诈活动的，依法追究法律责任。

第五十条 本法自 2010 年 1 月 1 日起施行。

部门统计调查项目管理办法

（中华人民共和国国家统计局令第22号）

第一章　总则

第一条　为加强部门统计调查项目的规范性、统一性管理，提高统计调查的科学性和有效性，减轻统计调查对象负担，推进部门统计信息共享，根据《中华人民共和国统计法》及其实施条例和国务院有关规定，制定本办法。

第二条　本办法适用于国务院各部门制定的统计调查项目。

第三条　本办法所称的统计调查项目，是指国务院有关部门通过调查表格、问卷、行政记录、大数据以及其他方式搜集整理统计资料，用于政府管理和公共服务的各类统计调查项目。

第四条　国家统计局统一组织领导和协调全国统计工作，指导国务院有关部门开展统计调查，统一管理部门统计调查。

第五条　国务院有关部门应当明确统一组织协调统计工作的综合机构，负责归口管理、统一申报本部门统计调查项目。

第二章　部门统计调查项目的制定

第六条　国务院有关部门执行相关法律、行政法规、国务院的决定和履行本部门职责，需要开展统计活动的，应当制定相应的部门统计调查项目。

第七条　制定部门统计调查项目，应当减少调查频率，缩小调查规模，降低调查成本，减轻基层统计人员和统计调查对象的负担。可以通过行政记录和大数据加工整理获得统计资料的，不得开展统计调查；可以通过已经批准实施的各种统计调查整理获得统计资料的，不得重复开展统计调查；抽样调查、重点调查可以满足需要的，不得开展全面统计调查。

第八条　制定部门统计调查项目，应当有组织、人员和经费保障。

第九条　制定部门统计调查项目，应当同时制定该项目的统计调查制度。

统计调查制度内容包括总说明、报表目录、调查表式、分类目录、指标解释、指标间逻辑关系，采用抽样调查方法的还应当包括抽样方案。

统计调查制度总说明应当对调查目的、调查对象、统计范围、调查内容、调查频率、调查时间、调查方法、组织实施方式、质量控制、报送要求、信息共享、资料公布等作出规定。

面向单位的部门统计调查，其统计调查对象应当取自国家基本单位名录库或者部门基本单位名录库。

第十条　部门统计调查应当规范设置统计指标、调查表，指标解释和计算方法应当科学合理。

第十一条　部门统计调查应当使用国家统计标准。无国家统计标准的，可以使用经国家统计局批准的部门统计标准。

第十二条　新制定的部门统计调查项目或者对现行统计调查项目进行较大修订的，应当开展试填试报等工作。其中，重要统计调查项目应当进行试点。

第十三条　部门统计调查项目涉及其他部门职责的，应当事先征求相关部门意见。

第三章　部门统计调查项目审批和备案

第十四条　国务院有关部门制定的统计调查项目，统计调查对象属于本部门管辖系统或者利用行政记录加工获取统计资料的，报国家统计局备案；统计调查对象超出本部门管辖系统的，报国家统计局审批。

部门管辖系统包括本部门直属机构、派出机构和垂直管理的机构，省及省以下与部门对口设立的管理机构。

第十五条　部门统计调查项目审批或者备案包括申报、受理、审查、反馈、决定等程序。

第十六条 部门统计调查项目送审或者备案时，应当通过部门统计调查项目管理平台提交下列材料：

（一）申请审批项目的部门公文或者申请备案项目的部门办公厅（室）公文；

（二）部门统计调查项目审批或者备案申请表；

（三）统计调查制度；

（四）统计调查项目的论证报告、背景材料、经费保障等，修订的统计调查项目还应当提供修订说明；

（五）征求有关地方、部门、统计调查对象和专家意见及其采纳情况；

（六）制定机关按照会议制度集体讨论决定的会议纪要；

（七）重要统计调查项目的试点报告；

（八）由审批机关或者备案机关公布的统计调查制度的主要内容；

（九）防范和惩治统计造假、弄虚作假责任规定。

前款第（一）项的公文应当同时提交纸质文件。

第十七条 申请材料齐全并符合法定形式的，国家统计局予以受理。

申请材料不齐全或者不符合法定形式的，国家统计局应当一次告知需要补正的全部内容，制定机关应当按照国家统计局的要求予以补正。

第十八条 统计调查制度应当列明下列事项：

（一）向国家统计局报送的制定机关组织实施统计调查取得的具体统计资料清单；

（二）主要统计指标公布的时间、渠道；

（三）统计信息共享的内容、方式、时限、渠道、责任单位和责任人；

（四）向统计信息共享数据库提供的统计资料清单；

（五）统计调查对象使用国家基本单位名录库或者部门基本单位名录库的情况。

第十九条 国家统计局对申请审批的部门统计调查项目进行审查，符合下列条件的部门统计调查项目，作出予以批准的书面决定：

（一）具有法定依据或者确为部门公共管理和服务所必需；

（二）与现有的国家统计调查项目和部门统计调查项目的主要内容不重复、不矛盾；

（三）主要统计指标无法通过本部门的行政记录或者已有统计调查资料加工整理取得；

（四）部门统计调查制度科学、合理、可行，并且符合本办法第八条、第九条和第十八条规定；

（五）采用的统计标准符合国家有关规定；

（六）符合统计法律法规和国家有关规定。

不符合前款规定的，国家统计局向制定机关提出修改意见；修改后仍不符合前款规定条件的，国家统计局作出不予批准的书面决定，并说明理由。

第二十条 国家统计局对申请备案的部门统计调查项目进行审查，符合下列条件的部门统计调查项目，作出同意备案的书面决定：

（一）统计调查项目的调查对象属于制定机关管辖系统，或者利用行政记录加工获取统计资料；

（二）与现有的国家统计调查项目和部门统计调查项目的主要内容不重复、不矛盾；

（三）部门统计调查制度科学、合理、可行，并且符合本办法第八条、第九条和第十八条规定。

第二十一条 国家统计局在收到制定机关申请公文及完整的相关资料后，在 20 个工作日内完成审批，20 个工作日内不能作出决定的，经审批机关负责人批准可以延长 10 日，并应当将延长审批期限的理由告知制定机关；在 10 个工作日内完成备案。完成时间以复函日期为准。

制定机关修改统计调查项目的时间，不计算在审批期限内。

第二十二条 部门统计调查项目有下列情形之一的，国家统计局简化审批或者备案程序，缩短期限：

（一）发生突发事件，需要迅速实施统计调查；

（二）统计调查内容未做变动，统计调查项目有效期届满需要延长期限。

第二十三条 部门统计调查项目实行有效期管理。审批的统计调查项目有效期为 3 年，备案的统计调查项目有效期为 5 年。统计调查制度对有效期规定少于 3 年的，从其规定。有效期以批准执行或者同意备案的日期为起始时间。

统计调查项目在有效期内需要变更内容的，制定机关应当重新申请审批或者备案。

第二十四条 部门统计调查项目经国家统计局批准或者备案后，应当在统计调查表的右上角标明表号、制定机关、批准机关或者备案机关、批准文号或者备案文号、有效期限等标志。

第二十五条 制定机关收到批准或者备案的书面决定后，在10个工作日内将标注批准文号或者备案文号和有效期限的统计调查制度发送到部门统计调查项目管理平台。

第二十六条 国家统计局及时通过国家统计局网站公布批准或者备案的部门统计调查项目名称、制定机关、批准文号或者备案文号、有效期限和统计调查制度的主要内容。

第四章 部门统计调查的组织实施

第二十七条 国务院有关部门应当健全统计工作流程规范，完善统计数据质量控制办法，夯实统计基础工作，严格按照国家统计局批准或者备案的统计调查制度组织实施统计调查。

第二十八条 国务院有关部门在组织实施统计调查时，应当就统计调查制度的主要内容对组织实施人员进行培训；应当就法定填报义务、主要指标涵义和口径、计算方法、采用的统计标准和其他填报要求，向调查对象作出说明。

第二十九条 国务院有关部门应当按《中华人民共和国统计法实施条例》的要求及时公布主要统计指标涵义、调查范围、调查方法、计算方法、抽样调查样本量等信息，对统计数据进行解释说明。

第三十条 国务院有关部门组织实施统计调查应当遵守国家有关统计资料管理和公布的规定。

第三十一条 部门统计调查取得的统计资料，一般应当在政府部门间共享。

第三十二条 国务院有关部门建立统计调查项目执行情况评估制度，对实施情况、实施效果和存在问题进行评估，认为应当修改的，按规定报请国家统计局审批或者备案。

第五章 国家统计局提供的服务

第三十三条 国家统计局依法开展部门统计调查项目审批和备案工作，为国务院有关部门提供有关统计业务咨询、统计调查制度设计指导、统计业务培训等服务。

第三十四条 国家统计局组织国务院有关部门共同维护、更新国家基本单位名录库，为部门统计调查提供调查单位名录和抽样框。

第三十五条 国家统计局建立统计标准库，为部门统计调查提供国家统计标准和部门统计标准。

第三十六条 国家统计局向国务院有关部门提供部门统计调查项目查询服务。

第三十七条 国家统计局推动建立统计信息共享数据库，为国务院有关部门提供部门统计数据查询服务。

第六章 监督检查

第三十八条 国家统计局依法对部门统计调查制度执行情况进行监督检查，依法查处部门统计调查中的重大违法行为；县级以上地方人民政府统计机构依法查处本级和下级人民政府有关部门和统计调查对象执行部门统计调查制度中发生的统计违法行为。

第三十九条 任何单位和个人有权向国家统计局举报部门统计调查违法行为。

国家统计局公布举报统计违法行为的方式和途径，依法受理、核实、处理举报，并为举报人保密。

第四十条 县级以上人民政府有关部门积极协助本级人民政府统计机构查处统计违法行为，及时向县级以上人民政府统计机构移送有关统计违法案件材料。

第四十一条 县级以上人民政府统计机构在调查部门统计违法行为或者核查部门统计数据时，有权采取《中华人民共和国统计法》第三十五条规定的下列措施：

（一）发出检查查询书，向检查单位和调查对象查询部门统计调查项目有关事项；

（二）要求检查单位和调查对象提供与部门统计调查有关的统计调查制度、调查资料、调查报告及其他相关证明和资料；

（三）就与检查有关的事项询问有关人员；

（四）进入检查单位和调查对象的业务场所和统计数据处理信息系统进行检查、核对；

（五）经本机构负责人批准，登记保存检查单位与统计调查有关的统计调查制度、调查资料、调查报告及其他相关证明和资料；

（六）对与检查事项有关的情况和资料进行记录、录音、录像、照相和复制。

县级以上人民政府统计机构进行监督检查时，监督检查人员不得少于 2 人，并应当出示执法证件；未出示的，有关部门有权拒绝检查。

第四十二条 县级以上人民政府统计机构履行监督检查职责时，有关部门应当如实反映情况，提供相关证明和资料，不得拒绝、阻碍检查，不得转移、隐匿、篡改、毁弃与部门统计调查有关的统计调查制度、调查资料、调查报告及其他相关证明和资料。

第七章 法律责任

第四十三条 县级以上人民政府有关部门在组织实施部门统计调查活动中有下列行为之一的，由上级人民政府统计机构、本级人民政府统计机构责令改正，予以通报：

（一）违法制定、实施部门统计调查项目；

（二）未执行国家统计标准或者经依法批准的部门统计标准；

（三）未执行批准和备案的部门统计调查制度；

（四）在部门统计调查中统计造假、弄虚作假。

第四十四条 县级以上人民政府有关部门及其工作人员有下列行为之一的，由上级人民政府统计机构、本级人民政府统计机构责令改正，予以通报：

（一）拒绝、阻碍对部门统计调查的监督检查和对部门统计违法行为的查处；

（二）包庇、纵容部门统计违法行为；

（三）向存在部门统计违法行为的单位或者个人通风报信，帮助其逃避查处。

第四十五条 县级以上人民政府统计机构在查处部门统计违法行为中，认为对有关国家工作人员依法应当给予处分的，应当提出给予处分的建议，将处分建议和案件材料移送该国家工作人员的任免机关或者监察机关。

第八章 附 则

第四十六条 中央编办管理机构编制的群众团体机关、经授权代主管部门行使统计职能的国家级集团公司和工商领域联合会或者协会等开展的统计调查项目，参照部门统计调查项目管理。

县级以上地方人民政府统计机构对本级人民政府有关部门制定的统计调查项目管理，参照本办法执行。

第四十七条 本办法自 2017 年 10 月 1 日起施行。国家统计局 1999 年公布的《部门统计调查项目管理暂行办法》同时废止。